Between Two People: Exercises Toward Intimacy

Mark E. Johnson, PhD
Jay B. Fortman, PhD
Christiane Brems, PhD

5999 Stevenson Avenue
Alexandria, VA 22304-3300

Order of authorship was determined randomly and does not reflect the relative contributions of the authors.

American Counseling Association
5999 Stevenson Avenue
Alexandria, VA 22304

Cover Design by Sarah Jane Valdez

Library of Congress Cataloging-in-Publication Data

Johnson, Mark E. (Mark Eliott), 1956–
    Between two people: exercises toward intimacy/Mark E. Johnson,
Jay B. Fortman, Christiane Brems.
      p.   cm.
    Includes bibliographical references.
    ISBN 1-55620-107-9
    1. Man-woman relationships.   2. Interpersonal communication.
3. Intimacy (Psychology)   4. Interpersonal relations. I. Fortman,
Jay B.   II. Brems, Christiane.   III. Title.
HQ801.J594   1993
306.7—dc20   92-42282
                                                      CIP

Printed in the United States of America (2nd Printing)

CONTENTS

PREFACE FOR COUNSELORS

Relationship counseling has become an important aspect of modern counseling practice. More and more clients choose treatment not merely for themselves, but for their relationships with intimate partners. We have observed in our own practices that more clients emphasize the need for intimacy and trust in their long-term relationships, yet that they do not always know how to go about establishing these traits. This book was designed for counselors who have recognized similar needs in their own clientele and who wish to embark upon the rewarding experience of helping people improve their relationships. *Between Two People* represents a collection of exercises we have developed over the years in our work with clients.

The exercises can be used by counselors of various theoretical orientations. In fact, the three of us represent three schools of thought: psychodynamic theory, family systems theory, and cognitive behaviorism. We believe that the exercises can be used successfully within each of these frameworks because the actual work of the clients can be presented in a manner consistent with the counselor's own preference. We cannot, nor do we, claim that the exercises are completely theory-free. Most likely they reflect our own belief that interpersonal processes are complex and are guided by childhood histories, experiences in families of origin, and by how people have learned to think, behave, and respond in certain situations.

The exercises in this book are best introduced by a counselor, especially early on in the treatment process. However, they can also be used by clients on their own, once both members of the couple have gained some counseling experience. We suggest that the counselor use the book initially as a personal reference and then introduce the exercises without using the book directly in session. If and when the couple seeking counseling responds positively to the exercises, the counselor may wish to introduce the book itself to the couple for use at home, perhaps in the form of assigned homework.

The exercises in sections 1 to 4 cover four major areas, and sections 5 to 8 are devoted to special topics. Within each section, exercises are presented in ascending order of difficulty. All instructions are written in such a way that clients can use them directly. Language has been chosen carefully to make this book usable with heterosexual as well as homosexual couples, and to be gender-free and culture-fair. The Preface for Clients contains detailed information about how to use the exercises and how to proceed when instructions are difficult. It also provides additional content information, therefore counselors are advised to read it as well.

We hope you will find this book and the exercises within it helpful to your relationship counseling practice. We would like to hear from you as you begin to use these exercises in your work. Your feedback may be helpful for future revisions of this manual and in our own work with clients. If you have any additional exercises that you have found useful in your practice, we would appreciate reviewing them and possibly including them in future revisions.

Christiane Brems
Mark E. Johnson
Jay B. Fortman

PREFACE FOR CLIENTS

Why Was This Book Written?

According to Webster's dictionary, communication is the exchange of information, and to communicate means to share and to make known. By the age of 3, most of us have learned to speak. Speaking to one another becomes a natural thing after this age. We don't take classes in how to communicate with our partners and other significant people in our lives, and there is no test that we have to pass before communicating. Communication is something we take for granted; we believe we know how to do it and that we can do it well.

Communication is not as easy as Webster's dictionary makes it sound, and it is particularly difficult with people you know very well and with whom you have an emotional tie. It is exactly with these people that miscommunications cause the most pain because they can result in hurt feelings and can break relationships. Furthermore, communication problems between two people tend to be self-perpetuating: Once you have developed a communication style with a person (regardless of how destructive it is), it can become a habit that is difficult, if not impossible, to break without help. Communication tends to be something we do, rather than something we examine and think about. This book is designed to help you think about your communication style with your partner to improve your ability to make yourself understood in your most intimate relationship.

Literally dozens of books, and even more textbooks for students, exist that address the topic of intimate relationships. Many of these books are written to help people end relationships and adjust to being single again. More recently, however, books with the purpose of helping people renew and improve intimate relationships have started to appear. It seems that various current social factors (e.g., AIDS; longer life expectancy; value of the nuclear family) have renewed people's interest in monogamous, satisfying, long-term relationships. Given the life expectancy of the average American and the early age at which she or he marries, there is the potential for an intimate, monogamous long-term relationship of over 40 to 50 years. To be able to live with one person in an intimate and meaningful relationship for such a long period of time, the two partners not only need to share common interests, but also need to know (or learn) how to keep romance alive and how to communicate effectively. This book was written to help you learn about the causes and contributing factors of relationship problems and to provide you with a practical program that will help you and your partner improve your intimate relationship.

What Does This Book Cover?

Part 1 of this book covers three areas that frequently contribute to problems in relationships: absence of romance, faulty communication, and family background issues. This part is designed to provide a practical guide for the improvement of the relationship by introducing the partners to ways of reintroducing romance in the relationship, improving communication, and changing the influence of family dynamics. Part 2 of this book provides additional exercises to help with problems within four domains, namely, household chores, finances, parenting, and sexuality. These exercises help in applying the skills gained through the book's previous sections to areas in intimate relationships that often cause difficulty.

For Whom Was This Book Written?

This book was written for people who are currently in an intimate relationship, not for people who are in search of one. The fact that you have this book indicates that you are in an intimate relationship and that you are interested in improving it. Having this book also indicates that you are willing to work hard to improve your relationship and that you are aware of the need of some long-term work to achieve this goal. The book is best used by the two partners in conjunction with a counselor, and cannot be used by one partner alone. Specifically, if only one of the two of you is interested in improving the relationship, whereas the other either does not feel improvement is necessary or feels it is too late even to attempt to work on the relationship, this book is not for you. However, if both of you have the commitment to give your relationship one more chance, the exercises in this book have the potential to help you.

What Is This Book Not Intended To Do?

This or any other book can never take the place of traditional counseling. It is designed as a complement to counseling, not a replacement. This book is not for you if you are looking for a fast and easy solution to your relationship problems. Following this program will require time, commitment, effort, practice, and the willingness to compromise. In fact, you should not attempt to do more than one exercise per counseling session or per day, and there are many exercises that you may need to repeat for several days before you are ready to move on to the next one. Some are best done only with your counselor present, at least for the first time you try them.

What Is the Format of This Book?

As you delve into this book you will realize that it is set up in a workbook format and provides you with a wide variety of exercises. This design was chosen because all of us were aware that despite numerous books about improving relationships, none provides the practical application of counseling exercises that we have found to be very helpful to couples in our private practices in relationship counseling. Thus, our primary focus is on a practical exercise program that the two of you will follow as a couple! As mentioned previously, these exercises are to be used under the supervision of a professional counselor.

You will notice that within the book, sections are arranged by topic. Within each section, material is arranged by level of difficulty. Therefore, the first few exercises may seem quite easy, but as you move along, you will be challenged more and more. Given that the sections are arranged by topic, you can go through them by topic, or you can go through various sections at the same time to stay at the same level of difficulty. We suggest that you follow the format of the book, but certainly, if you or your counselor have a different preference, you are welcome to try it. You should note, however, that some exercises have prerequisite exercises (identified at the beginning of the exercise). No matter how you move through the book, never do an exercise without having successfully completed its prerequisite. Furthermore, all exercises interconnect, and all exercises will involve all facets of a relationship to some degree; they are merely arranged according to which facet is most prevalent (hence the arrangement by topic).

Finally, some words of caution: If an exercise is too difficult, abandon it, go back to easier ones, and then try the exercise again later. There may be some exercises that you will never master—that's okay! Some exercises may need to be done several times before you get them "right"—that is to be expected and is no cause for despair. Just keep trying. Although the exercises are arranged from easy to difficult, this may be the wrong order for some couples. Make modifications to your program IF you deem them necessary and if your counselor agrees or recommends changes.

Is There Practical Advice About How to Use the Exercises?

As you begin working on your exercises, you will notice several repeated directives. Instead of discussing each of these individually in each exercise, some hints are given below on how to deal with these directives if you are uncertain about them. It is always best to consult your counselor when you are in doubt or don't understand a given set of instructions.

1. What to do when it says "take turns":

Whenever you receive the directive to take turns, the implication is that one of you goes first. If you have your own way of making this determination, use it! If you are uncertain about how to make this decision, use some random procedure to make it. For instance, toss a coin, draw straws (whoever gets the longer straw gets to go first), draw numbers (make up two slips of paper: one with a 1 and one with a 2; whoever draws the 1 gets to go first).

2. What to do when it says "pick one partner":

Whenever you receive the directive to pick one of the two of you, you can rely on your own strategy for selection or you can use the same strategies outlined under "taking turns." For example, whoever draws the longer straw is chosen.

3. What to do when there is a minimum or maximum length of time:

Don't try to time an exercise based on your internal sense of time. Use a timer with a buzzer, and set it to go off at the maximum time allowed for the exercise. As soon as the timer goes off, end the activity. Similarly, if there is a minimum, set a timer so you know when you have gone on long enough. If you are enjoying the activity, you may continue. Otherwise the buzzer is your signal that you may end.

4. What to do when it says "at a time convenient to both of you":

This is the toughest directive for most couples. It is often hard enough for one person to find a convenient time, not to mention two people trying to coordinate their busy schedules. If you already have a procedure for making such a decision, follow it. If not, we suggest the following, depending on whether the convenient time is to be negotiated or whether it is to serve as a surprise:

(a) When the time is to be negotiated, both of you should write down three time periods within the next 2 days that would be convenient for you. Then compare these times and see if there is any overlap. If so, your task is complete. If not, come up with two more times each, and compare again. Overlap means that now you are done. Otherwise you will need to sit down and go over all of the 10 times the two of you have listed so far. Each has to give a reason why you cannot meet at each of these times. Chances are that at least one of these times will work for you. If not, repeat the procedure for the next 2 days after the initially proposed days.

(b) When the time is the basis for a surprise, it is more difficult to come up with a convenient time because you will not have your partner's input. Try to use previous time schedules that your partner developed and base your decision on these. If this does not work, wait for a time when you know your partner is usually at home (e.g., after 8:00 P.M., on a Sunday afternoon). If your partner has extremely variable hours, plan the surprise during a time when you know your partner is supposed to be busy with some other activity that you can do for her or him (e.g., if your partner usually goes to do the laundry at 5 P.M. on Friday, do the laundry for her or him and use that time for the surprise).

Whenever an exercise asks you to write notes or other messages, please be advised that it is perfectly fine to use video- or audiotape instead. However, it tends to be better if both partners agree to use the same medium, unless using different ways of communicating is built into the exercise to provide a measure of surprise. In general, if one partner prefers taping, both should tape; if one prefers writing, both should write. It will be helpful to save the work you produced because many of these lists will be used again in later exercises or may come in handy for your personal future reference.

We realize that none of these tips will work all the time. However, they do tend to work most of the time and greatly reduce the amount of arguing couples tend to engage in over these types of decisions. Finally, to be able to move through the exercises without having to interrupt the process to gather necessary materials, try to have the following items at hand when you sit down to work on your relationship with the help of this book: small and large sheets of paper, pencils, pens, red and green highlighters, and a timer that buzzes. Occasionally you may need additional, more specific, items, and those will be mentioned in the exercise for which they are required (e.g., some of the family-of-origin exercises require large sheets of sturdy paper).

What Are Some of the Special Features of This Book?

In designing this book based on our experience in working with many different couples, we have found that our techniques work best when they are presented in a framework of equality, freedom, and absence of bias and prejudice. Thus, we decided that it was important in writing this book to use language that reflects these goals. In other words, as you go through the workbook, you will find that we have avoided words such as husband or wife, the generic "he," "his," "him," or "man," and the assumption that the two intimate partners are of opposite genders. Instead, you will find language that is neither sexist, racist, nor homophobic.

You will note that we refer to the people in intimate relationships as partners so as not to imply that people have to be married or of opposite genders to love each other and to be in a committed, stable, long-term relationship. We believe that this book will work for any couple willing to make an effort to work on their relationship, regardless of gender, race, or sexual orientation. It is recommended for married couples, cohabiting heterosexual couples, cohabiting homosexual couples, and any other couples who consider themselves in an intimate, long-term relationship.

To all of you, good luck as you embark on your road to intimacy, romance, and better communication. We hope this book will prove as helpful to you as the strategies within it have been to many of the couples we have seen in counseling.

Christiane Brems
Mark E. Johnson
Jay B. Fortman

AUTHOR BIOGRAPHIES

Christiane Brems, PhD, is associate professor of psychology and graduate studies coordinator at the University of Alaska Anchorage, as well as a licensed psychologist. She received her PhD in clinical psychology from Oklahoma State University.

Mark E. Johnson, PhD, is associate professor and chair of psychology at the University of Alaska Anchorage, and a licensed psychologist. He received his PhD in counseling psychology from the University of California at Santa Barbara.

Jay B. Fortman, PhD, is a licensed marriage, family, and child counselor in private practice in Goleta, California, and a school psychologist in Santa Barbara, California. He received his PhD in educational psychology from the University of California at Santa Barbara.

AUTHOR BIOGRAPHIES

PART ONE Communication, Romance, and Family-of-Origin Exercises

SECTION ONE   *Nonverbal Communication*

EXERCISES

1. Refocusing Your Attention: Nonverbal
2. Learning to Trust
3. Camera
4. Observation of Expression
5. Feedback on the Observation of Expression
6. Nonverbal Feelings Practice: Number One
7. Nonverbal Feelings Practice: Number Two
8. Nonverbal Feelings Expression
9. Watching Others: Nonverbal
10. I Have Feelings: Nonverbal
11. Labels For Feelings: Nonverbal
12. Automatic Nonverbal Feelings Expression
13. Nonverbal Needs Practice
14. Nonverbal Touching: Part One
15. Nonverbal Touching: Part Two
16. Nonverbal Touching: Discussion
17. Nonverbal Expression of Affection
18. Nonverbal Language for Social Situations
19. Aggressive Versus Assertive: Nonverbal
20. Saying "No" Nonverbally

The exercises in this section focus on nonverbal methods partners use to interact with one another. Thus, the first section of the book provides a fresh look at the relationship, but for now avoids some major pitfalls that can result from verbal interactions between two people. These exercises will help you discover interactions and feelings in your relationship that have been left unspoken, yet have had a profound impact. They are also designed to help you regain trust in your partner and develop a new awareness of and closeness to one another. Following the directions closely and not speaking are essential to the success of these exercises.

1 REFOCUSING YOUR ATTENTION: NONVERBAL

Purpose This exercise will help you refocus your attention on each other and develop greater closeness. It will also give you a greater awareness of how we communicate with one another through nonverbal means.

Benefit In many ways, the eyes truly are the pathways to the soul. Early in a relationship, two people will often gaze lovingly into one another's eyes. This is a way to get to know each other and to make an emotional connection. As relationships mature, often people do not take the time to focus enough attention on their partners. This may slowly cut away the emotional bonds between two people. By refocusing your attention on your partner, you will be able to strengthen your emotional connection and become closer with one another.

Directions **Step One:** Find two comfortable chairs and move them so they face one another. Now sit across from one another.

Step Two: Face each other and simply look into each other's eyes. Keep your mind as clear as possible and focus only on positive thoughts about your partner and your relationship.

Duration and Frequency The first time you do this exercise, spend only 15 to 20 seconds looking into each other's eyes. If you have a timer that measures seconds, use it to tell you when the time is up. Otherwise, try to estimate the time and stop sooner if either of you is feeling uncomfortable. Repeat this exercise several times. Each time you repeat it, spend more and more time looking into each other's eyes.

Suggestions Be as relaxed and comfortable as possible for this exercise. When looking into your partner's eyes, focus only on positive thoughts. Think of things that you like about your partner, perhaps how her or his eyes or face looks. It may help to think of some enjoyable moments that you have had with your partner. Think of anything about your partner or relationship, as long as it is positive.

Pitfalls Do not make this a contest to see who can stare at each other longer or to see who blinks first. The purpose is not to compete but rather to cooperate. At first, this may feel awkward and uncomfortable, but this will pass with time and soon you will gain the benefits of the exercise. Do not spend the time counting the seconds or thinking about something totally unrelated to your relationship. Instead, focus on positive thoughts about your partner and about your relationship. While doing this exercise, do not talk with one another—talking will neutralize the purpose of the exercise.

4

2 LEARNING TO TRUST

Purpose

This exercise will help you develop a greater sense of trust in one another. It will also allow you to become of aware of the feelings you experience when you rely upon another person.

Benefit

One of the main foundations of a healthy relationship is the ability to trust one another. Without trust, it is difficult, if not impossible, to be truly intimate and close with another person. Trust does not merely involve believing a partner will or will not engage in a certain behavior. Trust is the basic confidence that you can share who you are with your partner and that you will be accepted and loved. It is the belief that your partner cares for you and has your best interests at heart.

Unfortunately, the level of trust in many relationships may deteriorate over time, especially if there have been a lot of hurtful experiences in the relationship. This lack of trust leads to further alienation between partners, which, in turn, leads to even less trust in the relationship. It is important to break this cycle and start the healing process that leads to increased trust.

Directions

Step One: Select a partner who will start the exercise. It is best to do this exercise indoors for the first time, perhaps around your home.

Step Two: Using a handkerchief or scarf, blindfold the partner who will be first to be led relying solely upon the other partner. The other partner's role is to guide her or his partner carefully around the home. Be sure to give adequate verbal directions and instructions so your partner does not get hurt. As this exercise is being done, both partners should be aware of their feelings.

Step Three: After 5 minutes, switch roles and repeat step 2.

Step Four: After both partners have had the opportunity to be in both the role of guide and blindfolded person, discuss the feelings you experienced when you were blindfolded and when you were the guide.

Step Five: Repeat this exercise without any verbal directions or instructions either now or when you have time.

Duration and Frequency

This exercise should take approximately 15 to 20 minutes, including 10 minutes for discussion. Repeat this exercise as often as both partners wish. When repeating it, vary the location of the exercise, perhaps going outdoors at least once.

Suggestions The first time you do this exercise, select a familiar indoor setting such as your home. As you guide your partner, hold her or him by the hand, arm, or shoulder. Be sure to give thorough verbal directions and instructions and walk slowly. As your trust of one another develops, you will be able to walk faster and use fewer directions. When you repeat this exercise, use both outdoor and indoor locations and familiar and unfamiliar surroundings. Remember, you are trying to develop trust, so make sure your partner comes to no harm during this exercise.

Pitfalls Often it is difficult for a person to give up complete control, which is necessary for this exercise, and occasionally a person will be afraid of being blindfolded. If this is the case, do not push yourself or your partner, just go slowly and patiently. When you are the guide, never forget to give explicit verbal directions about what you are doing, where you are going, and what is in front of your partner. Failure to give thorough directions may result in less trust rather than more.

3 CAMERA

Purpose This exercise will further enhance the trust you have in one another. It will also give you an opportunity to view the world through your partner's eyes and help you recognize what she or he likes and appreciates.

Benefit The more you understand your partner, the more trust you will have in the relationship. However, sharing who and what you are with another person can be risky. There is the danger of being rejected or ridiculed. The fear of rejection often leads people to keep their thoughts and feelings private. Ironically, keeping feelings from your partner makes it harder for her or him to share feelings with you. As a result, two people who do not know each other very well will have little trust in one another.

By beginning to take risks and sharing some things with your partner, you are initiating the process of increasing trust in the relationship. Sharing things that you consider to be important, positive, or beautiful can be a major first step.

Prerequisite "Learning to Trust"

Directions **Step One:** Select one partner to be the "camera" and one to be the "photographer." When you first do this exercise, choose a familiar, indoor setting such as your house.

Step Two: The camera closes her or his eyes while the photographer leads the camera to different locations. The photographer's goal is to have the camera "take pictures" of things that the photographer considers beautiful or that the photographer considers to be an important and positive aspect of her or his life. Upon arrival at such a location, the photographer pushes an imaginary button on the camera's back, at which time the camera opens her or his eyes. When the photographer releases the button, the camera closes her or his eyes and is led to another location. When you are the camera, be aware of what you see and how you feel about it.

Step Three: After 5 to 10 minutes of this "photo session," switch roles and repeat step 2.

Step Four: After you have completed both photo sessions, discuss the experience and which photos you enjoyed. Focus on how you felt, both while you were the camera and the photographer.

Duration and Frequency   This exercise will last about 15 to 20 minutes, depending on how much time is taken photographing and discussing experiences. It should be repeated a few times on different days, varying the setting.

Suggestions   The first time you do this exercise, use a familiar indoor setting such as your house. When you repeat this exercise, use different settings, both indoors and outdoors. Guide the camera from place to place by holding her or his hand or shoulder. As the photographer, select scenes that evoke positive feelings from you. As the camera, keep your eyes closed and open them only when your "shutter release" is pushed. Neither of the partners should speak during this exercise until both have had a chance to be the camera.

Pitfalls   Because the camera has to keep eyes closed and be led around, the camera will have to trust the photographer. Both partners should be careful to ensure that the camera does not get hurt when being led around. The photographer should not select scenes that are likely to elicit negative feelings from the camera. This is not the time to show your partner a messy room or a broken window that needs repair. Do not use this exercise as an opportunity to hurt your partner. Do not criticize one another's selection of locations. When you are the photographer, do not use the same "pictures" that your partner used.

4 OBSERVATION OF EXPRESSION

Purpose
This exercise will help you become more aware of your partner without the use of words. Furthermore, but less important at this point, you might learn how you respond to your partner when no words are involved at all.

Benefit
Once people learn to use language, they largely begin to neglect the nonverbal aspects of themselves and others. In other words, they become less and less aware of their own and others' facial expressions, gestures, body posture, and so forth. All of these things are part of nonverbal communication and generally need to be relearned by adults. This exercise will help you get back in touch with your own nonverbal expressions and those of your partner. This can be tremendously helpful because it will open a whole new method of communication and understanding for the two of you. Besides, often when you stop using words, you also stop fighting.

Directions
Step One: Choose two comfortable chairs and move them so that they face one another. Now, without speaking, each partner needs to select a chair and sit down.

Step Two: While you sit across from your partner, observe all expressions and even the slightest movements she or he makes. Become aware of the smallest details.

Step Three: After having observed for at least 2 minutes, begin monitoring your own thoughts, feelings, and behaviors in response to your partner's expressions. Do not say anything aloud.

Duration and Frequency
Do this exercise for 5 minutes the first time you try it. Going any longer than 5 minutes for the first time may become somewhat awkward. Repeat this exercise as often as you like, but negotiate the length of time for each repetition before you engage in the exercise again. The exercise works best if it is no shorter than 3 minutes and never longer than 10 minutes.

Suggestions
During this exercise, just enjoy the newness of the situation. You may find that you need to repeat this exercise several times to gain its full benefit. Repeating the exercise should be easy enough because it takes no more than 5 to 10 minutes each time.

Pitfalls
Doing this exercise will probably be a completely new experience for you. Like anything new it may feel strange, odd, or even like a

waste of time. It would be a mistake to give up. Keep trying, because you will find that you learn things about your partner that you never noticed or knew before.

While engaging in this exercise, under no circumstances should you speak. Speaking would defeat the purpose, which is to relate in a completely new, nonverbal manner.

5 FEEDBACK ON THE OBSERVATION OF EXPRESSION

Purpose   This exercise is an extension of "Observation of Expression." It will help teach you about the impact of your own nonverbal expressions and behaviors on your partner. Equally important, this exercise will help you learn about how you are affected by the nonverbal behaviors of your partner.

Benefit   Even though as adults we do not often consciously use nonverbal means to express ourselves, we do so automatically. As a result, nonverbal expressions are likely to affect others, just as we are affected by others' nonverbal communication. Couples often have to learn to become more consciously aware of how they express things without words, and how they react to what the partner expresses nonverbally to them. With this increased awareness, partners become more able to understand one another and can avoid misunderstanding.

Prerequisite   "Observation of Expression"

Directions   **Step One:** Choose two comfortable chairs and place them so that they face one another. Now, without speaking, each of you should choose a chair and sit down across from each other.

Step Two: Choose one partner who will be the "verbal partner." The verbal partner then observes the silent partner for at least 1 minute. While observing the silent partner, the verbal partner tries to become aware of her or his own feelings, thoughts, and other reactions to the silent partner's nonverbal expressions.

Step Three: After 1 to 2 minutes of observing the silent partner, the verbal partner begins to say aloud what she or he is thinking and feeling in response to the other's nonverbal expressions. While the verbal partner is speaking, the silent partner must not talk, but only listen.

Step Four: Switch roles and repeat steps 2 and 3.

Duration and Frequency   This exercise should take approximately 5 minutes per turn. Repeat the exercise as often as you both wish.

Suggestions   As the silent partner, you may find that it is often difficult to hear a person speak while not being allowed to respond. However, for now it is important to follow the "no talking" rule. (There will be exercises later in the workbook in which you will get the opportunity to respond.) As the verbal partner, restrict your

11

comments to what you are feeling or thinking in response to the nonverbal communication of the silent partner. Do not use this time to criticize the partner. Do not focus on the physical appearance of your partner, but rather on the nonverbal communication she or he is expressing while you are observing.

Pitfalls   This exercise is not intended to lead to an argument about whether the verbal partner is responding or understanding correctly; it should merely help the partners identify that they react to one another even when no words are involved. Furthermore, this exercise could be abused as a mind-reading game. Once again, that is not the purpose. Just try to learn as much about your partner and your own reactions as possible. This is not the time to challenge and fight, but to learn to trust and understand.

One more word of caution: Being observed while not being allowed to speak may tempt an individual to exaggerate certain movements or nonverbal expressions. Resist this impulse and attempt to behave as naturally as possible!

6 NONVERBAL FEELINGS PRACTICE: NUMBER ONE

Purpose   This exercise will help you gain awareness of how difficult it is to express feelings completely without words. More important, it will demonstrate how arduous it can be to read another person's feelings if that person does not use words to express them.

Benefit   Sometimes people will say one thing but really feel something else, and usually this difference is communicated in their nonverbal behavior. Lack of awareness of this discrepancy can lead to misunderstandings with others, who may be aware that what you are saying and feeling are not the same. Sometimes people think they can read other people's emotions by looking at their faces. Be careful, it is not that easy and can actually be dangerous because you may draw the wrong conclusions. Finally, sometimes we express a feeling nonverbally and expect others to understand it. Realizing that this may not be an easy task for them helps prevent many fights among couples who expect their partners to be able to do such mind reading.

Directions   **Step One:** At the end of this exercise, you will find a list of feelings. Write each word on a separate 3″ × 5″ piece of paper, so that each "feeling card" represents one feeling. Select one partner to become the actor and to go first. This actor then selects one of the feeling slips, without the other person seeing which one it is.

Step Two: The actor's task is to try to express that feeling without words as naturally as possible, but without exaggeration, using all relevant facial expressions, gestures, or body posture.

Step Three: The observer tries to guess the feeling the actor is attempting to express. When the observer has guessed the feeling correctly, switch roles and start over.

Step Four: If the observer has not guessed the feeling correctly within 2 to 3 minutes, the actor finally tells the partner what the feeling was, and then the actor and observer switch roles.

Duration and Frequency   This exercise should last no more than 2 to 3 minutes for the selection of the feeling and the first expression per turn. Repeat this exercise for all the feelings on the list. You will need approximately 10 to 20 minutes to complete the entire exercise.

Suggestions   Before starting, you may want to add some of your own feelings to the list provided. In doing this exercise, try to be as realistic as possible when it is your turn to express a feeling. In other words,

13

do not exaggerate it, but rather express it as you think you would if you were really feeling this emotion. When it is your turn to guess the feeling, just do your best. Remember, the purpose of this exercise is to help both of you realize how difficult it is to read feelings without the help of words. Thus, if you cannot guess a feeling your partner is expressing, that inability is perfectly understandable, in fact even expected. Save the slips of paper for future exercises.

Pitfalls   Do not use this exercise to chastise your partner for not being able to read your emotions. Do not expect her or him to be a mind reader. Be careful not to turn this into a competition to see who can guess the most feelings correctly. Remember, this exercise is designed to demonstrate how unfair it is to expect others to know your feelings when you are not using words.

LIST OF FEELINGS

sadness	*delight*
jealousy	*grief*
anxiety	*love*
shock	*pain*
joy	*panic*
distress	*anger*
pity	*surprise*
fear	*compassion*
disappointment	*guilt*
happiness	*impatience*
frustration	*exhilaration*
affection	*boredom*
hysteria	*loneliness*

7 NONVERBAL FEELINGS PRACTICE: NUMBER TWO

Purpose

This exercise will further increase your awareness of how you and your partner express feelings without the use of words. It is not intended to teach you how to read each other's mind, but rather to help you gain a better understanding of your partner.

Benefit

Although it is usually not a good idea to expect your partner to be able to read your emotions, there are some situations in which it helps if the two of you can communicate feelings without words. This ability also helps the two of you feel closer to one another because it shows that you know each other so well that at times you can communicate without words.

Prerequisite

"Nonverbal Feelings Practice: Number One"

Directions

Step One: In this exercise, you will use the feeling cards from "Nonverbal Feelings Practice: Number One." Select one partner to start the exercise. This partner chooses a feeling slip that represents a feeling that she or he often experiences. Share this feeling slip with your partner.

Step Two: The partner who selected the feeling slip now tries to express that feeling without words, using only facial expressions, gestures, or body posture. This partner should try to express the feeling in the same way she or he expresses the feeling when really experiencing it.

Step Three: The other partner's task is to observe and try to remember how the other person expresses the feeling when not using words.

Step Four: When the observing partner feels confident that she or he understands how the expressing partner shows the chosen emotion, switch roles and repeat steps 1 to 3.

Duration and Frequency

This exercise should last approximately 5 minutes per turn, including selecting the feeling and expressing it. Repeat this exercise for all the feelings that each partner often experiences. The repetitions do not all have to be made on the same day; however, they should occur no more than 3 days apart. Each repetition should take approximately 5 minutes or less per turn.

Suggestions

In doing this exercise, try to be as realistic as possible when it is your turn to express a feeling. In other words, do not exaggerate it, but rather express it as you think you would if you were really feeling this emotion. Realistic expression is important because you are trying to teach your partner what to look for in the future.

Pitfalls Do not use this exercise to justify your expectation that your partner should always know what you are feeling. This practice is for the few times when it is impossible for you to say aloud what is going on inside you, for instance when too many other people are around, or when you are so upset you cannot speak. Never expect your partner to be a mind reader.

8 NONVERBAL FEELINGS EXPRESSION

Purpose   This exercise is designed as an extension of "Nonverbal Feelings Practice: Number Two." Its purpose is to help you determine whether you were able to identify your partner's nonverbal expression of particular emotions. It will also provide additional practice in understanding nonverbal expression.

Benefit   Practice makes perfect: With this exercise you will practice better mutual understanding and you will feel closer to one another as you realize that you can indeed communicate without words. It is an exciting feeling to realize that you can know another person that well.

Prerequisites   "Nonverbal Feelings Practice: Number One"
"Nonverbal Feelings Practice: Number Two"

Directions   **Step One:** Select one partner to start the exercise. Without the use of the slips of paper, this partner needs to choose a feeling that she or he has experienced at least occasionally while with the other partner. Without using words, express this feeling to the other partner, just as you did in previous exercises.

Step Two: The other partner now tries to identify the feeling and has to keep trying until she or he does so correctly, or until 3 to 4 minutes have passed.

Step Three: Switch roles and start over.

Duration and Frequency   This exercise should last approximately 5 minutes for the first selection of the feeling and the first expression, per turn. Repeat this exercise for as many feelings as are likely to be expressed in the relationship. The repetitions do not all have to be made on the same day; however, they should occur no more than 3 days apart. Each repetition should take approximately 3 to 4 minutes or less per turn.

Suggestions   When expressing a feeling, try to be as realistic as possible and express it in the way you usually do. At first, select feelings that you experience often in the company of your partner.

Pitfalls   Do not turn this into a competition in which you try to stump your partner or try to make correct guesses. Under no circumstances should either of you get angry at the other for not guessing correctly. This is the responsibility of both of you: If one cannot guess correctly, it could well be because the other does not express the feeling clearly enough. Remember that neither of you is a mind reader.

9 WATCHING OTHERS: NONVERBAL

Purpose This exercise will help increase your awareness of other people's body language and how much information is conveyed nonverbally. Knowledge of nonverbal communication through body language will help you communicate more effectively with your partner.

Benefit All kinds of information is conveyed by a person's body language. Often this nonverbal communication is the most honest form of communication between two people. By increasing your awareness and interpretation skills of this form of communication, you will gain greater sensitivity to and awareness of your partner's feelings. This, in turn, will lead to increased and more accurate communication between the two of you.

Prerequisites "Nonverbal Feelings Practice: Number One"
"Nonverbal Feelings Practice: Number Two"

Directions **Step One:** With your partner, begin to observe people in various situations: at a shopping mall, at work, on television, and so on. Together, identify one person to whom you pay particular attention. Pay close attention to the person's gestures, facial expressions, and body posture. Focus on the person's carriage and the "vibes" she or he radiates. As you observe, try to imagine or guess how the person feels about herself or himself and other people. Try to identify what cues conveyed these feelings.

Step Two: After a few minutes of observing, share with your partner your impressions of the person and what cues led you to these impressions. Discuss with your partner how your own body language compares or contrasts with what you observed.

Step Three: Repeat steps 1 and 2 as often as time permits.

Duration and Frequency There is no time limit for this exercise; anywhere from 5 to 45 minutes is appropriate. It may be repeated as often as you like.

Suggestions When out in public, at the beach, or in other similar locations, just relax and watch people as they go by. When you discuss your interpretation with your partner, do so quietly and go on. Do not try to convince each other. Also be aware of possible cultural differences in behavior patterns. You may want to begin doing this exercise by yourself as well. In this case, just as when you do the exercise with your partner, the goal is to focus on body language and what it might communicate. Try to relate the knowledge you gain from this exercise to your partner's and your own body language and what it may communicate.

Pitfalls   Avoid becoming frustrated by trying to observe too many people at one time. Instead, focus on one person at a time. When discussing with your partner, avoid trying to convince one another about the messages that the person's body language may communicate. The goal is to increase your general awareness of nonverbal communication, not to achieve consensus about the communication. In fact, it is likely that if you disagree about its meaning, neither of you is correct!

10   *I HAVE FEELINGS: NONVERBAL*

Purpose

This exercise is designed to help make you more aware of the feelings and emotions you yourself tend to experience.

Benefit

Perhaps the cornerstone of intimate communication is the ability and willingness to share one's inner thoughts and feelings. For most people, a major difficulty in attaining this level of communication with a partner is the inability to identify one's own feelings and emotions accurately. Thus, an important beginning is to take time to recognize the feelings that we ourselves tend to experience. The recognition and awareness of your own feelings can lead to greater self-awareness and more intimate communication in your relationship.

Directions

Step One: This exercise is to be completed individually by each partner. At regular intervals throughout the day, for example, once each hour, take a few minutes to review what is going on within your body and mind. Do this also after any specific situation or event in which you are aware of experiencing strong feelings or emotions.

Step Two: Focus on what you are feeling at any chosen moment, both physically and emotionally. At this point, do not worry about the accuracy of the label you decide to attach to the feeling or emotion; focus more on recognizing the physical or bodily experience of the feeling. If you are focusing on your feelings that arose in response to a specific event or situation, try to make a linkage between the event and the feeling you identified.

Step Three: At the end of the week, review the different feelings you experienced during this period of self-focusing. Examine the events that evoked your emotions during this time.

Duration and Frequency

This exercise should be carried out several times daily for 1 week. It may be repeated as necessary or desired.

Suggestions

Try to go through your day in the usual routine, but identify a regular time to focus your attention on your inner self. One possibility is to use the top of every hour to focus on yourself. Another good time to focus on your inner self is immediately after an event or situation in which you experienced strong feelings. Wait until you have privacy to pay attention to your feelings, but do not wait too long until after the event. If you experience difficulty choosing a label for your feelings, just listen to what your body communicates—perhaps your stomach hurts or your hands are shaking. Awareness of physical reactions is as, if not more, important as attaching a label to the emotion. The idea is to understand that you do have feelings and when you have them, not necessarily to find the perfect word to label them.

Pitfalls   Do not be discouraged by an absence of feelings or difficulty in recognizing and labeling feelings. Even if it seems as if you did not have any feelings, continue to do this exercise a few times and pay close attention to your bodily reactions. Do not be too quick to put a label on the emotions you experience.

11 *LABELS FOR FEELINGS: NONVERBAL*

Purpose   Once you are aware of your feelings and emotions and the events and situations that are likely to evoke them, it is helpful for communication to give a name to those feelings. This exercise is designed to help in this identification process.

Benefit   True intimacy between two people depends on the ability to share one's inner self with another. Before one is able truly to share this inner self with another, one needs to have an awareness of the feelings and thoughts that are experienced. Awareness of feelings and emotions is facilitated by the ability to recognize, identify, and label one's own feelings and emotions. Being able to label feelings is also helpful in the communication of feelings with another person.

Prerequisites   "Nonverbal Feelings Practice: Number One"
"Nonverbal Feelings Practice: Number Two"
"I Have Feelings: Nonverbal"

Directions   **Step One:** As with "I Have Feelings: Nonverbal," this exercise is to be completed individually by each partner. The first step is to become aware of and recognize the presence of your feelings and emotions. To accomplish this, as in the prior exercise, focus your attention on your body and mind. This could be at any time, or after an event or situation that evoked strong feelings.

Step Two: Once you are aware of the presence of feelings, examine the predominant emotion and try to give it a name. At first, it may be helpful to use the feeling cards from the "Nonverbal Feelings Practice: Number One" exercise to help you find labels for your feelings. Check each card until you find the one that best describes how you feel. If you cannot find an appropriate label and are unable to label the feeling yourself, you may want to wait for another feeling to emerge to complete this exercise.

Step Three: Repeat this exercise as often as possible and for as many feelings as you are able to recognize and experience. At the end of the day, review the emotions you have experienced and were able to label. This process will help you identify feelings in the future with greater speed and accuracy.

Duration and Frequency   Practice this exercise several times daily for 1 week, trying to recognize, identify, and label as many feelings as possible. This exercise can be repeated as often and for as long as you feel comfortable.

Suggestions   The purpose of this exercise is to have you look closely at your inner world. At this point, it is not necessary to share what you have learned with your partner. Indeed, for many people, this would make the exercise too threatening or difficult. Continue to practice this exercise until you can quickly and easily identify and label each feeling and emotion as you experience it.

Pitfalls   Many people have difficulty looking inward at their feelings. Often they are afraid of the feelings or have learned over the years to ignore or push them away. If you find it hard to examine your feelings closely, you may be tempted to quit. Try not to give in to this temptation, but instead push yourself to examine your feelings. Also, some people will not be able to differentiate carefully among various feelings and seemingly experience only a few feelings. It is important to keep looking inward to identify and label feelings and to discriminate among feelings.

12 AUTOMATIC NONVERBAL FEELINGS EXPRESSION

Purpose This exercise will help you learn more about your own nonverbal expressions and about how your partner interprets them.

Benefit Often we express a feeling nonverbally, and to us it is very clear what we are expressing. As a result, we expect others around us to recognize and understand the feeling we thought we expressed so clearly. However, sometimes the other person misreads what you expressed and you may feel hurt, let down, or misunderstood. This exercise will demonstrate how your expressions of feelings come across to your partner and will help clear up misunderstandings in this area.

Directions **Step One:** Select one partner (imitator) to start this exercise. This partner chooses a nonverbal expression that the *other* partner (observer) frequently demonstrates. The imitator then tries to duplicate that nonverbal expression.

Step Two: The observer watches and tries to identify the feeling that the imitator is expressing through nonverbal behavior. After identifying the feeling, the observer shares what the expression means and what it is like to experience that feeling.

Step Three: The imitator then discusses whether this is how she or he had interpreted and understood this expression in the past.

Step Four: Switch roles and repeat steps 1 to 3.

Duration and Frequency The entire exercise (one turn each) should take about half an hour, depending on whether there is consensus about the feeling expressed by the nonverbal behavior. Repeat the exercise as many times as there are typical nonverbal expressions for each partner. The repetitions do not need to take place on the same day, but should occur within 3 days of each other.

Suggestions Move from the most commonly or frequently expressed feelings to less likely ones. Try to capture all aspects of the nonverbal demonstration of the feeling.

Pitfalls Do not use this exercise to make fun of your partner, and do not imitate the nonverbal expressions in a sarcastic, exaggerated, or aggressive manner. Try not to challenge your partner's explanation of the expression; instead believe what the partner tells you the expression is intended to communicate.

13 *NONVERBAL NEEDS PRACTICE*

Purpose
This exercise will help raise your awareness about how difficult it is to express a need nonverbally. Although communicating feelings through nonverbal means can work well, expressing your needs without words is extremely difficult, if not impossible.

Benefit
This exercise will help you realize how difficult it is for your partner to figure out what you need if you do not verbalize that need directly. It helps you realize that although your needs may be clear to you, they may not be clear at all to your partner unless you talk about them.

Prerequisites
"Nonverbal Feelings Practice: Number Two"

"Nonverbal Feelings Expression"

Directions
Step One: Select one partner to start the exercise. This partner chooses a need from the list at the end of this exercise, and tries to express this need to the other person without using words. Add your own needs that may not be included in the list.

Step Two: Express the need through nonverbal communication, using gestures, facial expressions, and body posture. Do not use any words at all.

Step Three: The other partner observes the nonverbal expression of need and tries to guess what need is being conveyed.

Step Four: Switch roles and repeat steps 1 to 3.

Duration and Frequency
This exercise should last approximately 5 minutes for the selection and expression of the need, per turn. Repeat this exercise for all the needs on the list. You can add some of your own needs to the list. The repetitions do not all have to be made on the same day; however, they should occur no more than 3 days apart. Each repetition should take approximately 3 minutes or less per turn.

Suggestions
Be sure to choose at least one need from the list that is a need you commonly perceive within yourself.

Pitfalls
Do not mistake this as an exercise in learning how to detect your partner's needs from nonverbal expression. The intent is just the opposite: Use this exercise to become aware of how difficult, if not impossible, it is to know your partner's needs without verbal

communication. Do not criticize one another's needs choices or expressions.

LIST OF NEEDS

need for praise	*need for help*
need for feedback	*need for affection*
need for attention	*need for* _____
need for company	*need for* _____
need for solitude	*need for* _____

14 NONVERBAL TOUCHING: PART ONE

Purpose   This exercise will help you learn more about what feels good to you. It will also help you to become more comfortable with your own body.

Benefit   Often people believe that they know exactly what their partner likes and dislikes. In many cases they are correct, but sometimes they make faulty assumptions. Many people also believe that they know everything about their partner and have little or nothing else to learn. By exploring with your partner what she or he physically enjoys, you will get to know your partner in a unique and special way. This exercise will be an opportunity to get to know your partner physically without the pressures that often accompany lovemaking.

By becoming more aware of your partner's sensitive body areas, you will learn a nonsexual way of giving your partner pleasure through touch. This touching can be a very important way to communicate with your partner nonverbally because it conveys affection and love. You will also learn more about your own body areas that you enjoy having touched.

Directions   **Step One:** Choose a comfortable and private location where you will not be disturbed by others. Select a partner to be the receiver and the other to be the giver.

Step Two: The receiving partner lies or sits down comfortably on a chair, couch, or bed and closes her or his eyes. The other partner then gently puts her or his fingertips on different areas of the receiving partner's body. Begin at the top of the head or at the feet and then proceed up or down the body. Do not spend too much time focusing on any one part of the body.

Step Three: As the receiver, be aware of how touch on each part of your body affects you both physically and emotionally. If you feel uncomfortable with a spot being touched, move your partner's hand to another part of your body. The giver is supposed to explore the receiver's body gently with the fingertips, simply moving from one part of the body to another. During this exercise, neither partner is allowed to speak.

Step Four: After 5 to 10 minutes, switch roles and repeat steps 2 and 3.

Duration and Frequency This exercise should take about 15 to 20 minutes to complete. It can be repeated as frequently as both partners wish to participate.

Suggestions At least during the first time, do this exercise with both partners fully clothed. After several repetitions, you may feel more secure and relaxed, and either or both of you may wish to remove some or all of your clothing. Remember, different parts of the face and back may be very sensitive to the touch. This exercise may be sexually stimulating; it is best to refrain from sex during this exercise, however.

Pitfalls It is important to be very gentle in your touch. Remember to stroke your partner's body merely with your fingertips. The goal is for your partner to learn of the areas that are enjoyable to be touched. Do not use this exercise as an opportunity to stimulate your partner sexually. This will only neutralize the exercise and may result in an argument. Be sure to respect your partner's desires if she or he moves your hand from a certain spot. Do not get angry if your hand is moved; later you will be given an opportunity to discuss it. Try not to become embarrassed, and take your time with this exercise.

15 NONVERBAL TOUCHING: PART TWO

Purpose   This exercise helps you gain further understanding about the nonverbal language and messages of touching.

Benefit   Through this exercise you will come to understand how your partner expresses her or his feelings and needs without verbalization, merely through physical contact using the hands. It will help you understand that your partner at times attempts to communicate with you nonverbally when touching you. Thus, for instance, a quick kiss on the cheek may communicate, "I love you but I am busy right now," whereas a long kiss on the mouth may indicate, "I love you and I feel very close to you right now."

Prerequisites   "Nonverbal Feelings Practice: Number One"
"Nonverbal Feelings Practice: Number Two"
"Nonverbal Touching: Part One"

Directions   **Step One:** Use the feeling cards you prepared in "Nonverbal Feelings Practice: Number One" in this section, and add any new cards that express other needs or desires you tend to experience with your partner. For instance, you may develop cards that indicate that you wish your partner to give you a kiss, a cuddle, sex, and so on. Other cards may contain messages such as a request for delay of intimacy, immediate reassurance, or more patience. Shuffle the cards and choose one partner to be the "giver," and the other to be the "receiver."

Step Two: The giver selects a card and, using only her or his hands, tries to communicate the feeling or desire written on the card by touching the partner.

Step Three: If the receiver guesses the expressed need or emotion correctly, switch roles. If the receiver is unable to guess correctly within 3 to 4 minutes, the giver reveals the content of the card and you switch roles.

Step Four: After you have switched roles three times, stop and discuss what you have learned about each other.

Duration and Frequency   It will take about 30 minutes to complete this exercise, which should be repeated several times over the course of several days.

Suggestions   The receiver is best served by this exercise if she or he relaxes and enjoys the sensations this exercise produces. Nevertheless, the receiver needs to be aware enough of the giver to be able to distinguish the different emotions and needs expressed in the giver's touch. The giver must be gentle regardless of the message being expressed. If the shuffling of the cards resulted in the giver's receiving a feeling or need that feels incompatible with her or his current state, the giver is allowed to draw a new card. This exercise must feel comfortable for both partners to produce the desired benefit.

Pitfalls   It is important that both giver and receiver avoid using words (beyond the guesses the receiver has to make) while the giver is touching. Complaints about how the giver expresses feelings or needs through touch are not allowed at this time. This exercise is intended for the two partners to learn how the other communicates through touch, not to critique how she or he chooses to do so. Obviously, however, the expression must never be painful or extremely uncomfortable for the receiver.

16 *NONVERBAL TOUCHING: DISCUSSION*

Purpose   This exercise will help you become aware of which body areas your partner finds enjoyable to have touched. It will provide both of you with a nonsexual way to give each other pleasure.

Benefit   Sometimes it is challenging for partners to share feelings with one another. One reason for the inability or unwillingness to communicate is that many people believe that their partner should know something without having to be told. This type of reasoning can lead to misunderstandings and arguments. Instead, it is important to communicate to your partner what you like and dislike. In this way, your partner will get to know you better and will be able to be more responsive to you in the future.

Often the difficulty in communicating is complicated when it involves the giving and receiving of pleasure from one another. Some people are too uncomfortable or embarrassed to talk about these things, even with their partner. This, in turn, can lead to serious arguments and lack of trust in one another. By being able to share with your partner what you find pleasurable, she or he will be better able to meet your needs and to give you pleasure. This mutual sharing will lead to greater closeness and trust in the relationship.

Prerequisites   "Nonverbal Touching: Part One"
"Nonverbal Touching: Part Two"

Directions   **Step One:** Choose a comfortable and private location where you know you will not be disturbed by others or distracted from the exercise. Select a partner who will go first as the receiver; the other partner will be the giver.

Step Two: The receiving partner lies or sits down comfortably on a chair, couch, or bed and closes her or his eyes. Then, following the directions from "Nonverbal Touching: Part One," the other partner gently puts her or his fingertips on different areas of the receiving partner's body. Begin at the top of the head or at the feet and proceed up or down the body. Do not spend too much time focusing on any one part of the body.

Step Three: The receiver is to share her or his feelings as the exercise proceeds. As you are being touched, tell your partner what you like and what you do not like; what feels good, what does not feel good; what tickles, and so on. The giver is to explore the partner's body gently with the fingertips, simply moving from one part of the body to another. During this exercise, the giving partner is not allowed to speak.

Step Four: After 5 to 10 minutes, switch roles and repeat steps 2 and 3.

Duration and Frequency

This exercise should take about 15 to 20 minutes to complete and can be repeated as frequently as both partners wish to participate. In later repetitions, place more focus on parts of the body that your partner has told you feel good to be touched and less on areas from which the partner derived little or no pleasure.

Suggestions

The first time you do this exercise, neither rush nor linger on a particular spot, even if your partner likes it. Listen to what your partner says and accept it. If there is a part of the body your partner does not enjoy being touched, respect this and move on to another part of the body immediately.

Pitfalls

Be very gentle in your touch and stroke your partner's body lightly only with your fingertips. Listen carefully to what your partner tells you and under no circumstances criticize it. As the receiver, try not to become embarrassed and try to be as honest as you can about your feelings. Do not use this exercise as an opportunity to stimulate your partner sexually. This will only neutralize the exercise and may result in an argument.

17 *NONVERBAL EXPRESSION OF AFFECTION*

Purpose
This exercise will help you realize that affection can often be expressed better without words than with words. The exercise will help you see that nonverbal expressions of affection enhance your trust and the level of intimacy you feel and can be much more romantic than words can ever be.

Benefit
Expressing affection is very difficult for many people. Often we are afraid of saying something that the other person might not like or accept. The ability to express affection freely is crucial to a healthy relationship, however, and must be learned. This exercise begins to teach you how to express affection in the safest of all possible ways: without words. You will soon realize how good it feels to receive such affection. You will also be surprised about how nice it is to give it.

Directions
Step One: Choose a quiet location where you will not be disturbed or distracted. Lie or sit down comfortably next to each other and begin doing any number of behaviors and actions to express affection toward one another.

Step Two: Anything acceptable to both partners is allowed (e.g., touching, licking, cuddling, holding, kissing). During this exercise, keep your affections nonsexual. Do not talk at any time during this exercise, except to say that you want to end the exercise.

Duration and Frequency
This exercise should last no more than 15 minutes for the first time. After the first time, when you repeat the exercise, it can last as long as it is comfortable and desirable for both partners. Each partner has the right to call it quits at any time during the exercise, and the other partner must abide by this request immediately. This exercise can be repeated as often as desired by both partners, and can be done spontaneously at any time as long as both partners agree to it.

Suggestions
Do not attempt to do this exercise if you are angry with each other or if you have just had a fight that has not yet been settled. When engaging in the exercise, be as gentle and affectionate as possible. Both of you have the right to let your partner know if she or he is doing something you do not like, but do so without using words. Simply take your partner's hand and move it, and this will be the clue to try something different. It is best to do this exercise in a romantic atmosphere, in other words, dim the lights, use candles, sit on a soft couch or chair, or anything else that

works for you. However, the exercise will also work in almost any setting in which the two of you are alone.

Pitfalls   If you are not used to cuddling, touching, and caressing, this may be a tough exercise at first. Try it until it feels good. You may need to keep your first few sessions short if necessary. Never force your partner to do or endure anything she or he does not like. If your partner moves your hand, stop what you were doing and try something different. Do not give up on this exercise if it does not work right away. This can be a tough procedure, but it will be well worth the effort.

For many couples, expression of affection in this manner is difficult to differentiate from sex. At this point, do not have sex while doing this exercise.

18 *NONVERBAL LANGUAGE FOR SOCIAL SITUATIONS*

Purpose This exercise will allow you and your partner to develop a nonverbal signaling system that you can use in public and private situations to communicate immediate and important requests, desires, or commands.

Benefit Frequently in public situations, partners want to communicate privately. This exercise will allow you and your partner to evolve a signaling system so that you can communicate with your partner when needed without using spoken language. This agreed-upon signaling system can help partners avoid the pitfalls of mind reading because they will learn a private language both will come to be familiar with. Nevertheless, it is best reserved as a system for emergency nonverbal communication rather than one to replace verbal communication between partners.

Directions **Step One:** Sit down with your partner and devise specific and clearly recognizable nonverbal signs (e.g., a double blink with the left eye; scratching the right cheek with the left hand) to communicate needs, requests, or commands that tend to arise in situations where the verbal communication thereof may be uncomfortable or impractical. For instance, the following messages may be encoded nonverbally in this exercise: "I want to leave"; "Hello, I love you"; "I need help!"; "I want you"; and "Keep away!" Add any other situations you may need or want to the list.

Step Two: Prepare a written list of your new language and study and practice it for a week. After 1 week, evaluate its success and revise any signals that are awkward or cumbersome.

Step Three: Once you are comfortable with the signals you have developed, try them out in an actual social situation. Discuss the results of this trial and again make any necessary revisions.

Duration and Frequency Step 1 of the exercise should take only 10 to 20 minutes for the first session. Follow-ups as directed in steps 2 and 3 vary significantly in length depending on the success of the system developed in step 1.

Suggestions Keep the signals as simple as possible and as distinct from one another as is practical to avoid confusion. A special hand touch, finger sign, or eye signal may be best. Remind each other regularly of the signs, especially before the next few social engagements. Be aware that your partner may need some time to respond to your signal. It might be helpful to write down the signals and corresponding messages in case you want to refer back to them.

Pitfalls   Do not make the signals too complicated. You will probably make mistakes and misread signals a few times at first. Be patient with one another.

19 *AGGRESSIVE VERSUS ASSERTIVE: NONVERBAL*

Purpose
This exercise will increase your awareness of how your body language communicates feelings, particularly strong ones, to your partner.

Benefit
We do not always say what we really feel, but often our nonverbal expressions give us away. Mixed messages make for a poor exchange of information, so an awareness of your own body language will help make you a more effective communicator.

Prerequisite
"Observation of Expression"

Directions
Step One: Choose one person to be the actor and the other to be the listener.

Step Two: Decide on a situation that would cause you to be aggressive, for example, dealing with a rude salesperson, having to wait in line, or getting cut off in heavy traffic. Act out that situation without speaking.

Step Three: The listener pays close attention to the actor's stance, hand gestures, facial expressions, distance away from partner, and so on. The actor should also discern how the listener is reacting as this is going on.

Step Four: Now repeat steps 1 to 3, but act assertively rather than aggressively. If you are not clear about the difference between aggression and assertiveness, work with your counselor on this step of the exercise.

Step Five: Switch roles and repeat steps 1 to 4.

Duration and Frequency
This exercise generally takes between 20 to 30 minutes, allowing each person a chance to express both aggressive and assertive body language.

Suggestions
The selection of an appropriate situation is important and therefore may take some time. The actor should have the final say in the choice of situation because she or he is more likely to be most aware of her or his likely feelings in a given situation. Nevertheless, the situation preferably arouses a strong reaction in both partners.

Pitfalls
You may feel uncomfortable acting out the situation, but try to overcome your stage fright and concentrate on portraying your

feelings accurately. Situations that involve the partners' relationship are off limits for this exercise. This procedure serves to familiarize the partners with each other's aggressive and assertive body language, and it is not a good idea to address difficult emotions in the context of the relationship at this time. This is to be reserved for later exercises. If you have a tendency to be physically aggressive with one another, do not attempt this exercise without your counselor present.

20 *SAYING "NO" NONVERBALLY*

Purpose This exercise will develop your ability to say "no" by using hand gestures, facial expressions, and eye messages.

Benefit Often what we express verbally and what our body language indicates are not consistent, particularly when we are attempting to say "no." Intense sexual difficulties occur because a person may be saying "no," but the body language may be saying "yes" or vice versa. This exercise will highlight those body gestures that indicate agreement and those that express a strong refusal.

Directions **Step One:** Select one person to be the actor and the other to be the listener.

Step Two: The actor selects a situation that would cause her or him to say an emphatic "no." The "no" is then to be acted out nonverbally.

Step Three: The listener concentrates on the different gestures, expressions, and signals the actor is sending while saying "no." The listener should assess whether she or he truly believes the message that is supposed to be sent, in other words, evaluate the clarity of the nonverbal message.

Step Four: Discuss the episode with one another. The listener needs to share which particular gestures signaled a clear "no" and whether any particularly nonverbal signals resulted in an unclear message.

Step Five: Switch roles and repeat the exercise.

Duration and Frequency This exercise will take 20 to 30 minutes and should be repeated several times for different situations that differ in the level of emphasis about the "no" being expressed. The exercise may be repeated as often as desired or necessary.

Suggestions Be helpful to, not critical of, one another. As the listener, be sure to share your impressions about the clarity of the actor's "no" in a positive, noncritical manner. As the actor, you are not allowed to argue about the perceptions the listener expresses. Give her or him the benefit of the doubt: If the listener indicates that the message was unclear, believe it. If your partner misunderstood, other people are even more likely to do so. The actor does not have to (but may) share the imagined situation to which she or he is responding. This situation merely gives the actor an event to respond to in order to make the action of saying "no" more realistic.

Pitfalls   Take this exercise seriously and avoid teasing about your partner's performance. Do not argue about who is right or wrong. Again, do not choose situations that involve your current relationship. Instead choose neutral situations, perhaps work-related ones, that do not involve either partner in a personal or relationship-related way.

SECTION TWO *Verbal Communication*

EXERCISES

From the exercises in this section you will learn anew how to deal with one another on a verbal level. Verbal communication often becomes rigid and patterned out of habit. Partners respond to one another without carefully listening to each other and come to expect certain responses without checking out whether that was really what the other person intended. These exercises are designed to make verbal communication a more conscious and courteous process for both of you. They will not only teach you new speaking skills, but more important, the exercises will teach you how to listen to one another with respect and an open mind. Vicious cycles can thus be broken and more productive and caring means of verbal communication be established.

1 SIMPLE REFLECTION

Purpose   This exercise is designed to help you learn how to listen to another person actively. Doing this exercise will help you communicate that you have heard what the other person has said to you.

Benefit   Couples often think they know each other so well that they do not need to listen to one another closely because they already know what the partner is going to say. Although sometimes this may be true, usually this kind of attitude is dangerous. This exercise will help redirect you toward listening to your partner carefully.

Couples also often do not let each other know that they have heard or understood one another. This exercise teaches you one of the most basic ways of letting your partner know that you have heard what was said.

Directions   **Step One:** Select one partner as the "speaker," and one as the "reflector."

Step Two: The speaker expresses something aloud, such as a belief, a complaint, a problem, or a feeling. At this point, the speaker should keep it to one clear statement.

Step Three: When the speaker is finished, the reflector repeats word by word what the speaker has just said (e.g., "You said 'I am sometimes so tired when I come home from work that I would really like just to be left alone for an hour' "). Be sure not to add your own comments or judgments about the statement.

Step Four: Using the same statement, repeat steps 1 to 3 until the reflector has stated the speaker's point accurately.

Step Five: Using a few different statements, repeat steps 1 to 4 several times to give the reflector a chance to practice this new skill.

Step Six: Switch roles and repeat steps 1 to 5.

Duration and Frequency   This exercise should last at least 5 minutes per turn, for a total of 10 minutes. It should be repeated until the reflector accurately reflects back the speaker's statements. The exercise should be repeated for several days. It would also be a good exercise to choose if you want to refresh your memory later.

Suggestions   While you are the speaker, be honest in what you say—do not make anything up for the sake of saying something. By being honest, you will not only get the benefit of learning to hear and reflect each other, but you will truly learn something about your partner's feelings, beliefs, and attitudes. At the same time, try not to select statements that you know will anger your partner. Be accurate in your reflections when it comes time to take the reflector role. Be careful not to add your own comments or to pass judgment on the statement. This exercise may feel awkward, but it is designed as a building block for future exercises.

Pitfalls   At first, this exercise may seem phony because no one really reflects exactly what another person says. Remember, however, that the exercise is designed to help you learn a new skill. Just like when you learn any new skill, you start with an exaggerated version of what the end product will be like. If you are not used to giving each other this kind of attention, this exercise will be tough at first. Keep trying until it works, even if it takes several repetitions over several days. This exercise is an important stepping stone toward improving your verbal communication.

2 *ADVANCED REFLECTION*

Purpose   Like the "Simple Reflection" exercise, this exercise is designed to help you learn how to listen to another person and how to communicate that you have heard what the other person has said. This exercise, however, is designed to do this in the most realistic, practical, and useful manner possible.

Benefit   You will continue to reap the benefits of being able to listen actively and of learning how to let your partner know that you have heard. In this exercise, your partner will not only realize that you have heard, but that you are also beginning to understand clearly what she or he has said. This type of reflecting is the building block of verbal communication for any type of conversation, not only conversation with your partner. As such, you may find yourself beginning to use this technique successfully in many types of situations.

Prerequisite   "Simple Reflection"

Directions   **Step One:** Select one partner who will start the exercise as the "speaker"; the other partner will be the "reflector."

Step Two: Just as in "Simple Reflection," the speaker now is supposed to say something aloud, such as a belief, a problem, or a feeling. At this point, keep your expressions to one clear statement.

Step Three: This time when the speaker is finished, using her or his own words, the reflector repeats just the basic idea of what the speaker has said. In doing this, no longer repeat word by word, but rather express in your own words what you think you heard the speaker say (e.g., "I think what I am hearing you say is that sometimes you are so tired when you come home that you would just like to be left alone for a while").

Step Four: Repeat this task in the same roles several times until the reflector has become very good at capturing the speaker's idea.

Step Five: Switch roles and repeat steps 1 to 4.

Duration and Frequency   This exercise should last at least 5 minutes per turn, 10 minutes total. It should be repeated until the reflector has become very good at expressing the speaker's statement in her or his own words. This exercise is one of the most important ones to master well, and therefore should be repeated often for several days. It is one of the best exercises to practice again when you want to refresh your memory later.

Suggestions   Just as in "Simple Reflection," while you are the speaker, you need to be honest in what you say—do not make anything up for the sake of saying something. If you are honest, you will not only get the benefit of learning to hear and understand each other, but you will also learn much about your partner's true beliefs, feelings, and attitudes. Although the reflector needs to use her or his own words in the reflection this time, the feedback still needs to be accurate and can express only the speaker's original statement. Do not add your own ideas; merely use your own words.

Pitfalls   This exercise will feel much less phony than "Simple Reflection" because you are beginning to master a skill that is crucial in any situation involving people who speak to one another. However, it will be difficult and still will feel a little awkward at first. That is why it is so important to keep practicing this skill until it has become almost second nature. When you notice yourselves using this technique at times other than during your exercise, you will know that you have truly mastered it.

Not much can go wrong with this exercise, but be patient with one another. Although some people learn this skill very quickly, others need a little more time. With enough practice and encouragement, however, everybody can learn it. If one partner has a more difficult time than the other, rather than being critical of that person, try to help each other out.

3 EMPATHIC REFLECTION

Purpose
Like "Advanced Reflection," this exercise will continue to help you learn to listen, as well as to communicate that you have heard what the other person has said. However, this exercise adds an important element: You will learn how to listen empathically and how to become more aware of your partner's feelings and expressions.

Benefit
Being able to repeat your partner's verbal statements in your own words is an important skill that you will have mastered through the previous two exercises. The added component of becoming empathic and able to understand your partner's feelings will greatly enhance your communication as a couple as well as your level of intimacy. Empathy is the ability to understand what your partner is saying on an *emotional* level and from her or his point of view. It is the ability to take your partner's perspective, and it is the highest form of understanding. Developing mutual empathy is crucial to well-functioning relationships.

Prerequisites
"Simple Reflection"
"Advanced Reflection"

Directions
Step One: Select one partner as the "speaker," and one as the "reflector." Based on the previous two exercises, alternate who goes first as the speaker, that is, whoever went first as speaker in "Advanced Reflection" now starts as the reflector.

Step Two: As in the previous exercises, it is the speaker's task to express verbally a belief, a complaint, a problem, or a feeling.

Step Three: It is the reflector's task to repeat what the speaker has said. However, this time the reflector neither repeats word-for-word what has been said, nor merely expresses the speaker's basic ideas in different words. Instead, and this is much more difficult, the reflector repeats what the speaker said by adding her or his impression of the feeling (or need) that the reflector thinks accompanied the speaker's statement. This is called an "empathic reflection" and may be something like this: "I hear you saying that you feel exhausted when you come home from work and so worn out that you do not want any more demands placed on you when you're home."

Step Four: The speaker then needs to indicate if the reflector has perceived accurately. If not, the speaker should elaborate on the original statement and the reflector should try again. If the reflector was accurate, repeat steps 1 to 3 in the same roles.

Step Five: After successful completion of a second empathic repetition, switch roles and repeat steps 1 to 4.

Duration and Frequency

This exercise will last at least 10 minutes per turn, for a total of 20 minutes to complete the exercise. Be sure to not finish the exercise until both of you are reflecting your partner's feelings accurately. It is an exercise that needs to be repeated often.

This exercise is the best one to repeat occasionally even after you have moved on to more advanced exercises. It is the building block for most verbal communication tasks that will follow in your program.

Suggestions

As in the previous repetition exercises, when it is your turn to be the speaker, you need to be honest. However, keep in mind that in this exercise the repetition is much harder, so start with a feeling that is not too complicated or difficult to understand. As you repeat this exercise more often, you will not have to be concerned with how easy or difficult the speaker's statements are. The reflector should be able to handle most of them (but probably never all of them).

Pitfalls

Never expect always to be able to be completely empathic. Sometimes it is just too difficult. Do not turn this exercise into an expectation that both of you will always know exactly how the other feels or what the other needs.

This will be the most difficult exercise you will need to master in your entire program. Therefore, it is important that you feel very confident about having mastered this task before moving on to the next exercise. Moving on too soon may jeopardize your success because from now on most exercises will assume that you have mastered "Empathic Reflection."

4 ROADBLOCKS TO COMMUNICATION

Purpose This exercise was developed to help you determine your listening style and to identify things that you do that interfere with good listening skills. This will help you use better the reflecting skills you have learned from the previous three exercises by removing behaviors that get in the way of the practice of good listening. The exercise presents descriptions of the three most frequently used "helping attempts" when one person is listening to another. These three helping attempts often do just the opposite and become roadblocks to communication and listening. Thus, the exercise was designed to help you recognize your own use of these roadblocks so that you can learn to eliminate them from your communication with your partner.

Benefit Doing this exercise will help you become aware of how you listen to others, and how certain things you may do out of habit, or even helpfulness, get in the way of open and honest communication. This will ultimately improve your listening skills and will make you feel more at ease in situations where communication is important.

Prerequisites "Simple Reflection"
"Advanced Reflection"
"Empathic Reflection"

Directions **Step One:** Take a few moments to read the following descriptions of verbal exchanges or "helping attempts" that can occur between people and their related pitfalls or disadvantages:

1. Advising, giving solutions: "What I would do is . . ."; "Why don't you . . . ?"
   - can imply person is not able to solve own problems
   - can cause dependency or resistance

2. Probing and questioning: "Why . . .?"; "Who . . .?"; "How . . .?"
   - the person may feel judged or cross-examined
   - the person may not want to answer the question

3. Self-disclosure: "When this happened to me . . ."
   - taking focus of conversation away from the speaker
   - implies that the person's problems are unimportant

Step Two: Think of a recent communication with your partner that somehow was unsatisfactory or led to a fight. Think back to the

48

specifics that your partner was saying and to your own responses to these statements.

1. What did you say to your partner?
2. Did you show your partner that you were listening?
3. Attempt to identify the use of the roadblocks described in step 1 that you may have used during this interaction.

Step Three: Continue to explore your interactions with your partner, as well as with other people, according to how you respond to them and which roadblocks you may be using.

Step Four: Once you are certain that you have identified the one or two major roadblocks to communication that you use, try to avoid them in all subsequent interactions with your partner. Instead, use the skills you have learned in the previous three exercises in this section.

Duration and Frequency

This exercise does not depend on the presence of your partner and can therefore be done as often as you wish and in any situation. However, it is best to practice the exercise with your partner (the other person does not necessarily have to be aware of this) at least once a day for 1 week.

Suggestions

As you do this exercise, be aware of how you use the three roadblocks to communication and notice their effects on your attempts at active listening and reflection. You may also want to note where and when you use these roadblocks most commonly. In fact, it is not unlikely that you will find yourself using them especially often in emotionally charged situations, in other words, situations that do involve your partner.

Pitfalls

The main pitfall of this exercise is the inability on your part to recognize the roadblocks in your communication or to fail to notice their effects on communication with your partner, particularly in highly emotional situations. Refusing to look at the roadblocks can close doors to better communication.

5 *MY CONTRIBUTIONS*

Purpose

This exercise will give you an opportunity to tell your partner what you believe you contribute to your relationship. It will also give you a chance to hear of the things that your partner believes she or he contributes to the relationship.

Benefit

As a relationship matures, partners often come to take each other for granted. They tend to lose track of those things that the other partner contributes to the relationship and fail to acknowledge the importance or value of these contributions. This can lead to feelings of being neglected and not appreciated, and even to being angry and resentful. Also, when these contributions are taken for granted, a person can forget the many things that she or he is giving to the relationship. Consequently, the person can feel as though she or he is not doing enough; this may result in guilt and, eventually, anger. When both partners become aware of the contributions each makes to the relationship, they can regain an appreciation of one another and of themselves.

Directions

Step One: Both partners are to write down five ways in which they contribute to the relationship. For example, how do you contribute financially, emotionally, or through household tasks or parenting? Be honest in developing these lists and be specific in your statements.

Step Two: When you are both finished, exchange lists and read each other's lists.

Step Three: Each partner is to pick two of the five items on the other partner's list. It could be two that she or he completely agrees with, or any random two items.

Step Four: Taking turns, one partner states appreciation of the other partner's contribution in a format similar to the following: "I recognize that you _____ and I truly appreciate it." If you wish, you can improvise on the exact wording, but be careful to use the format.

Duration and Frequency

This exercise will take about 10 to 15 minutes to complete. It can be repeated as often as both partners wish. During repetitions, each partner should write down a new list of things that she or he contributes to the relationship.

Suggestions

When identifying your contributions, be honest with yourself and your partner. Try to be as specific as possible. Pick items from a variety of topics, including parenting, housework, or emotional, social, and financial contributions. Try not to place all of your items into one category. Be supportive of your partner and express true appreciation of her or his contributions to the relationship. You may want to save the lists that you develop in this exercise to help with future exercises.

Pitfalls   Do not use this as an opportunity to score points with your partner or to punish her or him. Do not put any hidden messages into your statements. For example, rather than, "I do *all* the housework," state, "I contribute to the relationship by doing a lot of the housework, such as doing the laundry and washing the dishes." Try to be specific about what you contribute—do not be vague. Avoid arguments about each other's contributions to the relationship. Do not argue with one another over the selection of items.

6 "I" MESSAGES

Purpose This exercise is designed to help you learn to take responsibility for your feelings, to help you stop blaming your partner for how you feel, and to learn about one another's feelings in a manner that is not defensive or argumentative. There are many tasks in this exercise, but they are closely related and best learned at the same time.

Benefit Often arguments occur between two people, especially partners in an intimate relationship, because one partner thinks that the other is to blame for her or his own feelings. However, most people fail to realize that they have control over how they feel and that others cannot make them feel a certain way. Learning to take responsibility for one's own feelings and stopping the blaming game will result in eliminating at least 50% of your arguments. Using "I" messages makes both of you more able to learn about the other's feelings without believing that you caused the feelings or that your partner is blaming you for how she or he feels. You will realize that eliminating blaming will make it much easier to talk about feelings and to learn about your partner.

Prerequisites "Simple Reflection"
"Advanced Reflection"
"Empathic Reflection"

Directions **Step One:** Select one partner to be the speaker and the other to be the listener.

Step Two: The speaker begins to talk about some feeling(s) she or he has about the relationship with the partner. But rather than saying, "You make me feel _____," the speaker says, "I feel _____ when you do/say _____."

Step Three: The listener's job is only to listen. At this point she or he does not respond to the feelings the speaker shares (you will learn how to problem-solve in a later exercise). In this exercise, just learn to use the phrase "I feel _____ when you do/say _____," instead of, "You make me feel. . . ." However, the listener can help the speaker if the speaker forgets to phrase things in terms of "I" messages (e.g., "Hold it, say 'I feel _____ when you _____,' not 'You make me feel _____' ").

Step Four: After approximately 3 minutes, switch roles.

Duration and Frequency	This exercise should last at least 3 minutes per turn, for a total of 6 minutes. You should repeat this exercise at least three times the first time you do this exercise. If you are doing very well with it, that might be enough. However, most people have a problem at first in using "I" messages. This exercise should be repeated several days in a row before you move on to the next exercise. Furthermore, this is a good exercise to repeat once you have moved on to more difficult exercises.

Suggestions

When you are the listener, pay close attention to your own reactions as the speaker speaks. Do you notice feeling less defensive when your partner says, "I feel angry when you read the paper at breakfast," rather than, "You make me so angry when you read the paper at breakfast"? What is the difference between these two statements? In the first, your partner merely states how she or he feels when you do one thing or another, without implying that you are causing the feeling. Somebody else might not get angry at all when you read the paper during breakfast. Maybe that is how everybody did it in your family. In the second statement, however, your partner is blaming you: "You *make* me angry." Your partner fails to realize that she or he has control over how to react to your newspaper habit. Being blamed for something is a sure way to begin feeling defensive and stands in the way of communication.

How would you respond to these two statements? You would be much more likely to start a fight after the "You make me angry" statement. You may respond with: "And you make me angry when you try to keep me from reading," and the fight is on. However, in response to the second statement, where you are not being blamed, you might say something like: "Oh, I did not know you were angry. I have always read the paper during breakfast. I am not doing it to make you angry." Now you are communicating. Problem solving would be the next step (do not worry, there will be an exercise for this).

Pitfalls

It is possible to disguise a blaming statement in what sounds like an "I" Message: "I feel angry *because* you read the paper during breakfast." Even though you are stating your feeling, you are still making the other person responsible for it. Therefore, avoid the "I feel _____ because _____" sequence.

7 POSITIVE "I" MESSAGES

Purpose This exercise is designed to help you apply what you learned in " 'I' Messages" in a manner that allows you to ask for what you want from your partner in a positive statement. The exercise helps you identify what you like and express this liking to your partner. Only if your partner knows what you like can that person respond and provide these things.

Benefit Being able to express what you like in a relationship or from a person in a positive manner, rather than through making demands, will help you get more satisfaction from the relationship. Furthermore, developing more appropriate ways to express positive wants and needs in your relationship will ultimately help you express concerns and disappointments better.

Prerequisites "Simple Reflection"

"Advanced Reflection"

"Empathic Reflection"

" 'I' Messages"

Directions **Step One:** Both partners should take a piece of paper and note several needs they experience in the relationship that are occasionally met by the partner, and that they appreciate about the partner. Careful preparation of this list of positive behaviors by the partner toward the self is very important and critical to the next step.

Step Two: Of the items on your list, choose one behavior of your partner that you like particularly. Then write down an "I" message that reflects this positive feeling about your partner. This message should reflect how positive you feel about your partner's behavior, and it implies that this is a behavior you would like the partner to engage in more often. For instance, you might write something like, "I like it and I feel loved when you hug me when I come home from work."

Step Three: Choose which partner should go first. Then take turns with the rest of this exercise.

Step Four: Read your positive "I" message to your partner; do not expect a response; certainly do not expect the partner to engage in the behavior you are praising. Merely tell the partner what it is you like. Then switch roles.

54

Duration and Frequency   When you first attempt this exercise you should reserve approximately 10 to 15 minutes to complete it. You should do this exercise only once at any given time. After you have practiced the exercise once and have developed a list of likes and wants, repetitions of the exercise will take only 2 to 3 minutes. This exercise can be repeated frequently, especially if it is clear to both partners that the positive "I" message is not a demand for the other partner to deliver the particular behavior that is being praised. The exercise may also be repeated spontaneously by one partner without expecting the other partner also to take a turn.

Suggestions   You must take the time and make the effort to recognize some things your partner does to you or with you that you really enjoy, and you must determine what you want from your partner. Do not discuss the content of the positive "I" messages; merely state your case and then switch roles. Keep your lists—they may be helpful in future exercises.

Pitfalls   In this exercise you need to take care not to be negative about your relationship. It is a pitfall to expect that the positive "I" message will always result in your partner's providing what it is that you like immediately. The positive "I" message is designed to communicate to your partner what you like, not to make a request of your partner. You will learn how to make requests later in this section.

8 TAKING TURNS: NONRELATIONSHIP ISSUES

Purpose
By having you place all your attention on your partner, this exercise will help you develop better listening skills. It will also give you an opportunity to experience what it is like to be truly listened to.

Benefit
When two people are talking with one another, much of what often occurs is not communication. The two people might be interrupting one another, finishing each other's sentences, not actively listening to what is said, getting ready to say something themselves, or thinking about something completely different. You will probably notice this when speaking with other people. You are thinking about what to say, or you will somehow take the focus off the other person and put it on yourself. Perhaps you will use what the other person says only as a launching pad for what you are going to say.

To communicate truly, two people need to listen to one another actively and carefully. This can be extremely difficult to do. However, because the ability to communicate well is a skill, it can be learned just like any other skill. The benefits of learning communication skills will go far beyond just helping your relationship, but will also help at work, with strangers and friends, and in other situations.

Directions
Step One: Select one partner to be the speaker and one partner to be the listener. Find two comfortable chairs and move them so they face one another. Sit comfortably across from each other.

Step Two: For the next 5 minutes (use a timer), the speaker shares an issue or feeling that is *not* related to the relationship. For example, the topic could be something that happened to you in the last week or could be about anything that has been on your mind recently.

Step Three: The listener just sits and listens; under no circumstances is the listener allowed to speak, no matter what the selected partner is talking about and no matter how emotional the listener's response is.

Step Four: After the 5 minutes are up, both of you need to get up and take a short break, about 5 minutes. Under no circumstances are you allowed to discuss anything that the speaker has brought up. In fact, it is best to not speak to one another during this break.

Step Five: After the 5-minute break, switch roles, and repeat steps 2 and 3. At this point, do not discuss anything that was brought up during either turn.

Duration and Frequency

This exercise will take approximately 15 minutes and should be done at least twice this week. The exercise can be repeated as often as both partners desire.

Suggestions

As speaker, select an issue or topic that may be of interest to your partner. Use an issue that your partner knows something about so you will not have to spend all your time giving background information. Be sure to select an issue that has personal meaning to yourself. As listener, focus carefully on what your partner is saying. Try to not become distracted with other thoughts. Be aware of how you are feeling both as speaker and as listener.

Pitfalls

The main danger is that the speaker might select a topic that is related to the relationship and may be difficult for the other partner to listen to without responding. Although it can be difficult just to listen for a long period of time, the success of this exercise depends on the listener's doing just that. Under no circumstances may the listener speak at this time.

9 *TAKING TURNS: DISCUSSION*

Purpose   This exercise builds upon the previous exercise to help you further develop more effective listening skills. It will give you an opportunity to give and receive feedback about what it is like to listen and be listened to.

Benefit   The continued practice and development of your listening skills will serve to enhance all relationships in your life. You will notice benefits from these skills almost immediately.

Prerequisite   "Taking Turns: Nonrelationship Issues"

Directions   These directions will be the same as in the previous exercise, with the exception of step 5.

Step One: Using the following procedure, select one partner to be the speaker and one partner to be the listener: The partner who started as the speaker in "Taking Turns: Nonrelationship Issues," will start this exercise as the listener and the other partner will be the speaker. Place two comfortable chairs across from one another and sit comfortably.

Step Two: For the next 5 minutes (use a timer), the speaker shares an issue or feeling that is *not* relevant to the relationship. Select a topic that was not used in "Taking Turns: Nonrelationship Issues." The listener's role is just to listen; she or he is not to speak at all.

Step Three: After the 5 minutes are up, both of you need to get up and take a short break, about 5 minutes. Do not discuss the topic that was brought up by the speaker.

Step Four: After the 5-minute break, switch speaker/listener roles, and repeat step 2.

Step Five: After both of you have had a turn, discuss with one another how it felt to listen and to be listened to. Focus on the experience of listening and being listened to, rather than the specific topic that was discussed.

Duration and Frequency   This exercise takes approximately 20 to 25 minutes and should be done twice in a 1-week period. Repetitions of the exercise are permitted as often as both partners wish.

Suggestions   As with the previous exercise, be sure to select an issue or topic that your partner might like to hear about and about which she or he has some background knowledge. As listener, remember to focus carefully on your partner and to not interrupt at all. While discussing the exercise, focus entirely on how you felt as listener or speaker. Do not discuss the content of what was said. That could result in arguments.

Pitfalls   Be sure to pick a topic or issue not related to the relationship. Otherwise, your partner may be too involved emotionally to listen carefully. As the listener, work hard on paying close attention to your partner and to not talk. Do not let yourself get distracted by other thoughts. A major pitfall also would be to focus on the content of what was said, rather than discussing how it felt merely to listen or to be listened to.

10 ADDING NONVERBAL CUES OF LISTENING

Purpose   This exercise continues to build on the listening skills learned and practiced in the prior two exercises. In this exercise, you will learn how to use nonverbal cues to enhance the communication between you and your partner.

Benefit   As you have learned in the previous section, nonverbal aspects of communication are critical. Indeed, some research suggests that up to 70% of all communication is through nonverbal means. By using nonverbal cues while listening, you will help your partner feel that she or he has your complete attention. This is another listening skill that will greatly benefit all relationships in your life.

Prerequisites   "Taking Turns: Nonrelationship Issues"
"Taking Turns: Discussion"

Directions   **Step One:** Select one partner to be the speaker and one to be the listener. Find two comfortable chairs and move them so they face one another. Sit comfortably across from each other.

Step Two: Using a timer set for 5 minutes, the speaker shares an issue or feeling that is *not* relevant to the relationship. Choose a topic that was not used in any previous exercise.

Step Three: The listener's role is to sit and listen without speaking whatsoever. As listener, be sure to add the following nonverbal cues of listening: (a) eye contact; (b) head nods every 30 seconds or as appropriate; (c) a smile every minute or as appropriate; and (d) a verbal "uh-huh" every 15 seconds or as appropriate.

Step Four: After the 5 minutes are up, both of you need to get up and take a short break, about 5 minutes. Under no circumstances are you allowed to discuss anything that the speaker brought up.

Step Five: After the 5-minute break, switch speaker/listener roles, and repeat steps 2 and 3.

Step Six: After both of you have had a turn, discuss how it felt to listen and to be listened to. Also discuss how the nonverbal cues felt both as listener and as speaker.

Duration and Frequency   This exercise should take about 15 to 20 minutes. It can be repeated as often as both partners like, but each repetition should be on a separate day.

Suggestions Remember to use only issues or concerns not related to your relationship. Be aware of how you feel when you are using nonverbal cues and when your partner is using them. Practice these nonverbal listening skills in several different situations, for example, at work, with friends, and with other family members.

Pitfalls At first you may feel awkward making nonverbal gestures. Keep at it—these nonverbal behaviors are crucial in demonstrating that you are actively listening to your partner.

11 TAKING TURNS: RELATIONSHIP ISSUES

Purpose This exercise is designed to improve your communication when it involves difficult topics. It helps break vicious cycles of communication (explained below), and is a good way for both partners to learn more about each other and about themselves.

Benefit Often couples have created what is commonly referred to as a "vicious cycle" of communication. What this refers to is the tendency to get caught in the same arguments over and over again and never to take the time to listen carefully to what the other partner is saying. What happens instead is that one partner will start complaining about something that she or he frequently complains about. The other partner, instead of letting the first partner finish the thought, will interrupt in self-defense and never give the partner the opportunity to finish her or his thought. The first partner then similarly interrupts, and the cycle of not listening and not allowing each other to finish thoughts continues. This cycle is extremely frustrating because neither partner ever gets to finish a thought without being interrupted and she or he has to keep bringing up this topic. As a result, the fight can continue literally for years.

This exercise breaks the vicious cycle by forcing you not to interrupt and to listen carefully to what your partner shares. Discussion is kept to a minimum. Sharing one's feelings and being able to finish sentences are the important goals in this exercise. Breaking vicious cycles is extremely important and one of the most necessary ingredients of better understanding and improved communication.

Prerequisites "Empathic Reflection"
" 'I' Messages"
"Taking Turns: Discussion"

Directions **Step One:** This exercise is spread out over 2 consecutive days. Before starting, set up a time on both days that is acceptable and convenient to both of you.

Step Two: Select one partner to be the speaker and one partner to be the listener. Sit facing each other in two comfortable chairs.

Step Three: For the next 5 minutes (use a timer), the speaker shares an issue or feeling that *is* relevant to the relationship.

Step Four: The listener is just to sit, listen, and not speak at all.

It is important for the listener not to interrupt, no matter what the selected partner is talking about and no matter how emotional the listener's response is.

Step Five: After the 5 minutes are up, both partners need to get up and go about their business. Under no circumstances are they allowed to discuss anything that the speaker brought up.

Step Six: On the second day, when your appointment time arrives, switch speaker/listener roles, and repeat steps 3 to 5. At this point, do not discuss anything that was brought up during either turn.

Duration and Frequency

Time spent each day will be no more than 5 minutes (excluding time spent to move chairs and select roles). The exercise can be repeated as often as the partners desire, but always requires a minimum of a 24-hour break before a repetition. This is an important exercise, so many repetitions are strongly encouraged.

Suggestions

Use this exercise wisely. For the speaker, it is a great opportunity to explore feelings and to share them with the partner, without being interrupted. For the listener, it is a chance to find out more about the partner without getting caught up in having to think of a clever response or defensive answer. Do this exercise often. The more often you do it, the more you will benefit.

Pitfalls

The worst thing the speaker could do with this exercise is to use the time to engage in partner bashing. It is not the purpose of the uninterrupted speaking time to criticize and humiliate your partner. It is time to speak about your own feelings, concerns, and attitudes about your relationship with your partner. This may include some negative comments about your partner, but remember to use "I" messages.

The worst thing the listener could do with this exercise is to break the silence. Remember, the exercise is intended to break vicious cycles in your communication patterns.

12 TAKING TURNS: MUTUAL SHARING

Purpose This exercise builds on the previous exercise by giving each partner a chance to discuss a topic without any interruption by the other partner. This process will help break the vicious cycles of communication that become habitual in a long-term, intimate relationship.

Benefit Often during arguments, couples will not truly listen to one another. Instead, each partner is too preoccupied with arguing her or his own point and being angry or defensive to listen to what the other partner is saying. If this vicious cycle can be broken in the middle of a discussion, then true communication and dialogue can be established.

Prerequisite "Taking Turns: Relationship Issues"

Directions **Step One:** As with "Taking Turns: Relationship Issues," this exercise is to be conducted over 2 consecutive days. Be sure to settle on two times that are acceptable for both of you.

Step Two: Using the following procedure, select one partner to be the speaker and one partner to be the listener: The partner who started as the speaker in "Taking Turns: Relationship Issues" will start this exercise as the listener, and the other partner will be the speaker. Place two comfortable chairs across from one another and sit comfortably.

Step Three: For the next 5 minutes (use a timer), the speaker is to share an issue or feeling that is relevant to the relationship. Try to choose a topic that is different than the one used in "Taking Turns: Relationship Issues."

Step Four: While the speaker talks, the listener is not to interrupt at all. She or he should just sit and listen without saying a word. After the 5 minutes are up, take a 10-minute break during which the two of you do not interact.

Step Five: After the break, switch roles and for 5 minutes (use a timer) the partner who was the listener gets a chance to respond to what the other person has shared. The other partner is just to listen and not speak at all.

Step Six: After 5 minutes are up, both of you need to get up and go about your business. Under no circumstances should you discuss anything brought up by either speaker or listener.

Step Seven: On the second day, when your appointment time arrives, the partner who started the exercise the day before as speaker becomes the listener and the other partner becomes the speaker. The speaker can continue the discussion from the prior day or start with a new issue or feeling. Repeat steps 3 to 6.

Duration and Frequency

The duration of the exercise for each day should be no longer than 20 minutes (5 minutes for each partner's discussion and 10 minutes for a break). The exercise can be repeated as often as the partners desire, but always requires a minimum of a 24-hour break before a repetition. Repeating this exercise several times is strongly encouraged. Furthermore, using the structure of this exercise is a good approach to use any time the two of you disagree on something.

Suggestions

Try to keep your cool during this exercise and be sure to listen carefully to your partner. This is not the time to solve the problem, just the time to listen to how your partner feels about the problem. As speaker, try not to provoke your partner with blame or accusations. Use "I" messages and be sure to own your feelings. As listener, remember just to listen and do not speak. Use the skills that you learned in the previous exercises, including reflection and empathy. Try to keep an open mind as you listen to your partner. Try putting yourself in her or his shoes and experience the situation from your partner's perspective.

Pitfalls

A danger of this exercise is the speaker's using the time to blame or provoke the listener. Remember that you are sharing your feelings and experiences, and that you are largely in control of how you feel. As speaker, just share how you feel and what you think about the situation without any blame or accusations and without trying to solve the problem. As listener, it may be difficult to hear your partner due to feelings of anger or defensiveness. Perhaps the speaker has brought up something that has been discussed time and time again. But remember that your partner would not have brought it up if it was not important to her or him; try to respect this by giving the topic your complete attention.

13 *I AM ANGRY (HOW ELSE DO I FEEL?)*

Purpose

This exercise will help you learn how to express your true feelings to your partner. It will give you an opportunity to learn how to listen to your partner as she or he shares feelings.

Benefit

One of the most difficult things partners face in a relationship is the honest communication of feelings. It can be risky to share your feelings because it puts you in a vulnerable position. But it is through honest sharing of feelings that trust develops and intimacy grows.

Prerequisites

"Taking Turns: Relationship Issues"
"Taking Turns: Mutual Sharing"

Directions

Step One: Select one partner to start the exercise. This partner will be the speaker and the other partner will be the listener.

Step Two: The speaker is to share a situation or occasion in which she or he felt angry. Be sure to choose a situation that is *not* connected to the relationship. The listener's role is only to listen to everything the speaker says.

Step Three: When the speaker is finished, the listener responds by asking, "How else did you feel?" The speaker then identifies and shares other feelings, while the listener just listens.

Step Four: When the speaker is finished, switch roles and repeat steps 1 to 3.

Step Five: When both partners are finished, discuss the exercise and how each of you felt both as speaker and listener.

Duration and Frequency

This exercise will take about 5 to 10 minutes for each partner's turn. It is an exercise that should be repeated several times before moving on to other exercises. When you repeat this exercise, be sure to do each repetition on a separate day.

Suggestions

Pay close attention to your partner when she or he is expressing feelings. Look at any verbal and nonverbal cues that reflect the partner's feelings. Be aware of how you are feeling when you share your feelings as well as when you listen to your partner share feelings. Use this as an opportunity to learn more about your partner, including what makes her or him angry. When you discuss the exercise, focus *only* on how you felt when you listened and talked. Do not focus on the actual problem the partner talked about. The important thing in this exercise is not the problem, but how the two of you communicate.

Pitfalls   When you are the listener, be careful to not get involved in what your partner is angry about. Do not argue with your partner about the problem. The goal is to learn how you communicate, not to solve a problem or start an argument. Be sure to pick a problem that does *not* involve your partner. This is not the time to share any feelings of anger you may have toward your partner. For this exercise, pick a situation that is completely separate from your relationship. Avoid responding to the problem area, and be careful to avoid using the roadblocks to communication identified in an earlier exercise.

14 *I AM ANGRY (HOW ELSE DO I FEEL?): RELATIONSHIP*

Purpose This exercise builds on the previous exercise by helping you learn how to express your true feelings about your relationship to your partner. It will also give you an opportunity to learn how to listen truly to your partner as she or he shares feelings about the relationship.

Benefit One of the most difficult emotions for people to share with one another is anger. It becomes even more difficult to share when the anger is over something that happened in the relationship. Some believe that expressions of anger in an intimate relationship indicate the absence of love; others believe that when anger is expressed, it will ruin the relationship; and still others believe that to prevent arguments, you should hide all feelings of anger from your partner.

The truth is that it is important to share the full range of your feelings with your partner, including anger. However, just as when airing all feelings, expressing anger needs to be done in a constructive, nonaccusatory manner. A person needs to recognize personal feelings as her or his own responsibility, rather than placing blame on the partner. When you are able to express the full range of feelings with your partner constructively, you will be able to experience a deep, intimate relationship. Similarly, it is crucial that you be able to listen to your partner's full range of feelings.

Prerequisite "I Am Angry (How Else Do I Feel?)"

Directions **Step One:** One partner will be designated to start the exercise as the speaker, and the other partner will be the listener. The partner who starts this exercise as the speaker should be the one who started the prior exercise as listener.

Step Two: The speaker is to share a situation or occasion in which she or he felt angry. In this exercise, choose a situation that *is* connected to the relationship. The listener's role is only to listen to everything the speaker says.

Step Three: When the speaker has finished talking, the listener responds by asking, "How else did you feel?" The speaker then has the opportunity to share any other emotions with the listener.

Step Four: After 5 minutes are up, both of you need to get up and take a short break, about 5 minutes. Under no circumstances should you discuss anything that the speaker brought up. In fact, it is best to not speak to one another during this break.

Step Five: After the break, switch roles and repeat steps 1 to 4. After the second break, discuss the exercise and share how each of you felt both as speaker and listener.

Duration and Frequency

This exercise should last approximately 5 to 10 minutes per turn. It can be repeated as often as desired. However, do not repeat this exercise more than once on any given day.

Suggestions

As the speaker, select a situation that has left you feeling angry. Choose a recent situation and be specific when you share it with your partner. Do not bring up old business at this point. Be sure to use "I" messages when you are the speaker. As the listener, listen carefully to your partner and become more aware of what makes her or him angry in your relationship. When you discuss the exercise, do not focus on the situation, but rather on the feelings you experienced as both speaker and listener.

Pitfalls

The greatest danger is that this exercise will be used to initiate an argument. The purpose of the exercise is not to start a fight, but rather to practice new communication skills and to explore your feelings when you communicate with your partner. Be careful to not get involved in what your partner is angry about, but rather focus on listening. Be sure not to speak while your partner is talking and to use "I" messages when it is your turn to speak. Do not use this as an opportunity to "beat up" on your partner. At the same time, be honest about your feelings.

15 *I UNDERSTAND . . .*

Purpose This exercise will help you develop another communication skill for self-expression that does not make your partner defensive, or require your partner to problem solve or respond in any particular way beyond active listening.

Benefit The exercise allows you the opportunity to share problems with your partner without making that person defensive and without creating the expectation that the partner will somehow take care of the problem. The exercise is similar to "I" messages, but focuses on communicating understanding of the other person, as well as revealing one's own feelings.

Prerequisites " 'I' Messages"

"Roadblocks to Communication"

Directions **Step One:** Select one partner to be the speaker, and the other to be the listener.

Step Two: The speaker is asked to select a concern or problem that has arisen in the relationship between the two partners that the speaker understands from the listener's point of view, but still does not feel good about.

Step Three: The speaker is asked to put this statement in a format similar to an "I" message, except that now the statement begins with "I understand" to communicate that the speaker understands why the listener is doing something or feels a certain way. Once the understanding is communicated, the speaker's feeling is added. Thus, the speaker may construct the following statement:

"I understand that it is difficult for you to leave your business meeting to call me and let me know that you will be late in arriving home. However, I feel very worried when I do not know where you are."

Step Four: Switch roles and repeat the exercise once.

Duration and Frequency This exercise can vary greatly in terms of how long it takes. The speaker will have a better sense of how much time will be needed because it is the speaker who knows how much information needs to be communicated. However, generally this exercise need not take more than 5 to 10 minutes. The exercise may be repeated frequently across several days or weeks; however, it should be limited to once per day.

Suggestions   In this exercise do not attempt to problem solve. That is not its purpose. It is merely to help you learn one more way of expressing yourself assertively without blaming the other person, and adding a component of understanding. Try to do this exercise 4 to 6 times before moving on to the next exercise. You can also practice this skill with friends, at work, and with other family members. If you begin to feel comfortable with this exercise, you may add a few minutes for the listener to respond with an "I" message to the "I understand" message of the speaker. However, if you find that this rebuttal leads to arguments, discontinue the attempt for now and try the exercise again later as you progress through this section.

Pitfalls   Never use this exercise to be sarcastic or blaming. Never put down your partner or make that person responsible for how you feel. In other words, be sure not to use a "You" message instead of an "I" message. Also, try to keep your message brief and clear so your partner will not misunderstand it.

16 REVERSING ROLES

Purpose   This exercise is included to help you develop a better understanding of how your partner views you and your role in the relationship. It will also provide insight about the impact of the role each partner plays and will help increase your empathy for one another.

Benefit   You will learn how your roles have developed in your relationship, and how they feel to the person who plays them. Furthermore, the exercise will result in increased empathy about what your partner goes through in fulfilling a particular task or role in the relationship. Finally, you will learn to discuss the roles you hold in your relationship.

Prerequisites   " 'I' Messages"

"Roadblocks to Communication"

Directions   **Step One:** Sit down opposite one another and choose one of the themes from the list provided at the end of this exercise. Select the theme according to how many problems you have in that particular area. Start with the least conflictual area, and use the more conflictual ones when you repeat the exercise later.

Step Two: From within the area chosen in step 1, choose one particular interaction that both of you engage in with one another on a regular basis. Then take turns describing in detail your role in that interaction. Include detailed descriptions of the behaviors in which you engage, feelings you may have, expectations you hold, and thoughts that tend to run through your mind when you do these things. Note the most important components of your role on a piece of paper and give it to your partner.

Step Three: Enact the situation you discussed in step 2, *but switch roles*. In other words, play-act that typical situation from your partner's perspective, taking your partner's role. As you role-play, become aware of your feelings toward your partner and of how you feel being in the other person's role.

Step Four: After you finish the interaction, discuss what happened and how you felt. Use "I" messages, "I understand" messages, empathy, and reflection. Avoid roadblocks to communication.

Duration and Frequency   The duration of this exercise depends on the area and roles that are being acted out. Sufficient time must be allowed to glean a true appreciation and understanding of the partner's role. The first attempt at this exercise may require as much as an hour. This exercise can be repeated often and at any time, as long as both partners agree. Repetitions are not allowed if one partner does not want to engage in this exercise.

Suggestions   A thorough and realistic description of your own role is crucial to the success of this exercise. Your partner must understand exactly what your behaviors and feelings are during a given interaction from your perspective. Be honest in your attempt to play the partner's role and take this task seriously. Listen to your feelings as you do your partner's tasks or chores and try to imagine how your partner feels in the real situation. Add new roles that you can switch as you both become aware of them. If a particular role becomes suddenly important or salient in an interaction with your partner, you may suggest to do this exercise spontaneously so that you can gain a better appreciation of what it feels like to be in your partner's shoes.

Pitfalls   No matter what role you have to play, do not exaggerate it or mock the partner. Failure to take the role seriously and inability to empathize honestly with what the partner usually experiences in playing this role will defeat the purpose of this exercise. Also, do not start arguing with your partner about minor details that are role-played incorrectly. Only correct major, or salient errors. Although you may feel uncomfortable role-playing or acting at first, this will get easier, so do not give up because of initial discomfort with the task.

LIST OF PROBLEM AREAS

household cleaning	*parenting*
dinner preparation	*hobbies*
dinnertime activities	*discussing the day*
yard work	*social activities*
coming home from work	*elder care*

17 *TAKEN FOR GRANTED: VERBAL COMMUNICATION*

Purpose   This exercise will help you gain a better understanding of what your partner does for you on a regular basis. It will also help you become aware of some areas in which your partner may be experiencing resentment and anger.

Benefit   This exercise results in greater appreciation of your partner's contributions to the relationship. It also provides a positive opportunity to express frustrations about feeling unappreciated in the relationship with the partner.

Prerequisites   "My Contributions"
"'I' Messages"
"I Understand . . ."

Directions   **Step One:** Each partner will make a list of things that he or she does in the relationship for the other partner, but which the other person does not seem to appreciate. The list should contain an agreed-upon number of items, and must have a detailed outline of what is done for the partner.

Step Two: When both partners have finished their lists, select one partner to be the speaker and to start the exercise. Taking turns, each partner will be asked to share one item from the list in the following format: "I feel unappreciated when I do _____ for you/us and you do not seem to notice."

The blank is to be filled in with the particular details noted in step 1 about the item that one partner identified as a contribution or thing done for the other partner that tends to remain unappreciated.

While the speaker is presenting the specifics about the unappreciated contribution, the listener is merely to listen and not to say anything. Both partners should be aware of their feelings, while in the role of both speaker and listener.

Step Three: After both of you have shared your lists, stop the exercise and go on about your business.

Duration and Frequency   Completion of this exercise will require approximately 20 to 30 minutes the first time when the lists have to be prepared. Repetitions are quicker because the same list can be used. However, in any repetitions, new items may need to be added occasionally. This exercise should not be repeated if one partner runs out of items. It can be repeated if necessary at a later time when a new issue comes up in the relationship.

Suggestions The first time you do this exercise, it is best to start with no more than two items on each partner's list. In subsequent repetitions, the number of items can be increased as long as both partners agree on the number. In preparing statements about not being appreciated, use your skills learned through "I" messages and "I understand" messages, and remember to remain empathic. Listen to your partner without being defensive and without feeling blamed or responsible to solve the "problem."

Pitfalls It is not going to help the purpose of this exercise to refuse to listen or to accept your partner's statements. Remember that "I" messages reflect the feelings of your partner and that they need to be taken seriously even if their impact was not planned or intended by the partner. Do not be argumentative—try to understand the statements and concerns from your partner's perspective.

18 *I SEE (HEAR), I THINK, I FEEL*

Purpose This exercise is designed to help you learn how to distinguish between information that comes from outside of you (actual events) and what comes from inside of you (e.g., your thoughts and feelings). Once that has been mastered, the exercise helps you understand how your thoughts can lead to your feelings. Ultimately, the exercise will help you learn about how your mind makes connections between events and feelings.

Benefit People often believe that things that happen around them cause them to have certain feelings. However, the fact is that it is how you interpret these events that results in your feelings. This idea is similar to the one you learned about in " 'I' Messages." This exercise will help increase your awareness and understanding of important components of communication that often lead couples to arguments, unjust accusations, and misunderstandings. Once you have understood that it is how you interpret events that leads you to experience certain feelings, you will be much less likely to accuse and blame your partner and more likely to cooperate and explore differences peacefully.

Prerequisites "Empathic Reflection"

" 'I' Messages"

"Taking Turns: Mutual Sharing"

Directions **Step One:** Select one partner as the speaker and the other as the listener.

Step Two: The speaker will focus on an issue relevant to the relationship. In relating this issue to the listener, the speaker makes a statement that includes the sequence, "I see (or hear) _____, I think _____, and I feel _____." For example: "*I heard* you slam the door when you came home from work, *I think* that it means that you were angry with me for not opening the garage for you, and *I feel* angry that you think that."

Step Three: The listener's task is to listen and to help the speaker with the "I think" part of the statement because that is the crucial and most difficult part.

Step Four: The speaker and the listener discuss the reality of the speaker's statement. For instance, for the above example, the listener may point out that she or he slammed the door because she or he had just had a fight with a boss and was taking the anger out in this way. In other words, the anger had nothing to do with the speaker, who therefore had no reason *based on reality* to be angry.

Step Five: Once you have successfully analyzed the speaker's statement, switch roles and start over.

Duration and Frequency

This exercise will probably require no more than 1 minute per statement and 2 to 3 minutes per discussion. You should repeat the exercise at least three times, for a total of no more than 15 minutes to complete this exercise. Doing this exercise again later is highly recommended because this is another exercise that serves as a building block for later exercises on problem solving and compromising skills.

Suggestions

While doing this exercise, focus your statements on issues relevant and important to the here-and-now. In other words, do not use it to bring up old issues. Furthermore, make sure that the issues you raise are relevant to the relationship with your intimate partner.

Pitfalls

Do not use this exercise to blame or argue with your partner. This is not a time to fight over an issue, but rather to work together on your communication. Remember, the task is to take responsibility, the opposite of blaming.

To complete the exercise with success, you have to make sure that you understand the difference between perceiving (i.e., seeing or hearing), thinking, and feeling. If you do not distinguish among these three, you will miss the purpose of the exercise, which is to differentiate between external (perceiving) events, and internal (thinking and feeling) events.

19 "ALWAYS" AND "NEVER"

Purpose   This exercise helps you to examine the use of the words "always" and "never" in your communications with your partner and other people. It will also help you understand the message you are sending when you use these words as well as effective alternatives.

Benefit   Certain words in our language can act as roadblocks or impediments to effective communication. Their overuse can create such a negative response in individuals that they prove to be counterproductive and destructive when used in conflict or problem-solving situations. This exercise will help to make you aware of how often you use such words in everyday communication. The awareness and elimination of the use of these words will lead to more effective communication with your partner and others.

Directions   **Step One:** During the next week, each partner should pay close attention to conversations with others, especially the other partner. Be alert to the use of the words "always" and "never." Make a written or mental note of the situations in which you use them and the reactions they produce in others.

Step Two: At the end of the week, discuss what you discovered with your partner. Explore common situations in which each of you used the two words and the reactions that they elicited.

Step Three: Individually or with your partner select alternative words to use in place of "always" and "never." Some examples are "often, sometimes, several times, usually, typically," and so on. For the following 2 weeks, practice using these alternative words. Pay attention to whether they are more effective in getting your point across or are more effective in reducing conflicts.

Step Four: After 2 weeks review the situation with your partner. Assess whether you were able to communicate more effectively with your new vocabulary.

Duration and Frequency   Changes in our patterns of speech need time to be assimilated. It may take some weeks for both of you to become aware of this behavior and to make changes in your vocabulary. Do not be discouraged by your mistakes; persevere and gradually the new words will become a habit.

Suggestions   Because using new words in place of "always" and "never" is a new behavior, you will occasionally forget or slip and use the old words. If this happens, do not worry. Just become aware of your lapses and, if possible, correct yourself by saying, "I am sorry, I meant sometimes."

Pitfalls   Remember not to correct your partner's slipups in a negative way. This is not an opportunity to criticize one another, but rather a chance to help each other. Maintain an awareness of your vocabulary; it is easy to revert to old habits after a few weeks.

20 ASSERTIVE VERSUS AGGRESSIVE: VERBAL

Purpose   This exercise will help to teach you how to state your feelings effectively without being offensive. It will give you the skills to share your feelings with your partner and others in a direct, honest manner.

Benefit   The ability to communicate feelings effectively is extremely important in a relationship. Frequently, however, because our emotions are involved, feelings can be expressed too strongly and destructively, and the reaction from the partner can be equally destructive. The lack of effective communication can result in defensive and aggressive responses that serve as roadblocks to further communication.

Prerequisites   " 'I' Messages"
"I Understand . . ."

Directions   **Step One:** Select one partner to start the exercise. This partner will be the speaker, and the other partner will be the listener.

Step Two: The speaker selects a situation that has occurred about which she or he feels angry. At first, the situations should not directly involve the other partner. The speaker clearly and honestly states her or his feelings about the situation. In stating these feelings, the speaker uses "I" messages. It is critical that the speaker focus on her or his feelings and not accuse or criticize the other partner. At this point, the listener concentrates on hearing what is being said and does not respond verbally. Instead, the listener is paying close attention to what she or he is feeling and how she or he would like to respond.

Step Three: After the speaker is finished, using "I" messages and "I understand" messages, the listener shares her or his responses and feelings. While this partner is speaking, it is imperative that the first partner just listen.

Step Four: After the second partner finishes speaking, the two partners then discuss how the exercise went. Be sure to discuss the conversation and how it went, not the situation that triggered the speaker's anger. The speaker should focus on sharing how she or he felt sharing the anger and whether she or he felt listened to and understood. The listener should focus on how she or he felt while listening to the speaker.

Step Five: Reverse roles and repeat steps 1 to 4.

Duration and Frequency   You should plan on this exercise taking at least 15 to 30 minutes. Repeat the exercise as necessary until both of you feel comfortable sharing your feelings with one another and until both of you feel you have been heard and understood.

Suggestions   When first practicing this exercise, keep the problems relatively minor and unrelated to the relationship. As you become more adept at the process, you will be able to tackle more complex problems including those that have occurred within the relationship. Throughout the exercise, it is crucial that both partners use "I" messages and "I understand" messages. As both speaker and listener, pay particular attention to how you are feeling. Also, be aware of one another's body language during the exercise. Save your lists for use in a future exercise.

Pitfalls   Often the speaker may not take responsibility for her or his feelings but instead may externalize them by accusing others. This is where "I" messages become particularly important. Be sure not to get too angry or volatile during this exercise. That is, if either partner becomes angry or aggressive, it is time to stop the exercise for the time being.

21 *PROBLEM SOLVING*

Purpose   This exercise is designed to help you develop better problem-solving skills that can be used for positive interactions with the partner, while focusing on searching for solutions to problems in the relationship. It will help you apply the skills learned up to this point in a practical way to problems ranging from minor, everyday issues to major issues in your relationship.

Benefit   Although this exercise will help you find solutions to problems with your partner, these skills will also come in handy with other people and in work settings. You will learn new ways of looking at things, how to increase your flexibility, and how to compromise.

Prerequisites   "Empathic Reflection"
"'I' Messages"
"I Understand . . ."
"Taken for Granted: Verbal Communication"

Directions   **Step One:** Select one partner who will start this exercise. Do the exercise only once per day. This means that the other partner will not be able to take a turn until the next day.

Step Two: Choose a problem that was presented by the starting partner in "I Understand . . ." or "Taken for Granted: Verbal Communication." Restate this problem in the same constructive, nonblaming way as was done during these prior exercises, paying attention to good communication skills. The listener should take an active listening stance, trying not to feel attacked or blamed, and remembering good listening skills.

Step Three: Once the problem has been restated, the speaker has to rephrase it according to the following format:

1. Definition: What is the problem? Be as specific as possible without placing blame; merely describe the situation.
2. Solutions: What are the possible solutions? Write down all solutions the speaker can come up with; do not evaluate them according to how realistic or "good" they are—just be creative for now.

Step Four: Once the problem has been defined and possible solutions have been offered by the speaker, the listener should restate the problem, showing that the speaker was heard and understood. Then the offered solutions should be restated, again without evaluating them or showing preferences. Then the listener needs to create a list of possible solutions as well, again without evaluating—just being creative.

Step Five: Now that a long list of solutions has been created, see if either of you has any more ideas. If so add them to the list. Now draw straws to see who goes first in the next step.

Step Six: The first partner now is asked to evaluate the possible solutions, discussing each listed solution according to how that partner thinks and feels about it and according to how realistic it seems to her or him and how much compromise it would require. Good communication skills learned previously must be used here to avoid blaming. All along the second partner only listens, using good (nonverbal) listening skills, and not interrupting. Once the first partner has thus evaluated all solutions, switch roles and repeat.

Step Seven: Based on the evaluations conducted in step 6, sort the solutions according to the preferences of each partner. Identify as many solutions as possible that are high in both partners' evaluations. Choose one of these and call it your solution. Implement it for a specified time period (usually 10 to 20 days) and then stick to it to give the solution a fair chance. Remember that no solution has to be either perfect or permanent. It facilitates compromise to know that a solution will be tried out for 2 to 3 weeks and can then be renegotiated using this same process if it is not satisfactory.

Step Eight: After the specified time period negotiated in step 7 has lapsed, assess how the solution is working. If it is not successful, discuss why not and determine new solutions by repeating this exercise.

Duration and Frequency

The first time, this exercise will require great care and hence a big chunk of time. Plan on at least an hour. Once these skills have been practiced frequently and have become more automatic, the time required for this task will decrease drastically. Repetition of this exercise is indicated each time the partners face a problem-solving issue, which may occur daily. At first, only one problem-solving task should be mastered per day. However, as you encounter success with this procedure, you may use your own judgment about how often to repeat it.

Suggestions

This exercise must begin with easily solved problems to guarantee success. Nothing impedes progress more than repeated failure. In coming up with solutions and compromises, attempt to be creative. Try to come up with new solutions that neither of you ever considered before. Do not be afraid to be a bit outrageous.

Pitfalls   Starting with problems that are deeply ingrained and highly charged emotionally for both partners will result in failure. Refusal of one partner to cooperate with the process and to compromise or consider novel solutions also will cause frustration and failure. This is perhaps the most difficult exercise encountered so far, so do not expect too much the first time. Be willing to compromise and wait for success.

SECTION THREE *Romance Recreated*

EXERCISES

1. The First Meeting
2. The First Love Note
3. Take a Peek
4. Take a Peek: Discussion
5. Being Friends Again
6. Physical Attractiveness
7. Psychological Attractiveness
8. The First Date: Remembering
9. The First Date: Recreating
10. The Special Treat
11. The Photo Show: Reexperiencing Memories
12. The Photo Show: Creating Memories
13. The Innovative Date
14. The Special Affection
15. The Favorite Romantic Fantasy
16. The Romantic Reality
17. The Romantic Surprise
18. Sharing Likes
19. Sharing Dislikes
20. Confirming Likes
21. Refuting Dislikes
22. Giving a Compliment

The exercises in this section are focused on rekindling romance and attraction in your relationship. Often partners in an intimate relationship forget to focus on the positive aspects of their interactions and have developed patterns of relating that have become trite and commonplace. Romance is an important motivator for relationships—it makes working on a relationship worthwhile and keeps partners together. It helps smooth rough water because partners tend to be more forgiving and tolerant of one another if romance is alive in the relationship. These exercises will help you rekindle romance and awareness of attraction, thus giving you a reason to maintain your relationship. Furthermore, this process will help both of you feel better about one another and yourselves—you will feel more valued, cared for, and desired.

1 THE FIRST MEETING

Purpose
This exercise is designed to help you remember what attracted you to one another and how you felt about your partner when you first met or recognized that you were attracted to her or him.

Benefit
In the hassles of everyday life, couples often forget what they like about each other. Indeed, many couples cannot even remember why they fell in love in the first place. Remembering these positive feelings about a partner helps the relationship endure difficult times and gives people a reason for trying to save the relationship.

Directions
Step One: Recall the first time you met your partner; try to remember as many details about that person in that setting as possible.

Step Two: Based on what partners remember of their first meeting, each partner individually notes at least three things that attracted her or him to the other and what she or he liked about the person. Focus on positive aspects only.

Step Three: After both of you have finished making notes, verbally share those three positive initial impressions with one another. Take turns for this step of the exercise.

Duration and Frequency
This exercise lasts approximately 15 to 30 minutes (or much more if you like). Repeating the exercise is not encouraged now, but certainly this is a task that can be fun when it happens spontaneously at any point in your lives.

Suggestions
Take your time remembering everything about this first meeting or the first time you realized you were attracted to your partner. Try to reexperience the feelings you had at that time. Remember how excited and hopeful you were in anticipation of time together with this person. Do your remembering in private, and then share only the most positive things with your partner.

Pitfalls
Do not try to do this exercise too quickly. Sometimes when you are used to thinking negatively about a person, it takes a while to remember the positive aspects. Do not say anything negative to your partner.

2 THE FIRST LOVE NOTE

Purpose   This exercise is designed to help you put down in words what you initially liked about your partner. It will remind you of what you like about your partner and what your partner likes about you.

Benefit   Often we can say something positive to a person, and yet she or he does not hear us or quickly forgets what we said. Similarly, sometimes we have a positive thought about someone and we never say it and end up forgetting it altogether. In this exercise, you will benefit from putting in writing or recorded format something that attracted you to your partner. This will not only help your partner understand that you have a positive feeling about her or him, but will also serve as a reminder for you that there is something you like about your partner.

Prerequisite   "The First Meeting"

Directions   **Step One:** After having verbally shared the positive information in "The First Meeting," write or record a love note to your partner, outlining what you previously shared verbally.

Step Two: Although you should be under no time pressure for this task, set a deadline that you can both agree on for when the notes are to be exchanged.

Step Three: Exchange the notes or recordings at the specified deadline. Neither of you is allowed to turn in a creation early and neither of you should miss the deadline.

Duration and Frequency   How long it takes to create a love note or recording varies greatly from individual to individual; however, no less than 30 minutes should be spent on this task. In fact, for some people it may be necessary to set the deadline of exchange for the next day. Generally, you should not set a time frame exceeding 24 hours. This exercise can be repeated as often as either of you desires. Neither of you will ever get tired of receiving these notes from your partner. Variations on this exercise are also recommended if you decide to repeat the exercise (e.g., a romantic or meaningful greeting card, a poem, etc.). Only your own creativity will limit the possibilities.

Suggestions   If you have trouble agreeing on a deadline, go with 24 hours. It is not worth a fight to try to negotiate a timeline. If you try variations on the task, do so after the first time.

Pitfalls   Do not try to say everything at once, and under no circumstances say anything negative in your message. If you decide to repeat the exercise on your own, do not expect your partner to do the same—you will only set yourself up for disappointment. If you cannot do that, do not repeat the exercise without telling your partner that you are planning on it and that you would like her or him to do the same. If your partner does not want to repeat the exercise now, accept that.

3 TAKE A PEEK

Purpose This exercise will help you focus attention on your partner and give you a chance to observe your partner without her or his being aware of it.

Benefit One of the greatest dangers couples face is that of taking one another for granted. Partners get so used to each other that they no longer are aware of each other's specialness and uniqueness. It was this specialness that first attracted you to each other. When you refocus your attention on your partner, you will remember the special traits that she or he has, which will help you gain a new appreciation of your partner.

Directions The directions for this exercise are simple. For the next few days, take every opportunity you can just to observe your partner. Do this without your partner's knowledge or awareness. Watch all her or his expressions and movements. Make mental notes about what your partner does and keep track of your own thoughts and feelings toward your partner. Look specifically for things about your partner that you like. When you are alone, make notes about what you saw, thought, and felt.

Duration and Frequency For the next few days, just observe one another and make mental notes about what you see and how you feel. You do not have to do this every moment you are together. Just be sure to do it at least two or three times a day for a few minutes each time.

Suggestions Try to observe your partner in a variety of situations and settings. Observe how she or he interacts with other family members, with children, and sales clerks. Look at the clothes your partner wears, how she or he carries out a chore, or just how your partner relaxes. Focus on finding attributes and traits that you like about your partner. Try to remember what it was about your partner that first attracted you. Look for these behaviors today.

Pitfalls Be careful to not watch your partner with a critical eye. The purpose of the exercise is not to find faults but rather to find positive qualities. Try not to be too obvious in your observations—this will only make your partner self-conscious. At this point, do not discuss your observations with your partner. For now, try to ignore negatives, and by all means refrain from writing negatives down.

4 *TAKE A PEEK: DISCUSSION*

Purpose   This exercise will help you share the observations, thoughts, and feelings you experienced during "Take a Peek." Its purpose is to discuss what you observed about your partner in that exercise.

Benefit   This exercise will help you learn ways to express a better understanding of your partner; such expression is often forgotten in the hustle and bustle of a hectic day. This exercise will help you recognize what is special about your partner and thus will enhance both your relationship and your partner's self-esteem. Nothing boosts one's confidence like a partner's compliments. Both of you will once again learn what is special about the other and why you decided some time ago to share your life.

Prerequisite   "Take a Peek"

Directions   **Step One:** Find two comfortable chairs and move them so they face each other. Now sit comfortably across from each other.

Step Two: Choose one partner to start the exercise, the speaker. The other partner becomes the listener. Using the written notes, this partner will share what she or he saw, thought, and felt during the previous few days of observation. This partner will share only positive things experienced during "Take a Peek."

Step Three: Switch roles and repeat step 2. After you are both finished, carry on with your own business without further discussion of what was shared.

Duration and Frequency   It should take about 5 to 10 minutes for each partner to share her or his experiences, for a total of 10 to 20 minutes. You may decide to spend more time sharing information, but not to spend time discussing it. The two "Take a Peek" exercises can be repeated as often as both partners wish.

Suggestions   Be sure that the listening partner does not speak when the speaker is sharing her or his experiences. As the speaker, focus exclusively on positive observations, thoughts, and feelings. The purpose of the exercise is not to find traits that you do not like about your partner, but rather to remember things that first attracted you to her or him. When sharing experiences, the speaker must be honest and not sarcastic or ironic. The listener must accept the speaker's positive statements without disagreeing or arguing.

Pitfalls   Do not be critical or judgmental in your observations and sharing. It would be counterproductive to criticize or ridicule your partner. Be patient with one another in the sharing of feelings—people have different comfort levels in sharing feelings with one another.

5 BEING FRIENDS AGAIN

Purpose   This exercise will help you reexperience some aspects of the good friendship that the two of you had earlier in your relationship. It will help you focus on the positive qualities that attracted you to each other in the first place.

Benefit   When couples first meet, they spend hours and hours talking to one another to learn more about each other. They try to find out the other person's likes and dislikes, political views, childhood experiences, what he or she does for a living, and so forth. After couples have been together for a while, they often get caught up in everyday activities and spend less time talking to one another. In fact, some studies have shown that couples spend as little as 5 minutes per day talking to each other. By breaking this habit of talking with each other only about mundane, everyday matters, you may renew the friendship you had earlier in the relationship.

Prerequisite   "The First Meeting"

Directions   **Step One:** Find a quiet time when you will not be disturbed or feel pressure to be doing something else. It might be late at night after other responsibilities have been met or on a weekend afternoon. Block out 15 minutes to complete this exercise.

Step Two: Either partner may start this exercise simply by initiating a conversation. Make sure the topic of the conservation is something neutral. That is, avoid any topics that might start an argument. The focus of the conversation may range from international politics to something that happened at work that day.

Step Three: Throughout the conversation, listen carefully to your partner and also keep track of how you are reacting and feeling. Enjoy the conversation and have fun sharing your ideas, thoughts, and feelings.

Step Four: After the 15 minutes have passed, the exercise is completed, so it will be time to stop the conversation.

Duration and Frequency   This exercise will take 15 minutes and can be repeated as often as both partners wish. During repetitions partners can keep the 15-minute time frame or can set any other time frame that they both agree on. However, be sure to set a time limit and use a timer to tell you when the time is up.

Suggestions It might help to recall the conversations that you had when you were first dating. Perhaps there is something on your mind about what happened to you during the day that is not related to the relationship. Or perhaps you saw something on television that really started you thinking. If the conversation drifts to a topic that will make one or both of you angry or upset, stop talking about the topic and move on to another, completely different one. Try to have fun with this exercise and do not let the conversation get too serious. Be respectful of one another and practice your best listening and conversation skills. Treat your partner as you would any friend with whom you are having a conversation. If you have difficulty defining a topic of conversation by yourselves, talk about what you did the day before, perhaps describing your day from morning to evening.

Pitfalls The main danger is that the conversation will drift in a direction that will result in an argument. The purpose of the exercise is to have a casual conversation, so do not try to solve any current relationship problems during this exercise. The goal is to have a conversation with your partner as any good friends would have. This exercise will invariably feel contrived at first. Hang in there—it will begin to feel natural very quickly.

6 PHYSICAL ATTRACTIVENESS

Purpose This exercise is designed to help you see each other's bodies in a new and different light. It will help you focus away from the negative aspects of the partner's appearance and will reorient you toward the positive.

Benefit Often when people in a close relationship run into problems, they become focused on the negative aspects of the partner. Sometimes, just simply refocusing your attention on the positive aspects of the other person can be of tremendous help. It helps you realize that your partner appreciates you, and it will help your partner realize that you still appreciate her or him. Physical attractiveness is an important characteristic of an intimate relationship. Partners tend to be more forgiving with one another if they feel that the other is attractive and vice versa. Often partners forget to compliment one another. This exercise will bring you back into the habit of doing so.

Directions **Step One:** Find two comfortable chairs and move them so they face one another. Now sit comfortably across from each other.

Step Two: Take a few moments to look at one another, focusing on what you like, not what you dislike, about what you see. Take turns and say out loud what you like about the other person that you can actually *see*.

Step Three: Say only one nice thing about the other's physical features at a time, but take at least two turns each.

Duration and Frequency Take at least 10 minutes for this exercise when you do it for the first time. Repeat it as often as desired, and vary the length of time devoted to it as needed. This can be a great exercise for times when you want to connect to one another but do not have a lot of time. It can also be done spontaneously.

Suggestions Try to pick physical characteristics of the other person that you truly do like. In other words, be genuine and do not lie. Do not say, "I love the way your hair looks" if you do not believe that. Do not say, "I love your ears" if the person is in the process of having them surgically altered. No irony, please.

It is impossible not to find something beautiful about another person; you just have to take the time to look for this beauty. Therefore, do not give up easily.

Pitfalls   No matter what you do, do not criticize. This exercise is there to help you see your partner's beauty, and nothing else. You have probably criticized one another often enough, and your partner knows exactly what you dislike about her or him. Do not undo your compliments: Do not say, "I like how you look in this shirt, but the pants are awful." Just stick with the positive.

7 PSYCHOLOGICAL ATTRACTIVENESS

Purpose Just like "Physical Attractiveness," this exercise is designed to help you see each other in a new and different light. However, in this exercise, the focus is not on physical features, but rather on emotional and psychological ones. This exercise will help you see the positives about your partner's values, ideas, beliefs, actions, and feelings.

Benefit In this exercise you will become aware of one another's positive character traits, a process that is often of great help in getting along better. As soon as we realize we like *something* about the other person, it is harder to hate her or him or to put the person down. Therefore, the benefits of this exercise are virtually limitless.

Prerequisite "Physical Attractiveness"

Directions **Step One:** Set up your chairs as you did in "Physical Attractiveness" and then sit comfortably across from one another.

Step Two: Take some time to look at your partner and to think about some of her or his character traits, values, ideas, beliefs, or feelings that you like, appreciate, or admire. After a few moments of thinking, take turns and say aloud what you like about the other that you *cannot* see (no physical features, but any emotions, attitudes, values, beliefs, or personality characteristics that you like).

Step Three: Say only one thing about the other's psychological attractiveness at a time, but take at least three turns each.

Duration and Frequency You will need to take at least 15 minutes for this exercise when you do it for the first time. As in "Physical Attractiveness," repeat this exercise as often as desired, and vary the length of time devoted to it as needed. This is another great exercise for times when you want to connect to one another but do not have a lot of time.

Suggestions Pick characteristics of the other person that you truly do like. Do not lie and do not use irony or sarcasm. Do not say something that the other person knows you cannot really mean because it clashes with your own beliefs or because you have criticized your partner about it many times before. It is impossible not to come up with something that you admire or appreciate in your partner. Take your time, and be honest.

Pitfalls   No matter what you decide to say, do not criticize. You have probably taken many opportunities in the past to tell your partner what you do not like about her or him. This is the time to focus on the good points. A negative, ironic, or smart remark will completely undo the benefits of this exercise.

8 THE FIRST DATE: REMEMBERING

Purpose This exercise is designed to help you remember the specialness of your first date: the things you liked about it and the things that were exciting or romantic to you. This exercise will help you get back in touch with and reexperience some of those feelings.

Benefit Over time, in relationships the partners forget what they once enjoyed doing together and how exciting activities carried out together can be. The benefit of this exercise rests in its purpose to help you remember these things about your own relationship when it was still in its earliest stages. Remembering these positive aspects of togetherness will help motivate you to work on the relationship and will give you a reason to try to improve or salvage it.

Directions **Step One:** Take a quiet moment and individually remember your first date with your partner. Try to recall what you did and how you felt. Focus on the positive aspects of the date.

Step Two: Each of you individually is to write down what you remember about the date and what you liked the most.

Step Three: Now verbally share with one another what you remembered about the date. Try to be specific about what you liked and how you felt.

Step Four: After sharing your notes with one another, try to agree on at least two or three things that either both of you wrote down or that you can agree on as being important and positive about that first date.

Duration and Frequency The length of this exercise varies greatly from couple to couple; however, never expect to spend less than 30 minutes on the sharing and negotiating parts of the exercise.

Suggestions Each of you should try to remember as much as possible about the first date. You may find that you remember things very differently. That is common and has to do with how people experience and remember things differently. Nevertheless, you will have some overlap. Focus on what you have in common.

Pitfalls Do not argue about who remembers "correctly" and who remembers "incorrectly." Memories differ, and the main goal here is to find something (even the smallest item) that you both agree on. Focus on the positive aspects of the date.

9 THE FIRST DATE: RECREATING

Purpose
This exercise is designed to help you recreate the specialness of your first date to help you reexperience some of the positive feelings you had about your partner earlier in your relationship.

Benefit
The benefits of this exercise are similar to those of "The First Date: Remembering." That is, the exercise will help you recall and reexperience the positive aspects of togetherness that the two of you enjoyed when your relationship was just beginning. Remembering these positive aspects can help put the relationship in more of a historical perspective and give both partners more motivation and interest in the relationship. Recreating the first date serves as a more salient reminder of feelings that were present earlier in the relationship.

Prerequisite
"The First Date: Remembering"

Directions
Step One: Go over the positive items that you agreed on in "The First Date: Remembering." Be sure that both of you agree on these aspects of the first date.

Step Two: Plan a date similar to your first date; set a time that both of you find acceptable.

Step Three: Set up the date, and share the responsibility for making arrangements; clearly delineate who does the necessary chores associated with the date. For instance, specify who is in charge of the logistics of the date, such as reservations, driving, tickets, baby-sitter, house sitter, elder care, and errands.

Duration and Frequency
The length of this exercise will vary depending on the nature of the first date. Repetitions of the exercise are encouraged, at least until one *successful*, that is, enjoyable, date has been experienced.

Suggestions
Even if your original first date included other people, do not include anyone else in this date. Others can distract you from your primary task—getting to know and enjoy each other's company.

Pitfalls
Do not think that this date has to be perfect and exactly like the first date. Especially if your first date was elaborate or impossible to recreate (e.g., prom night), try merely to capture the spirit of the original date. It would be frustrating and harmful to think that it has to be "right" the first time you try it. In fact, it may take several attempts before you complete this exercise and feel good about it. Do not despair—it will happen. Do not try to set up a date so elaborate that you have to work very hard on getting everything prepared. Remember, this is a new task—keep it simple.

10 THE SPECIAL TREAT

Purpose
This exercise is designed to engage you in more activities in which you do things for one another.

Benefit
Doing special things for one another makes partners appreciate one another more. The partner who receives the treat is grateful, and the partner who gives the treat feels good because of having done something nice. No one can lose.

Directions
Step One: From the list on the following page pick at least five special treats (add your own if necessary) that you would enjoy receiving from your partner.

Step Two: On a separate sheet of paper, write down your choices and give the list to your partner.

Step Three: Read your partner's list and pick two items that are realistic and within your means to provide.

Step Four: Do one of the items within the next 48 hours.

Step Five: Do the other item within 5 days after having done the first one (try to build in an element of surprise).

Duration and Frequency
The preparation of the list should involve careful thought and planning; thus, at least 30 minutes should be dedicated to it. Carrying out the task itself, however, may not require much of your time at all. This exercise is a great one to repeat often because as it is inexpensive, not very time-consuming, and often extremely effective.

Suggestions
Put a lot of thought into your list of special treats. Do not put items on your list that you are already receiving, or that you know are impossible for your partner to provide. Save your lists of choices for future exercises.

Pitfalls
Do not expect perfection the first time and do not be impatient. Give your partner plenty of time and credit even just for trying.

SPECIAL TREAT IDEAS

giving a small gift, e.g., mug, plant, cologne

drawing a bubble bath for the partner

arranging a baby-sitter to have a night alone

sending a romantic greeting card

bringing a cup of tea or coffee　　*taking a bath together*
doing the dishes out of turn　　*writing a love note*
preparing a surprise dinner　　*doing the shopping*
washing your partner's hair　　*giving chocolates*
throwing a surprise party　　*giving a massage*
doing a chore out of turn　　*buying flowers*
going on a shopping spree　　*bringing candy*
serving breakfast in bed　　*saying "I love you"*
taking a shower together

_____

_____

_____

11 THE PHOTO SHOW: REEXPERIENCING MEMORIES

Purpose   This exercise is designed to help you remember the good times that you have had together and the things that you have shared. It will provide you with a reminder of times to come.

Benefit   It is very human to forget how much we have shared with family, friends, and life partners. Sometimes it takes an external clue to remind us of our shared history. This exercise will help you benefit from the past experiences you have shared with your partner—both good and bad. It will help remind you of the things you have already been through together, and will help give you the motivation to continue facing life together.

Directions   **Step One:** Get out any photo albums you might have and find pictures that you have taken since becoming a couple.

Step Two: Go through the photos together, focusing only on pictures that were taken when you were with each other.

Step Three: For each picture, share with each other what you remember about the picture. Remember what the picture is of, when it was taken, what the two of you were doing, and how you were feeling at the time. Focus on the pictures for which there are pleasant and positive memories, skipping any pictures that may bring back negative memories.

Duration and Frequency   The duration of this exercise varies greatly, depending on how absorbed you become in the task and how many photographs you have. Take your time and enjoy this task. In fact, it is okay (perhaps preferable) to spread this exercise over several days. Repeat this exercise as often as you both wish.

Suggestions   Focus on pictures that bring back positive memories, perhaps pictures of vacations or family events. Try to reexperience your feelings when the pictures were taken. Go on to the next photo only when both of you are ready.

Pitfalls   Many events hold both positive and negative memories. As you go through the photos, resist any temptation to dredge up negative memories. Do not focus on what you should be doing now, but rather on what you have done together.

12 THE PHOTO SHOW: CREATING MEMORIES

Purpose This exercise is designed to help provide you with an ongoing reminder of all that you have shared together.

Benefit Too often, people focus on negative experiences and memories and push aside positive and pleasant memories. Painful and unpleasant memories can have a lot of power and lead us to forget or ignore positive memories. Often it helps couples to have an external reminder of positive and pleasant memories. Such a reminder will be created through this exercise and will help you keep positive memories from being pushed too far away.

Prerequisite "The Photo Show: Reexperiencing Memories"

Directions **Step One:** From your photo collection, together find pictures of you as a couple. If you do not have a lot of pictures, see if friends or families can help you out. In any case, find as many pictures of yourselves as possible.

Step Two: Take your favorite pictures of you as a couple out of the albums, and make a collage together. Each of you should choose a few favorite pictures; you don't have to choose the same pictures to include them.

Step Three: Hang the collage in a place where you often find yourselves together and where you will see it often.

Duration and Frequency The duration of this exercise will vary depending on how many photographs you have. Repetitions of the exercise in the sense of creating new collages and collecting new photographs are encouraged, but only if *both* of you are interested.

Suggestions Try as much as possible to share the work on this exercise equally. It can be an enjoyable task if both of you can agree to be open-minded and not at all perfectionistic. Remember, the pictures are to serve as reminders, and therefore do not have to be beautiful or artistically valuable. Choose from a wide variety of pictures. Vacation pictures work especially well. Make duplicates of photos if necessary. When you make the collage, consider a large cork board rather than the traditional cut-and-paste approach. That way it is easy to exchange pictures and rearrange them later. For hanging the collage, find a highly visible place that both of you are likely to see regularly.

Pitfalls Like any task that requires some degree of cooperation, this exercise may lead to some disagreements. It is not yet your task to resolve these kinds of disputes. Later exercises will have this as their focus. For now, both of you have to take some responsibility in not being too critical and in being willing to compromise. Try it, it will be worth the effort. If a partner strongly objects to a certain photo, don't include it.

13 *THE INNOVATIVE DATE*

Purpose

This exercise is designed to encourage you to do things together again in an atmosphere of leisure and specialness, in which one person does the planning and the other can merely enjoy.

Benefit

This exercise will help you recreate the atmosphere of your relationship when it was still in its early and more romantic stages. Romance is important because it gives you a reason to try to work out differences with one another.

Directions

Step One: Each partner needs to write down on a separate piece of paper at least two items from the list of dating ideas that follows (you can add to the list if you wish).

Step Two: Compare notes to find at least one activity that both of you like and find exciting or pleasant.

Step Three: Choose a time convenient for both of you.

Step Four: Pick one partner who will agree to make all the necessary arrangements to set up this innovative date at the time the two of you have chosen.

Step Five: Repeat the exercise 1 week later, switching roles.

Duration and Frequency

This can be a lengthy exercise and takes some dedication by the person responsible for the arrangements. Take your time, spend at least 1 to 2 hours preparing for the date, then choose an evening or day for the actual event. Repeating the exercise is encouraged, as long as both of you are interested.

Suggestions

Plan this activity at a time you are certain is convenient for both of you. Avoid times or activities you know are difficult for your partner. For example, do not plan a late night dinner on the evening before your partner has an important business presentation. Save your list of preferences for future use.

Pitfalls

Never force your partner into this type of activity when she or he is not in the right mood. However, do not always turn down the activity for that reason. Try to find a happy medium.

DATING IDEAS

seeing a performance (theater, opera, symphony)

renting and watching a movie (alone at home)

window-shopping, not planning to buy anything

enjoying a dinner at a favorite restaurant

watching the sunset from a special place

taking a long walk at a favorite place

watching a movie (at a movie theater)

having a romantic dinner at home

going for a scenic driving tour

bowling or playing tennis

touring through museums

ice- or roller skating

enjoying a new band

exercising together

going for a picnic

going to a dance

taking pictures

flying a kite

windsurfing

bicycling

fishing

golfing

exploring a new place

_____

_____

_____

14 THE SPECIAL AFFECTION

Purpose
This exercise is designed to help bring affection and tenderness back into your relationship.

Benefit
Feelings of affection and tenderness for your partner are an important component of a loving relationship. They can soften the blow of inevitable mistakes, make partners more tolerant of one another, and make them more likely to forgive one another for small transgressions.

Directions
Step One: From the list at the end of this exercise, pick at least four forms of affection that you particularly enjoy (add your own if the list does not include what you like, but keep the affections nonsexual).

Step Two: Write down or record the items you have chosen and give your list to your partner.

Step Three: Read your partner's list and give your partner a form of affection as defined in her or his list at least once in 2 days for the next 10 days (i.e., a total of five affections).

Step Four: Always pick a time that is convenient to both of you.

Duration and Frequency
The preparation of the list should involve careful thought and planning. Execution of the task itself, however, may not require much of your time at all. After the 10 days are over, you should decide whether to repeat this exercise. It is a great one to repeat often because it is inexpensive, not very time-consuming, and often extremely effective.

Suggestions
Respect one another: If one partner is not in the mood, do not force the affection. Be sure to include only those items on the list that you really want to receive from your partner now. Feel free to revise your list after each set of 10 days. Remember that for the time being, the affection must remain nonsexual. Save your lists of preferences for future use.

Pitfalls
Forcing the partner to cooperate when that person is not in the mood ruins the purpose of this exercise. Also, trying to go beyond the special affection when the other partner is not ready or interested will spoil the effects of this exercise.

SPECIAL AFFECTION IDEAS

massage

foot rub

kissing

hugging

cuddling

joint shower

being tickled

joint bubble bath

nonsexual touching

having hair combed

_____

_____

_____

_____

_____

_____

_____

_____

_____

_____

15 THE FAVORITE ROMANTIC FANTASY

Purpose　This exercise is designed to help you decide what your favorite romantic fantasy is and to share it with your partner.

Benefit　Couples often assume that each partner knows what is romantic to the other. As a result, they often do not share their ideas about romance with one another. This leads to misunderstandings and misconceptions, but most of all it often contributes to the absence of romance in relationships. Knowing what the other person considers romantic helps each partner create an environment in which romance can flourish.

Directions　**Step One:** Think about things you find romantic and that you would consider doing with your partner.

Step Two: Choose several of these romantic activities and write them down. Be sure to write down at least two to three activities. At this point, try to come up with specific and short activities that you consider romantic.

Step Three: Verbally share your notes with your partner. Give specific information on what the activity would be like and how it would be romantic. When this is done, exchange notes with one another.

Duration and Frequency　You should probably spend at least 30 minutes preparing your lists and another 20 to 30 minutes sharing the lists with one another.

Suggestions　Think carefully about your romantic scenarios. You and your partner may use these in the future, and therefore they should be accurate and well thought out. Make your fantasies realistic and easy for your partner to accomplish. Save your lists of fantasies for future use.

Pitfalls　Take your time. Do not argue about who came up with the most romantic scenarios. Romance has different definitions for everyone, and no one can judge what is more or less romantic.

16 *THE ROMANTIC REALITY*

Purpose

This exercise is designed to help you recreate the romantic atmosphere that your relationship might have had when it was in its early stages. It is to remind you that romance is an important part of a relationship, regardless of how long you have been together.

Benefit

This exercise will bring some romance back into your relationship, thus helping you remember why you fell in love to begin with. It is likely to bring back some old (positive) feelings you had for one another that have gone unnoticed for some time.

Prerequisite

"The Favorite Romantic Fantasy"

Directions

Step One: Review the list of romantic ideas that the two of you generated in "The Favorite Romantic Fantasy."

Step Two: Identify one idea that is romantic and acceptable to both of you. Optimally, this scenario would have been included on both partners' lists.

Step Three: Create the situation by following the next step.

Step Four: Share the responsibility for making arrangements. Clearly delineate who is responsible for the pragmatics of the situation that are appropriate, such as reservations, errands, arrangements, food, tickets, shopping, and so on.

Duration and Frequency

This can be quite a lengthy exercise and takes some dedication on both your parts; take your time—spend at least 1 to 2 hours preparing for the fantasy enactment, then add an evening for the actual event. Repeating the exercise is encouraged, as long as both of you are interested. On any repetition, try to come up with a new romantic fantasy that is acceptable to both of you.

Suggestions

Choose a time convenient for both of you. Be thorough in your planning.

Pitfalls

Do not expect perfection on your first attempt or you are sure to feel cheated. Failure on the first try is common and merely means that you need to give yourselves another chance. Even romance needs to be practiced.

17 *THE ROMANTIC SURPRISE*

Purpose This exercise is designed to help you learn to create romantic situations in a way that surprises your partner, and thus takes on a specialness that a jointly planned event cannot have.

Benefit It is hoped that surprise romance will spark the old feelings of excitement that may have existed in your relationship at one time. Surprises are a great way of livening up a relationship and of showing that partners care about one another.

Prerequisites "The Favorite Romantic Fantasy"
"The Romantic Reality"

Directions **Step One:** Each partner is to choose one of the items on the partner's list created in "The Favorite Romantic Fantasy."

Step Two: Keep your item choice secret from your partner.

Step Three: Create the situation at a time within the next 2 weeks that is convenient for both of you and surprise your partner with it.

Duration and Frequency This can be a short, or lengthy and involved, exercise and takes some dedication on the planner's part. Take your time—spend at least 1 to 2 hours preparing for the fantasy enactment, then add the time needed for the actual event. Repetitions are encouraged, as long as both of you are interested.

Suggestions Pick an easy item on the list the first time you try this exercise. Take plenty of time to prepare and be ready to put your partner's needs ahead of yours during the exercise.

Pitfalls Do not expect perfection and certainly never complain about the choice of romantic event. If it was on the list, it was fair game and appreciation is in order. Do not argue or nag, just try to enjoy the moment, or at least the intent behind the situation. It does not matter who created the first situation. Both of you will have a turn. Do not compete about who can or did create the better romantic event. The intent is more important than the actual success of the exercise. If one of you absolutely hates surprises, you may need to skip this exercise.

18 SHARING LIKES

Purpose   This exercise (and the next three) is dedicated to building trust in your intimate relationship by asking you to share sensitive information about yourselves with one another.

Benefit   Trust is a basic building block in a well-functioning intimate relationship. Without trust partners grow apart and stop sharing themselves with one another. This is one of the most common reasons why relationships become problematic.

Directions   **Step One:** Take 5 to 15 minutes to write down a list of at least five things that you like about yourself.

Step Two: Give the list to your partner (without talking about it). Under no circumstances should the lists be discussed—this will occur in a later exercise.

Duration and Frequency   This is a very brief exercise, and it needs to be done only once.

Suggestions   Think carefully about what to put on your list. Do not shortchange yourself; you are bound to have many good features—write them down. If you have difficulties, think of compliments others have given you. Stand in front of a mirror and look at yourself. What do you see that you like? Focus on different aspects of your life such as how you interact with your friends and what you do well on your job. Save this list—you will use it again.

Pitfalls   Talking about the lists prematurely could defeat the purpose of this exercise. Do not criticize or question your partner's list under any circumstances.

19 SHARING DISLIKES

Purpose
As mentioned in the previous exercise, this exercise is also dedicated to building trust in your intimate relationship by asking you to share sensitive information about yourselves with one another. It increases your vulnerability by asking you to disclose negative information about yourself.

Benefit
As was mentioned before, trust is a basic building block in a well-functioning intimate relationship. Without trust partners grow apart and stop sharing themselves with one another. This is one of the most common reasons why relationships become problematic.

Prerequisite
"Sharing Likes"

Directions
Step One: Write down a list of no more than five things that you *do not* like about yourself. Do not spend more than 10 to 15 minutes developing this list.

Step Two: Without discussing it, give this list to your partner. There will be an opportunity to discuss the lists later.

Duration and Frequency
Just like "Sharing Likes," this is a brief exercise that does not need to be repeated. The time involved is only the time spent developing the list and reading your partner's list.

Suggestions
Be as honest as possible in preparing your list, but do not feel as though you have to include everything. You may skip some things if you feel that you would make yourself too vulnerable at this point. However, if you do skip an item now, think about revising your list later as your relationship becomes more trusting and open. Save your lists of dislikes—you will be using them in a future exercise.

Pitfalls
Talking about the lists prematurely could defeat the purpose of this exercise. Do not criticize or question your partner's list under any circumstances.

20 CONFIRMING LIKES

Purpose

This is the third in the series of four exercises dedicated to building trust in your intimate relationship. It asks you to talk about sensitive information with your partner in the most positive way.

Benefit

Again, remember, trust is a basic building block in a well-functioning intimate relationship. Without trust partners grow apart and stop sharing themselves with one another. Learning to trust is crucial to attempts at saving a relationship.

Prerequisites

"Sharing Likes"
"Sharing Dislikes"

Directions

Step One: From your partner's list given to you in "Sharing Likes," pick at least one item with which you completely agree (in other words, you agree that this is a nice thing about your partner).

Step Two: Select one partner to start the exercise. This partner explains to the other why she or he agrees with this item and why she or he likes this trait.

Step Three: After the first partner has finished discussing the item, switch roles. Repeat this for as many items as you like, but be sure that both partners agree beforehand on the actual number of repetitions.

Duration and Frequency

This exercise is short and can be repeated as often as you wish. Decide on the number of repetitions beforehand.

Suggestions

Be honest in your feedback to your partner, that is, do not say you like something if you do not. Insincerity is likely to be detected.

Pitfalls

Do not say anything negative or critical. Do not use sarcasm or irony.

21 *REFUTING DISLIKES*

Purpose This is the final exercise in the series of four dedicated to building trust in your intimate relationship. It is the most difficult one because it involves information that has made your partner quite vulnerable.

Benefit By now you know how important trust is to a well-functioning intimate relationship. Without it, partners grow apart and become strangers. This exercise is the most difficult one in the series and requires the strongest level of trust from both of you.

Prerequisites "Sharing Likes"
"Sharing Dislikes"
"Confirming Likes"

Directions **Step One:** From your partner's list given to you in "Sharing Dislikes," pick at least one item with which you completely *disagree* (in other words, you *do not agree* that this is a problem trait in your partner).

Step Two: Select one partner to start this exercise. This partner should be the one who did not start in "Confirming Likes." This partner explains why she or he disagrees with this item and why she or he does not think that it is a bad trait (it could be that you do not think that it is a bad trait to begin with, or it could be that you do not think it is a trait your partner has).

Step Three: After the first partner has finished discussing the item, switch roles. Repeat this as many times as you like, but be sure that both partners agree beforehand on the actual number of repetitions.

Duration and Frequency Again, this is a very short exercise, especially given its value to both partners and to the relationship. The number of repetitions can range from zero to the total number of items on your lists. However, the number of items to be covered should *always* be settled before you begin the exercise.

Suggestions Be honest with one another. Be sensitive to one another's vulnerabilities. Do not spend too much time on each repetition.

Pitfalls Never, under any circumstances, use this exercise to agree with items on your partner's list. Never use this exercise as a way to get at your partner or to criticize your partner.

22 GIVING A COMPLIMENT

Purpose   This exercise will help you share with your partner the things that you like about her or him.

Benefit   Sometimes in relationships people lose track of their partner's positive qualities. It was many of these positive attributes that first attracted you to your partner. But, somehow through the everyday grind of life, people forget the positive aspects of their partner, and perhaps even focus on the negative. By acknowledging the positive aspects, partners will gain a greater appreciation of the other person, as well as a greater appreciation of themselves.

Prerequisites   "Physical Attractiveness"

"Psychological Attractiveness"

"Sharing Likes"

"Confirming Likes"

Directions   **Step One:** Write down a list of seven things that you like about your partner. These can be physical, emotional, or personality traits. Be specific about the things you like and write the sentences in the following format:

- I appreciate _____ because _____
- I like _____ because _____
- Thank you for _____ because _____

Step Two: Find two comfortable chairs and move them so they face one another. Now sit comfortably across from each other.

Step Three: Select one partner to start the sharing portion of this exercise. This partner will then read one of the things on her or his list. The other partner should just listen to the compliment, being aware of how she or he is reacting to the compliment. Afterwards, the receiving partner is just to say, "Thank you," nothing else!

Step Four: Switch roles and repeat steps 1 to 3. Continue to go back and forth with each partner giving one compliment per turn until you have shared all the compliments. Remember, after receiving a compliment, say only, "Thank you," and move on to presenting your own positive statement about the partner.

Duration and Frequency   This exercise should take about 10 to 15 minutes to complete. It can be repeated as often as both partners wish. For any repetitions, each partner should make a list of seven (or any other prearranged number) new things that she or he likes about the other person. The number of compliments can be negotiated, as long as both partners agree on the number and as long as a limit is set.

Suggestions   Try very hard to be honest with yourself and with your partner. It may help to recall when you first started dating and some of the positive thoughts you had at that time. If you get stuck thinking of compliments, it may help to look back at the partner's list of what she or he likes about the self and at the items you chose to confirm for the partner. Be as specific and concrete as possible in your statement. Save your lists of compliments for future use.

Pitfalls   This is not the time to be sarcastic or ironic. Do not give a compliment unless you really believe it to be true. Try not to be vague or ambiguous in your compliment. State a specific attribute of your partner that you like. Do not qualify or negate your compliment with statements like "When you want to be . . .," "You used to be . . .," or "With everybody else. . . ." When you are receiving the compliment, do not argue with your partner, just accept it and say, "Thank you."

SECTION FOUR *Family of Origin*

EXERCISES

The exercises in this section are concerned with the partners' families of origin. People learn about relationships, even intimate ones, from messages and observations within their own family of origin as they grow up. Many of these observations and messages result in lifelong attitudes and values that carry over into the person's own intimate relationships. These unexplored attitudes can serve to hinder or facilitate relationships. These exercises are designed to help you take a look at the attitudes you have carried forth into your current relationship from your family of origin. Once you have recognized where your attitudes and opinions originated, you can choose whether you want to maintain or change them.

1 FAMILY TREE

Purpose This exercise is designed to help each partner build her or his own individual "family tree." A family tree lets you lay out your family on paper to see the relationships between family members and to look at your "roots." Your individual family trees can be useful in later exercises to help you identify and describe the quality of the relationships that your family members have.

Figure 1 represents an example of a completed family tree. This example is provided to give you an idea of how to build your own family tree. Your own family tree will probably be much more detailed than this example. Feel free to be creative in doing your own family drawing. Use a large sheet of paper to make sure that you do not run out of space.

Benefit This process will help both of you get an overview of your own and your partner's family members. By developing your family trees, you will gain a clearer understanding of your family members and hence who may have had an impact on your development. Furthermore, surprisingly many couples rarely talk about their extended families, leaving partners guessing about the number of siblings, aunts, uncles, and so forth, and the number of family-like relationships, such as those with foster parents or stepchildren.

Directions **Step One:** Get two very large pieces of paper and colored marking pens. Begin drawing your individual family trees about three-fourths of the way down on the page. Each partner should start her or his family tree by placing the two partners onto the page, as exemplified in Figure 1. Draw a circle around your name if you are a woman, and a square if you are a man.

Step Two: In each of your individual family trees, place all your brothers and sisters on the sheet. Place these siblings on the same row as yours. Use the sample family tree to help show you how to lay these names out. Include any stepbrothers and stepsisters as well as any deceased siblings. Remember to use names, as well as a circle or square to indicate whether it is a brother or sister.

Step Three: Place any children on the row below the two of you. This will include any adoptive children, stepchildren, and any children that are no longer alive. Place your brothers' and sisters' children on this row as well, connecting their names with their respective parents.

Step Four: Place any grandchildren on the row below the children.

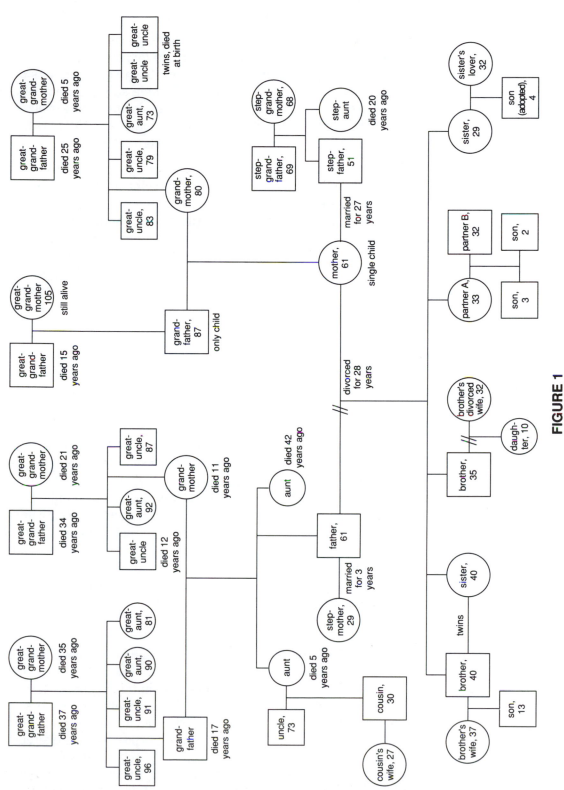

FIGURE 1
Partner A's Family Tree

Include any adoptive grandchildren, stepchildren, and any grandchildren that are no longer alive.

Step Five: Now place your parents above yourself. Include any stepparents, and any parents that are no longer alive. Above your parents, place your grandparents—both from your mother's and father's side. Again, do not forget to include stepgrandparents, foster grandparents, and so on. If a person is no longer living, you should still include her or him, but somehow indicate that the person is no longer alive (perhaps by drawing an × across the name).

Step Six: Continue adding all the people in your respective and combined families that you can possibly remember—the more the better. Include up to five generations: grandparents, parents, you, children, and grandchildren. Use the sample family tree as a reference. For each generation, include as many relatives as you can remember. At this point, however, all you are putting on your paper are names (and possibly familial relationships) in their appropriate gender symbol. Further details about the persons in your family tree can be added through the exercises that follow, if you wish.

Duration and Frequency

Plan to spend at least a couple of hours on this task. Be thorough; there will not be a need for repetition.

Suggestions

Use as large a piece of paper as you can find (2 × 3 feet would be great) to give yourself plenty of space to fill in all the names and possibly other details during later exercises. If you have step-, adoptive, or foster relatives, you may want to draw their gender box in a different color to differentiate them from your biological relatives. Use Figure 1 to guide your drawings, but feel free to alter them in any way that makes this task easier or more enjoyable for you. You can do this exercise in two different ways: You can choose one partner to go first, and together draw that person's family tree, then repeating the exercise for the second partner. Or you can each draw family relationships that belong in the same row at the same time. In other words, both of you may draw your children at the same time, each in your respective family tree; both of you may draw your siblings at the same time; and so on.

Pitfalls

If you choose to do the exercise simultaneously, do not make this a task where you do not collaborate or talk. If you choose to do the same row for each of you, one goes first in talking about the appropriate families, then draws, and then allows the partner to do the same on her or his family tree. Not talking about your families while drawing the tree counteracts the purpose of this exercise, which is for both of you to get a sense of each other's family members and relationships. Although this exercise has no real pitfalls other than lack of thoroughness or paper that is too small, you should still take the task seriously and collaborate with your partner.

2 *THE FAVORITE SIBLING*

NOTE: If neither of you has any siblings, skip this exercise. If one of you does not have any siblings, skip step 4.

Purpose

This exercise is designed to help you begin a detailed exploration of your family by focusing your attention on your favorite sibling.

Benefit

It is perfectly okay to identify one sibling as more liked than another. We all have such preferences. Most generally what they mean is that this particular sibling is more like us than our other siblings. That similarity is what makes this exercise of particular benefit to you. Most likely, you will identify some traits in your sibling that are also true for you, even though you have never thought of them as pertaining to you. As a result, you will probably not only learn new information about each other's family relationships, but also about your own characteristics.

Prerequisite

"Family Tree"

Directions

Step One: Select one partner to start this exercise. This partner identifies her or his favorite sibling from among the ones that *lived in the same household* during the childhood years. Share with your partner that person's name, your familial relationship, and her or his profession.

Step Two: Describe this person to your partner in detail. Cover everything you can remember, focusing primarily on that sibling's behavior, beliefs, attitudes, ideas, interests, hobbies, friends, school performance, involvement with you, and involvement with other family members. Talk about what you like and do not like about this sibling.

Step Three: The other partner should help you in your recollections by asking questions, reflecting information, responding empathically, and maintaining interest. That partner may even take some notes as you are talking to prevent you from forgetting important details.

Step Four: Once the first partner has shared all the information that can be remembered about this sibling, switch roles and repeat steps 1 to 3.

Duration and Frequency

As for all family-related exercises, the time frame for this exercise is difficult to predict; however, it is best to restrict yourselves to no more than 30 minutes per sibling. Furthermore, one of you may need some more time than the other to complete this task relative to your part of the family.

Suggestions   Remember to choose from all your siblings, whether they are full siblings, half siblings, adoptive siblings, foster siblings, or unrelated other children who lived in your household when you were growing up. The more detail you can come up with about your favorite sibling the better. Focus primarily on her or his traits as a child, though toward the end you may also explore present-day characteristics. Cooperate with and help your partner by using the communication skills you have learned by now. If you wish, you can put your notes directly onto the family tree.

Pitfalls   There are few pitfalls that you will face in this exercise because you are focusing your attention on a person you like and enjoy. The major problem perhaps is the failure to take the exercise seriously. Remember, however, that any looking back on family relationships can result in some painful memories. Stop the exercise if things are too painful. You may even want to involve your counselor to a large extent to help you deal with any old, hurtful feelings. Furthermore, it is important that the two of you be supportive of one another, and that you *never* minimize your partner's pain that may result from childhood memories or recollections of family members.

3 OTHER SIBLINGS

NOTE: If neither of you has any siblings, skip this exercise. If one of you does not have any additional siblings, skip step 4.

Purpose

This exercise will help you continue your exploration of the dynamics and attributes of the members of your family of origin. It serves to fill in some more detail by looking at the rest of your siblings.

Benefit

This exercise continues your analysis of the family members of your family of origin. It asks you to take a look at siblings other than your favorite one because all siblings are likely to have made an important contribution to your development. Assessing all your siblings according to their likes, dislikes, beliefs, attitudes, and so on can provide interesting insights about your family's influence on all of you and about patterns in your family.

Prerequisite

"The Favorite Sibling"

Directions

Step One: Select one partner to start this exercise. For all of your siblings not covered in the previous exercise who *lived in your household* during your childhood years, go through the following steps, covering them one by one. For each person, give her or his name, the relationship to you (biological, foster, adoptive, etc.), and profession.

Step Two: Describe each sibling individually and in some detail. Cover everything you remember, including what you liked and disliked about this person, special traits and physical features, special interests or hobbies, and what kinds of friends this person had.

Step Three: The other partner helps in these recollections by discussing the information presented, asking questions that convey interest, and by responding empathically and supportively if painful memories emerge.

Step Four: Once the first partner has covered all the information that can be remembered about her or his siblings, switch roles and repeat steps 1 to 3.

Duration and Frequency

The time needed for this exercise can vary greatly for different people; however, it is best to limit discussions to 30 minutes per sibling. Furthermore, one of you may need a bit more time than the other to complete this task, especially if one of you has significantly more siblings than the other.

Suggestions

Be sure to include all children in your childhood household, regardless of blood relationship. Half, adoptive, or foster siblings are as important as full biological brothers and sisters. Again, the more detail you can use in describing these children, the better. Focus on childhood, but add adult traits if you wish. Cooperate with and help your partner by using the communication skills you have learned by now. You may want to take some notes about the siblings directly on your respective family trees.

Pitfalls

The danger exists that this type of looking back at your families may bring about some hurtful memories. It is important that the two of you be supportive of one another, and that you *never* minimize your partner's pain. Be sure not to seem bored or uninterested. Finding out about your partner's siblings can help you understand her or him better. Being bored in this task may signal a lack of caring for the partner, whether this is intended or not.

4 *EASY PARENT*

Purpose   This exercise will guide you in how to begin an exploration of your relationship with your parents by considering the parent with whom you got along the best. It helps you identify attributes about this parent, and encourages you to explore how these characteristics have affected you and how you yourself may be carrying them on.

Benefit   As we grow up, our parents serve as role models to us. As a result, we adopt many of their attitudes, values, ideas, and behaviors. Gaining a better understanding of our parents often helps us understand our own behaviors and feelings. It can also help us to see patterns in our families. For instance, abusive parenting behavior tends to run in families. That is, if your parent disciplined you by hitting you, you are at higher risk of using that same technique with your own children. Understanding this pattern can be helpful in breaking the cycle. Finally, this type of exploration will help you and your partner understand one another better and can lead to significant improvement in your relationship because you will have more tolerance and understanding for your partner, and significantly improved communication.

Prerequisite   "Family Tree"

Directions   **Step One:** Select one partner to go first. This partner will identify the one parental figure in her or his childhood with whom she or he got along best. This can be any parental figure, including a mother, father, stepmother, stepfather, grandparent, aunt, or uncle. Share with your partner that person's name, your relationship, and her or his profession (including that of homemaker).

Step Two: Use as much detail as possible in describing this parent to your partner. Cover everything you can remember through your own personal memory and from stories others tell you about this parent and about your relationship with her or him in early years. Do not forget to include your parent's beliefs about life, attitudes toward children and work, ideas, interests and hobbies, and, most important, her or his involvement with you. The relationship of this parent with your other parent(s) is also important to note.

Step Three: The other partner will help you in your recollections by asking questions that show interest and caring and by being supportive if painful memories should emerge. That partner should take some notes, perhaps directly onto the family tree, as you are talking to prevent both of you from forgetting important details.

Step Four: Once the first partner has shared all the information she or he can remember about this parent, switch roles and repeat steps 1 to 3. If the first part of the exercise took too much time, you may want to wait until another time to go over the other partner's easy parent.

Duration and Frequency

The time frame for this exercise can vary from a few minutes to a few hours per partner. Discuss beforehand how much time you are willing or able to spend, and then share it equally between the discussion of your two respective parents.

Suggestions

Remember to choose from all your parental figures if there are more than just biological parents. Include in your selection adoptive parents, foster parents, step parents, or others. But in the end, choose the one that you remember as being the one with whom you got along the "easiest." Be very thorough in your description of this parent and her or his characteristics. Help each other by using the communication and listening skills you have learned by now. Support and caring are particularly important to exercises that involve the exploration of relationships with parents.

Pitfalls

Looking back at your families, especially your parents, may bring about some hurtful feelings, painful memories, and surprising reactions. It is important that the two of you be very supportive of one another, and that you *never* minimize the pain a partner may express as she or he discusses this "easy" parent. Just because this parent was the easier one to get along with does not mean that she or he was a great parent who always did the right thing.

5 DIFFICULT PARENT

Purpose   This exercise is designed to continue your exploration of your relationships with your parents. It challenges you to think about your relationship with your more difficult parent to help you analyze that person's attributes and her or his continued impact on you.

Benefit   As discussed in "Easy Parent," our parents serve as role models as we grow up, and we often become like our parents in regard to attitudes, values, ideas, and behaviors. This is true not only for "easy" parents, but also for "difficult" ones, and not only for positive behaviors but also for inappropriate ones. Because we model ourselves after our parents, exploring memories of our parents helps us gain a better understanding of who we are and why we behave the way we do. This, in turn, can often help to explain issues we face in current intimate relationships. Such insights can lead to significant improvements in your intimate relationship because both of you will have greater understanding for each other's behavior and therefore will be more tolerant of one another.

Prerequisites   "Family Tree"
"Easy Parent"

Directions   **Step One:** Select one partner to start this exercise. This partner needs to identify the parental figure in her or his childhood with whom she or he had the most difficulty getting along. Share with your partner that person's name, your familial relationship, and her or his profession.

Step Two: Describe this person with as much detail as possible. Cover what you can remember from personal memories as well as what you remember from statements about this parent by other people. Many of these memories may be unpleasant; try to find a few, if at all possible, that are pleasant or neutral. Think of how other people may describe this person to gain an objective perspective. Also include in your discussion how this parent related to other parental figures in your life.

Step Three: By asking questions, reflecting information, responding empathically, and maintaining interest, the other partner helps as much as possible in this process of exploration. Caring, support, and concern will be critical in the discussion of this difficult parent. Here, more so than in any other exercise,

129

painful emotions may emerge that must be responded to appropriately by the partner. Use your best listening and communication skills. Do not forget to take some notes as the partner is talking.

Step Four: Once the first partner has shared all the information she or he can remember about the difficult parent, switch roles and repeat steps 1 to 3. If the first part of the exercise took a lot of time, you may want to wait until another time to go over the other partner's difficult parent.

Duration and Frequency   As for the previous exercise, the time frame for this exercise is difficult to predict and could vary from a few minutes to a few hours. It is best, however, for you to attempt to split your available time evenly between the discussion of your two respective difficult parents.

Suggestions   As indicated in "Easy Parent," remember to choose from all your parental figures if you had more than your biological parents. Be thorough in your description of your most difficult parent and her or his characteristics. Cooperate with your partner by using the communication skills you have learned by now. As you do this exercise, you may choose to make some notes on the family tree itself. Be willing to make yourself a little vulnerable with your partner by admitting any sad or angry feelings that come up as you discuss your difficult parent. If you are the listener, acknowledge the partner's vulnerability and help her or him feel safe and protected.

Pitfalls   A danger exists that this type of looking back at your difficult parent may bring about some hurtful emotions and reactions. It is most important that the two of you be supportive of one another, and that you *never* minimize your partner's pain that may result from childhood memories or recollections of difficult parents. If the discussion of the difficult parent becomes too painful for the disclosing partner, consider ending the exercise and seeking help from your counselor to deal with any unfinished business there might be with this parent.

6 *FAMILY-OF-ORIGIN ROLES*

Purpose   This exercise is designed to help you recognize the roles your various family members, including yourself, played within your family of origin.

Benefit   Often roles people take on early in life are carried into adulthood and profoundly influence how we relate to others. Exploration of early life roles can help us understand why we do what we do and provides us with a springboard for change.

Prerequisites   "The Favorite Sibling"
"Other Siblings"
"Easy Parent"
"Difficult Parent"

Directions   **Step One:** Select one partner to go first. For all of your family members *covered so far*, identify how they fit into your family and what role they played by looking at the following aspects of functioning:

- role (e.g., money earner, clown, party organizer)
- function (e.g., keep everyone happy, distract from problems)
- type (e.g., happy-go-lucky, serious, distracted, sad)
- conflicts (e.g., argumentative with parent, truant, fighter)
- add your own dimensions as necessary and appropriate

Step Two: Describe each family member to your partner in detail. Cover everything you can remember, focusing primarily on the above categories.

Step Three: The other partner should help you in your recollections by keeping you on task and by maintaining and communicating interest. That partner should take some notes as you are talking because many details are easily forgotten if not recorded while the memory is discussed.

Step Four: Once the first partner runs out of memories and analyses about various family members, switch roles and repeat steps 1 to 3.

Duration and Frequency   Try to keep this exercise to approximately 10 to 15 minutes per family member discussed. If you talk any longer than that about any one person, the task may become too tedious. The total length of the exercise will depend on the number of relevant family members.

Suggestions   Cooperate with and help your partner by using the communication and listening skills you have learned by now. Allow for plenty of time and be supportive and patient with one another. Make some of your notes directly on your respective family trees, if you wish. Focus on the dimensions outlined in step 1, so as not to make this exercise repetitive with previous ones that covered the same family members. In this exercise, you are not so much describing the person as exploring the person's role in your family.

Pitfalls   Do not get sidetracked by describing the person all over again; that was the task of previous exercises. Instead, focus on her or his role in your family. Be aware of your own and your partner's feelings as these roles are discussed. If you begin to notice patterns, you may note these (verbally or in writing), but for now, refrain from discussing them as they pertain to your relationship. Such discussion is reserved for later exercises.

7 UNDERSTANDING MOTHER'S BACKGROUND

Purpose

This exercise is designed to continue your exploration of the dynamics and attributes of the members of your family of origin. It serves to fill in detail about your extended family on your mother's side.

Benefit

Knowing more about one's family across the generations often provides helpful insights into why certain things take place in our families. It helps us develop more empathy with our family members and understand ourselves in relationships much better. Such self-knowledge makes us more able to change and more willing to be tolerant of others' quirks and interactional styles.

Prerequisite

"Family-of-Origin Roles"

Directions

Step One: Select a partner to begin this exercise. This partner will identify all family members on her or his mother's side who can be remembered. Look at your family tree to make sure you include everyone.

Step Two: Share with your partner each person's name, your familial relationship, and her or his profession. Describe each person to your partner in some detail. Include information about the person's role in your mother's life, and focus particularly on recognizing patterns or specific life-styles that seem to reemerge in different generations.

Step Three: The other partner helps by asking relevant questions, by pointing out interesting tidbits that emerge, and by listening for patterns and life-style choices. That partner may take some notes directly on the family tree, if desired.

Step Four: When the first partner is finished, switch roles and repeat steps 1 to 3.

Duration and Frequency

A minimum of 30 minutes per partner should be allowed. If you want to use more time, be sure to agree upon a time frame before you start the exercise. Both partners should have approximately equal time.

Suggestions

Help your partner's exploration through using the listening skills you have learned by now. Listening is important in this exercise because often we discover patterns by listening, not by talking. The listening partner has a heavy responsibility in this exercise in this regard. Be supportive and patient with one another, as well as understanding and caring.

Pitfalls Looking at roles, patterns, and life-styles in your mother's, and hence your own, life may reveal painful realities. Patterns of abuse or neglect may emerge; life-styles of unconcern and hostility may be discovered. Such recognition can be very painful, and recognizing these patterns in your own life often is overwhelming. Be careful not to overburden yourselves. Feel free to take breaks as necessary and consider doing this exercise only in the presence of your counselor if you expect a lot of unfinished business to arise or if you have a history of abuse.

8 UNDERSTANDING FATHER'S BACKGROUND

Purpose   This exercise will continue your exploration of your family of origin by filling in detail about your extended family on your father's side.

Benefit   Patterns tend to repeat themselves across generations, and recognizing such patterns provides helpful insights into why certain things take place in our families. This, in turn, helps us understand ourselves better in our intimate relationships and paves the way for change. It is impossible to change behaviors, attitudes, or beliefs if we are not aware of having them. Exploring families will help us recognize these patterns in ourselves.

Prerequisite   "Understanding Mother's Background"

Directions   **Step One:** The partner who did not start "Understanding Mother's Background" begins this exercise by identifying all family members on her or his father's side who can be remembered from childhood.

Step Two: For each person a name and familial relationship is provided. Also identify the person's profession. Move on to describe each person in some detail. Cover everything you can remember including but not limited to typical behaviors, general beliefs and attitudes, interests, and goals. Focus also on each person's role in and contribution to the extended family. Explore the impact on your father. Look for patterns that seem repetitive and life-styles passed on across generations.

Step Three: The other partner needs to help you in your recollections by asking questions and reflecting or summarizing information. Such reflection and summary serves to help you recognize patterns, to provide support, and to signal interest. The partner may even take some notes as you are talking to capture all necessary detail.

Step Four: Switch roles and repeat steps 1 to 3 when the first partner has depleted her or his fund of information about the father's family.

Duration and Frequency   Allow at least 30 minutes per partner, but feel free to use more time. If you want to use more time, set a limit per partner before you begin.

Suggestions   Again, patterns are best detected through careful listening. Hence, the listening partner has the difficult job of summarizing and making sense of a lot of material that is being covered here. Be patient and supportive.

Pitfalls   The discovery of patterns and life-styles serves to clarify our current reactions and relationships. Despite this positive effect, the discovery of the passage of styles from generation to generation can be painful and exhausting. If you already have a strained relationship with your father, or if there is a history of abuse in your relationship with him, consider doing this exercise only in the presence of your counselor. It is possible that pain will overwhelm you and that new memories may emerge that you did not know you had.

9 *YOUR PARTNER'S PARENTS*

Purpose   The goal in this exercise is to identify and discuss any common characteristics or qualities each partner shares with her or his own parent(s). It is intended to continue your exploration of the effect of the dynamics and attributes of the members of your family of origin on you personally and on your current intimate relationship.

Benefit   As a child, your parents most likely had a profound influence on your development. Children often strive to be like their parents and, as a result, take on similar qualities and characteristics. This process is an inevitable aspect of growing up and does not stop on reaching adulthood. Indeed, much of who a person is, her or his characteristics, values, morals, ideas, and so on will be quite similar to those of her or his parent(s). By identifying these similarities, you can gain a better understanding and awareness of the influences that helped make you who you are today. This, in turn, will help you gain a better awareness of who you are within your relationship with your partner.

Prerequisites   "Understanding Mother's Background"

"Understanding Father's Background"

Directions   **Step One:** Separately, both partners are to write down as many characteristics as they can recall that their partner shares with her or his parents. These qualities include such things as values, morals, thoughts, physical appearance, and behaviors. As you write these lists, try to be objective and unbiased and avoid being critical and disparaging of your partner or her or his parents.

Step Two: Once both partners have completed the first step, select one partner to start the sharing portion of this exercise. This partner will share what she or he perceives as similarities between partner and partner's parent(s). In sharing the list, the partner will simply read each characteristic one at a time.

Step Three: While the first partner is sharing her or his list, the other partner should just listen. The only speaking on this partner's part should be limited to questions to help clarify one of the characteristics. This is not the time to agree or disagree.

Step Four: This process continues until the first partner has shared her or his entire list. At this point, switch roles and repeat steps 1 to 3. If the first part of the exercise took a long time, you

137

may want to wait until your next meeting time to complete the other partner's family tree.

Duration and Frequency

As for all family-of-origin exercises, the time frame for this exercise is difficult to predict and could vary from a few minutes to a few hours per partner. Furthermore, one of you may need significantly more time than the other to complete this task relative to your part of the family. Talk about a reasonable time frame beforehand and try to stick to it.

Suggestions

As you develop your list, be as objective and unbiased as possible. Do not use this exercise as an opportunity to criticize your partner or her or his parents. The purpose is to identify similarities, not to point out faults. Be sure to include positive similarities, not just negative ones. Be as specific about the similarities as possible; it will help your partner in seeing the similarity her- or himself.

Pitfalls

Perhaps the greatest danger is for one partner to take this exercise as an opportunity to criticize her or his partner or her or his partner's parents. This will do nothing except completely ruin the value and effectiveness of this exercise. Another potential pitfall is focusing exclusively on either positive or negative characteristics. Instead, it is important to identify both positives and negatives. Last, for the listener, it is important to try to remain open and receptive and not to become angry and defensive.

10 YOUR SIBLINGS' COMMITTED RELATIONSHIPS

NOTE: If you don't have any siblings, skip this exercise. If one of you does not have a sibling, skip step 4.

Purpose   This exercise is designed to continue the exploration of patterns and dynamics specific to your family of origin. It does so by asking you to fill in detail about your siblings' committed relationships.

Benefit   Knowing more about our siblings' committed relationships often provides helpful insights into our own intimate relationships. After all, it is likely that of all the adults in our lives, we are most like our siblings. By looking closely at our siblings' committed relationships, we may learn to understand ourselves in relationships much better because there may be important parallels and similarities.

Prerequisites   "The Favorite Sibling"

"Other Siblings"

"Understanding Mother's Background"

"Understanding Father's Background"

Directions   **Step One:** Select a partner to begin. This partner identifies all siblings and the committed relationships that they are currently in or have been in during adulthood. The partner will share all that she or he knows or can remember about these relationships.

Step Two: In discussing these relationships, cover everything you can remember, including displays of affection, arguments, activities they shared, areas of agreement and disagreement, and similarities and dissimilarities. Be sure to include any other committed relationships that you can recall, for example, prior and subsequent relationships.

Step Three: The other partner helps by asking clarifying questions and through reflection. If the partner knows the siblings and the relationships under investigation, she or he is allowed to add information from her or his perspective once the first partner has recalled everything from her or his perspective. The listening partner may take some notes to record details.

Step Four: After the first partner has gone through all of her or his siblings, switch roles and repeat steps 1 to 3.

Duration and Frequency   This exercise will last about 15 minutes per sibling. Total time will depend on the number of siblings and relationships that need to be discussed.

Suggestions   Cooperate with your partner by using the communication skills you have learned by now. As always, be as open and honest as possible. Listen for patterns and similarities across relationships.

Pitfalls   There are few pitfalls in this exercise. It is a little bit easier to talk about siblings' than parents' or one's own relationships. Avoid discussing similarities with your own intimate relationship for now. This will happen later.

11 *YOUR PARENTS' RELATIONSHIP*

Purpose   This exercise continues the exploration of intimate relationship patterns in your two respective families. Now that siblings' relationships have been scrutinized, it is time to take a look at the intimate relationship of your parents.

Benefit   Knowing more about our parents' relationship with one another often provides helpful insights into how we formulated our opinions about what a committed relationship should be like. After all, childhood is a time of great learning, including learning about what relationships between adults are like. By looking closely at our parents' relationship (or relationships), both from our childhood and our current adult perspective, we learn more about ourselves and our own attitudes about intimacy and adult relating.

Prerequisites   "Understanding Mother's Background"

"Understanding Father's Background"

"Your Siblings' Committed Relationships"

Directions   **Step One:** Select a partner to go first. This partner begins by identifying and listing in chronological order all the committed relationships for each of her or his parents. For some people, this will include only the mother's and father's relationship. For others, it may include previous and subsequent relationships. The first partner will share all that she or he can remember about these relationships, with the strongest emphasis on the intimate relationship of the parent(s) with whom most of her or his childhood was spent.

Step Two: To be sure that you include all relevant detail, discuss everything you can remember about your parents' displays of affection, arguments, shared activities, areas of agreement and disagreement, similarities and dissimilarities, and so forth. If there is more than one committed relationship per parent, pay particular attention to how the intimate relationships of the same parent varied or stayed the same across different partners.

Step Three: The other partner helps you in your recollections by reflecting information, responding empathically, and asking questions. That partner should take some notes, perhaps directly on your family tree.

Step Four: Once the talking partner cannot recall any additional information, switch roles and repeat steps 1 to 3.

Duration and Frequency   Plan at least 15 minutes per committed relationship that will be discussed. Calculate the total time you should plan for this exercise by multiplying 15 minutes by the number of committed relationships your parents had.

Suggestions   This is a tough exercise. Take your time and be tolerant of one another. Ask each other questions if you think the partner is leaving out information. Be sure to think of your parents' committed relationships not only from your current perspective, but also from your childhood perspective. Things that may make sense to you now may have startled you when you were a child; things you may have taken for granted as a child may seem inappropriate from your current adult perspective. Do not hide any facts; trust your partner to be responsible in how she or he handles the information you share.

Pitfalls   This exercise can derail if you try to do it too quickly or if you compare your parents' relationships to your own. Stick to the task of recounting what you remember. A major problem with this exercise can be that one partner may not be sensitive to the painful feelings that can be evoked in the other person as details of parents' intimate relationships are recounted. Lack of honesty also will destroy the purpose of this exercise.

12 *RELATIONSHIP PATTERNS*

Purpose   This exercise is designed to compile and make sense of the information you have gained in your exploration of the committed relationships of your parents and siblings. It serves to identify any common relationship patterns that your siblings and parents may share.

Benefit   Being able to identify and examine patterns in the committed relationships of your siblings and parents often provides valuable information about your own relationship. By looking closely at your siblings' and parents' relationships, you may gain a better understanding of what you have learned from your family of origin about relationships. This, in turn, will help you understand your current relationship much better.

Prerequisites   "Your Siblings' Committed Relationships"
"Your Parents' Relationship"

Directions   **Step One:** Select one partner to start this exercise. This partner will identify any patterns that she or he noticed about the *other* partner's siblings' and parents' relationships. That is, the first partner should see if there are any similarities or patterns among the committed relationships of her or his partners' siblings or parents. In identifying these patterns, the partner should focus on all aspects of the relationships, including both constructive and destructive patterns. Use any notes you took in "Your Siblings' Committed Relationships" and "Your Parents' Relationship" to facilitate your task.

Step Two: While the first partner is talking, the other partner should focus on listening and remaining open to the information. This is not the time to dispute or argue over the presence of patterns.

Step Three: After the first partner has identified as many patterns as possible, take a few moments to discuss these patterns and add any more patterns that may come to mind. When this has been done, switch roles and repeat steps 1 and 2. If the first part of the exercise took a long time, you may want to wait until your next meeting time to complete the other partner's turn.

Duration and Frequency   Plan on approximately 30 minutes, though this may be a relatively short exercise for some.

Suggestions Do not challenge what your partner has identified as a pattern. Be honest with your partner—it is important to your relationship to identify as many patterns as possible.

Pitfalls Because one partner will be sharing her or his impressions about the other partner's family, there is a risk of the receiving partner's becoming defensive or even angry. This partner should work hard at just listening and trying to remain open and receptive to the information. At the same time, the discussing partner should not take this opportunity to criticize or lambaste her or his partner's family. The purpose is to identify objectively patterns among relationships, not to identify weaknesses or faults.

13 *REENACTING THE PAST*

Purpose   This exercise continues the exploration of patterns in intimate relationships for your family of origin by assessing how you yourselves may be recreating your parents' relationships in your own intimate relationship with each other.

Benefit   Previous exercises, including "Relationship Patterns," asked you to identify patterns among your siblings' and parents' relationships. This exercise will have you examine whether these patterns exist within your own relationship. This knowledge will give you greater insight into the forces that have affected your relationship. This knowledge, in turn, will help empower you to become free from your past.

Prerequisite   "Relationship Patterns"

Directions   **Step One:** Select one partner to start this exercise. This partner will take the information learned from the previous exercise on "Relationship Patterns" and apply it to the current relationship with her or his partner. In so doing, she or he will take the identified patterns one at a time and share them with her or his partner to assess whether the pattern holds true in their current relationship.

Step Two: While the first partner is sharing her or his perception of the pattern(s), the other partner merely listens. This is not the time to agree or disagree. However, the listening partner will take ample notes during the sharing process.

Step Three: This continues until the first partner has shared each identified pattern. At this point, switch roles and repeat steps 1 and 2.

Step Four: Select any pattern(s) both of you noticed and agreed upon as being present in your intimate relationship with one another. For each pattern, rate it with regard to whether you find it positive, negative, or neutral. If it is a positive pattern, no change is necessary; if neutral, ignore it for now, but perhaps come back to it later; and if negative, allow each partner to talk about how it affects her or him.

Step Five: Together, outline the role each of you plays in a given negative pattern. Problem-solve how each of you could change her or his behavior to change the overall pattern. Use the skills you

145

learned previously to problem-solve and compromise. Keep this up until you have reached a solution.

Step Six: Repeat step 5 for each negative pattern. Repeat step 5 for each neutral pattern both of you agree you would like to change.

Duration and Frequency

This is a most important and very lengthy exercise. Depending on how many negative patterns you identify, this exercise may last several days or weeks.

Suggestions

Do not discard or refute an identified pattern too easily. Look at each one carefully and try to be as objective as possible about its presence or absence in your present relationship. In problem solving and compromising, go back to the verbal communication section of this book and reread appropriate sections to ascertain whether you are using good communication and listening skills. Give yourselves plenty of time because this is one of the most important exercises in this book. Be willing to do this exercise exclusively in the presence of your counselor if you have difficulty negotiating compromises or if you feel yourselves getting excessively angry with one another. The fact that you have reached this point in the exercises makes it very likely that you can succeed with this exercise. Be patient.

Pitfalls

A possible danger is the denial of the existence of any identified patterns within your current relationship. Because it is likely that at least some of the patterns are present in your relationship, you should take your time and carefully consider each pattern. This exercise should not be taken as an opportunity to blame one another for any relationship problems. The goal is not to ascribe blame but rather to gain understanding. A big problem that could arise in this exercise is insufficient time. This is one of the longest exercises. Be willing to spend several weeks if necessary.

14 THE PICTORIAL FAMILY TREE

Purpose
This exercise is designed to add an additional piece to your exploration of your families of origin.

Benefit
Pictures add a different component to our recollections—sometimes they confirm what we remember, sometimes they contradict our memories. In any case, they add one more component of information.

Directions
Step One: Select one partner to start this exercise. This partner will go through family albums to try to find pictures of her or his family members discussed in previous exercises. While doing this, it is important to pay attention to any additional information you might gather from this task about your family.

Step Two: The other partner should help you in this task by asking questions and pointing out features that either support or contradict what you have revealed about your family so far.

Step Three: Once the first partner has picked out pictures of family members, switch roles and repeat steps 1 to 4. If the first part of the exercise took a long time, you may want to wait until your next meeting time to go over the other partner's family albums.

Duration and Frequency
This exercise can be quick if you have few pictures, or can take a lot of time if you have many. Set a predetermined maximum time limit; then split it evenly.

Suggestions
Avoid conflict or fighting by using the communication and listening skills you have learned by now. If you have space, you may want to add some pictures to your family tree. However, you may keep them separate from your family album in some other manner as well (e.g., in a collage).

Pitfalls
There are few pitfalls for this exercise because it merely involves additional data gathering. However, some pictures may bring back sad memories or may evoke angry feelings. Be willing to end the exercise if these feelings become overwhelming. Ask your counselor for help if necessary.

15 THE FIRST FAMILY MEMORY

Purpose   This exercise will provide further help in getting you to think back to your childhood and your family during those days. It will help you get back in touch with the feelings you experienced as a child within your family of origin.

Benefit   The first step in learning about how events that happened in your childhood influence your present-day relationships is to try to understand how you felt and what you and your family did when you were very young. Getting back in touch with these feelings will help you understand yourself and your reactions to your partner. As you remember, through earlier exercises, you learned that the way you react to your partner is greatly affected by how you interpret her or his behavior. The next step is for you to learn that how you interpret your partner's behavior is strongly influenced by your family background. As a result, by becoming more aware of your feelings and memories in the context of your family of origin, you will be able to understand your current relationships better and to avoid unnecessary conflict.

Directions   **Step One:** Choose a partner to start the exercise. This partner starts talking about her or his childhood within the family of origin, slowly working backwards toward earlier and earlier memories.

Step Two: The other partner helps this process of remembering by asking questions, by reflecting (remember "Advanced Reflection" and "Empathic Reflection" in section 2), and by paying close attention and listening.

Step Three: Once the first partner has arrived at what is believed to be the earliest memory, she or he needs to describe in detail everything that is remembered. Focus on what happened, how it felt, whom it involved, and what happened afterwards. The other partner helps by asking questions, listening, and using reflection.

Step Four: Explore the memory to see what relevance it holds for your life experiences today. For example, perhaps the memory was of being left by a parent, resulting in the child's being afraid of having been permanently abandoned. Maybe this experience is related to the adult's fears today of being alone and concern that the partner may want to leave. Try to see how your childhood memories are connected to your feelings in the present.

Step Five: Switch roles and repeat steps 1 to 4.

Duration and Frequency	The duration of this exercise is difficult to estimate. It depends on how long it takes each individual to remember early childhood memories. As a result, it could take anywhere from a few minutes to a few hours for each partner. Repeating this exercise is unnecessary, unless the partners want to explore other childhood memories.

Suggestions Take your time in thinking back to the very earliest family-of-origin memory you have. For most people, the first thing that comes to mind is not the very earliest remembered event. So keep trying to think back to younger and younger ages until you are reasonably sure that you cannot remember any further back. It might help to use landmark events such as birthdays, moves, accidents, and so on to push your memory further and further back. Sometimes it helps to call a brother, sister, cousin, or friend to see what they remember about you and your family during your early childhood.

Pitfalls It happens occasionally that as people recall their early childhood they remember something very painful, such as being left by a parent, being abused, experiencing a death in the family, or similar events. If this happens, talk to your partner about the memories. In rare circumstances, the memory may be so overwhelming and painful that a person may need to stop the exercise and work with her or his counselor on this memory. But do not let this possibility frighten you from doing the exercise. If you have such a strong, painful memory, you will need to deal with it at some point because it probably has a significant impact on your feelings and actions today.

It will probably present more problems if you cannot remember anything at all. This might indicate that something was so painful in your childhood that your mind has responded by blocking out any memory of the events. In this case, after you have followed the suggestions given above, skip to the next exercise.

16 *WHAT I'M HANGING ONTO— UNFINISHED BUSINESS*

Purpose   This exercise will help you identify negative situations and events that occurred within your family of origin about which you still have strong feelings.

Benefit   Much happens to us, both positive and negative, during our childhood within our family of origin. Although families can be a vital source of happy events and pleasant memories, they can also be the source of unhappy events and unpleasant memories. When unpleasant events occur and the feelings and reactions they produce remain unresolved, the events can continue to have an impact on our lives and color our outlook. The first step in eliminating or minimizing this impact is to identify the events that have caused hurt or painful feelings and emotions.

Directions   **Step One:** Independently, each partner should take some time and think back over her or his childhood. Choose a quiet time when you are unlikely to be disturbed.

Step Two: Try to remember as many important events of your childhood as possible. Focus on recalling events that caused hurt or painful feelings at the time they occurred. As you recall these painful events, try to remember what happened, who was involved, and how you felt at the time. Write this information down as soon as possible.

Step Three: Keep this list private and at this time do not share it with your partner.

Duration and Frequency   This exercise could take anywhere from 30 minutes to 2 to 3 hours. It may also take several different attempts to complete it.

Suggestions   One approach is to think slowly backwards through your life to your earliest memories and then to work forward from there. Another approach is to identify landmarks within each year of your life such as birthdays, first day of school, or graduation. Using these landmarks as starting points, try to recall what else occurred around these times in your life. Include as many negative events as you can recall, including everything from major life crises to minor hurt feelings. At this point the goal is to identify the events, not to evaluate their importance or impact.

Occasionally people have difficulty remembering much of their childhood. In these cases, it may be helpful to look at photographs, diaries, yearbooks, and similar sources to jog your memory. It may also be helpful to talk to people who knew you when you were a child and ask them to recall some events in your life. Often when people begin to spend some time recalling their childhood using landmark events, the memories start rolling back.

Pitfalls   Perhaps the most worrisome danger is that you may recall some traumatic event that was previously hidden from your awareness and that this recollection may cause you severe distress in your present life. If this occurs, you should immediately let your counselor know. Another pitfall is the possibility that you will not be able to remember much about your childhood. In this case, use some of the approaches mentioned in "The First Family Memory" to stir your memory. A final pitfall might be the inability to identify any negative events whatsoever in your childhood. Negative events occur in everybody's childhood; this is a part of life and of growing up. Perhaps you are trying too hard to identify extremely traumatic events and are overlooking the everyday, mundane occurrences in childhood that nonetheless cause painful feelings. Remember, the pain or hurt is not based on how you would react today, but rather how you reacted as a child.

17 SHARING NEGATIVE EXPERIENCES

Purpose   This exercise is designed to help you share with your partner the negative events you identified in "What I'm Hanging Onto—Unfinished Business."

Benefit   What your partner experienced in her or his childhood, both negative and positive, may have a significant impact on who she or he is today. Thus, a better understanding of your partner's childhood will lead to a greater understanding of your partner. This increased understanding can provide greater insight into what each partner brings to the relationship which, in turn, can lead to a better understanding of the relationship itself.

Prerequisite   "What I'm Hanging Onto—Unfinished Business"

Directions   **Step One:** Select one partner to start this exercise. This partner should review the list that she or he developed during "What I'm Hanging Onto—Unfinished Business" and select one of the events to share with her or his partner. Both partners should agree on how many items to review during this exercise.

Step Two: The speaking partner should share this event with her or his partner, relating what occurred, who was involved, and how she or he felt. Focus on only one event at a time and share with your partner as much detail about it as possible.

Step Three: While the first partner is sharing the item from her or his list, the other partner should be just listening. The only speaking on this partner's part may be questions to help clarify details about the event. The listening partner should practice the active and empathic listening skills that were learned in earlier exercises. This is a time for sharing and listening, not for critiquing or discussing.

Step Four: After the speaking partner has shared her or his first item on the list, switch roles repeat steps 1 to 3. Continue this process, going back and forth, until you have either shared all your items or reached the predetermined time limit.

Duration and Frequency   Before starting, decide on a time limit for this exercise. It is recommended that no more than 30 to 45 minutes be spent on this exercise at any given time. You may need to repeat the exercise several times to make it all the way through the lists.

Suggestions   As the speaker, you may want to start off with one of the less painful events. In this way, you will slowly work your way to the more painful and hurtful events that occurred in your childhood. As the listener, it is important not to evaluate or critique the event but rather just to listen. What is painful for one person is not necessarily painful for the next; however, this does not lessen the pain for the person who does experience the event as painful or hurtful.

Pitfalls   It is important to be supportive of one another throughout this exercise. Do not criticize or ridicule your partner for her or his feelings or for the events that occurred in her or his life. Be honest about the negative events in your life. However, if there is something that you just do not want to share with your partner at this time, do not pressure yourself to do so for the time being. At the same time, take some risks with your partner and share as much as you possibly can. Avoid hidden criticisms or blaming, including statements such as, "Why didn't you try harder to resist?"

18 CLARIFYING

Purpose This exercise is designed to help you use the information you gained in exploring your negative childhood events to improve your present relationship. The goal is to identify what, if any, impact the negative events have on your present relationship.

Benefit Being able to identify and discuss negative events that occurred in your childhood is the first step in clarifying their effects. The final step is to identify any ways in which these events continue to affect your present life and your relationship with your partner. Often people are able to use this information to gain greater insight into the difficulties with their relationship.

Prerequisites "What I'm Hanging Onto—Unfinished Business"
"Sharing Negative Experiences"

Directions **Step One:** Select one partner to start this exercise. This partner will identify any current relationship difficulties that she or he believes may be related to her or his own childhood experiences. The focus at this point is exclusively on the speaking partner's childhood experiences.

Step Two: While the first partner is talking, the other partner should focus on listening and remaining open to the information. She or he should be using the communication skills learned in previous exercises to help facilitate the other partner's exploration. This is not the time to dispute or argue over the presence of problems or patterns.

Step Three: After the first partner has identified as many relationship problems associated with childhood experiences as possible, switch roles and repeat steps 1 and 2. If the first part of the exercise took a long time, you may want to wait until your next meeting time to continue the exercise.

Step Four: After both partners have had an opportunity to share their ideas about how their own negative childhood experiences may be related to present relationship difficulties, the focus shifts to each partner talking about the other partner's childhood. Thus, the first partner identifies any of the other partner's childhood experiences that she or he thinks may be related to present problems. This is not a time to criticize or ridicule, but rather to speculate and hypothesize.

Step Five: During this time, the other partner should just listen and use her or his communication skills to facilitate the other partner's task. This is not a time to argue and be defensive, but rather to cooperate and explore together. After the first partner has identified as many relationship problems associated with her or his partner's childhood experiences as possible, switch roles and repeat steps 4 and 5.

Step Six: After both partners have completed their turns, take a few minutes to discuss what has been shared.

Duration and Frequency

This is another important and lengthy exercise. Do not start it unless you have at least 1 hour right then. You will probably spend several days on this exercise.

Suggestions

Do not challenge what your partner has identified as a problem in the relationship. Be honest with your partner—it is important to your relationship to identify as many problems that may be related to your childhood experiences as possible. This is a difficult exercise; both partners must be patient and must persevere to identify any situations related to earlier experiences.

Pitfalls

Because one partner will be sharing her or his impressions about the other partner, there is a risk that the receiving partner may become defensive, or even angry. This partner should work hard at listening to the information with an open and receptive mind. At the same time, the discussing partner should not use this time as an opportunity to criticize or lambaste her or his partner. The purpose is to identify objectively relationships between childhood events and current relationship difficulties, not to ascribe blame for the difficulties.

19 SOLVING CHILDHOOD-RELATED PROBLEMS

Purpose This exercise instructs you to solve the problems identified in "Clarifying." It is designed to help you walk through the problems each of you perceives in the relationship that are clearly tied to your respective childhood experiences.

Benefit By now it has become clear to both of you that your childhood is not in the past, but rather ever-present in your current day-to-day life. You have identified several areas in your intimate relationship in which you have problems that are directly related to childhood experiences. Having knowledge of this reality is not enough—now you need to take the time to change these problems. It is probably true that the problems you identified in "Clarifying" were not new to you. However, it may be true that you had never placed them within the context of your childhood before. Having created this context will make problem solving much easier now, and this exercise will help you do so.

Prerequisite "Clarifying"

Directions **Step One:** Select one of the problems identified in "Clarifying." Sit down, each of you individually, and think about why this problem exists and how it is manifested in your relationship.

Step Two: Share your thoughts from step 1. Attempt to reach a consensus on how the problem is manifested and why it is a problem.

Step Three: Begin the problem-solving process by discussing how each of you is willing to compromise in an attempt to tackle this process. Write down these compromises and assess whether they are sufficient to solve the problem. Continue this process until you find a potentially viable solution. Implement the solution. Proceed as you learned in the communication section of this book.

Step Four: Repeat steps 1 to 3 for each problem identified in "Clarifying."

Duration and Frequency This is another lengthy exercise. Count on an hour per problem to arrive at a solution, and a week per problem to implement the solution.

Suggestions Go back to section 2 and reread exercise 21 on problem solving. Proceed as described there for each individual problem. Pay particular attention to the special fact that these problems arise from childhood experiences, and therefore are more ingrained and longer-term than many other problems you may have encountered so far. Hence you need an extra dose of patience and willingness to compromise. Be supportive of one another and listen empathically.

Pitfalls   The major pitfalls are not taking enough time and not being tolerant and patient. This exercise is critical, and trying to rush now will result in failure. Ignoring the ingrained and long-standing nature of the problems discussed here is a major problem and must be avoided.

20 CONCLUDING EXERCISE

Purpose

This exercise is designed to bring closure to your family exploration tasks. It is less of an exercise designed for you as a couple to do together than it is an exercise for each of you to learn more about the self and apply that knowledge to the intimate relationship that you are currently working on together.

Benefit

Summarizing and applying information is a necessary ingredient of self-exploration. It brings closure and solidifies your understanding of your self in your relationship.

Directions

Step One: Set aside some time for yourself, when you can be alone, and when you feel comfortable to just sit and think.

Step Two: Get out your family tree and family pictures and look at them, all the while thinking about what this information means to you and what you have learned about yourself through that task and other exercises.

Step Three: Try to apply what you have learned about yourself to your intimate relationship with your partner.

Duration and Frequency

As for most of the exercises in this section, the time frame for this exercise is almost impossible to predict accurately and can vary significantly. Furthermore, one of you may need much more time than the other to complete this task in a manner that makes it most meaningful and helpful to you individually. Because you are doing this exercise by yourself, however, this should not pose a problem.

Suggestions

Give yourself plenty of time and do this exercise alone, in a quiet place without interruptions. Unplug the phone and, if necessary, hang a "do not disturb" sign on the door.

Pitfalls

Do not expect everything to make sense immediately. Sometimes information has to incubate in our minds before it comes to mean something. Do not expect immediate changes in your relationship, or expect suddenly to feel like a changed person yourself. Insight alone does not create change—only hard work and persistence will do that. It may still take some time—persevere.

PART TWO *Special Topics*

SECTION FIVE *Household Chores*

1. Chores in the Family of Origin
2. Understanding Each Other's Family: Chores
3. Identifying Chores
4. Reversing Roles
5. Going on Strike
6. Chore Expectations
7. Dividing Chores
8. Dividing Chores: Let's Try Again
9. Hiring Outside Help
10. Surprise Chores

The exercises in this section serve to help partners deal with an area of relating that is often full of anger and feelings of being taken advantage of. Discussing household chores often is neglected in relationships, and patterns usually develop because one person may be more tolerant or intolerant of how things are run than the other. Often household chores are not discussed because of stereotypical beliefs that certain chores fall to a certain partner merely because of gender. In this section it will be important for both partners to evaluate the chores in their household and how to share them equitably. Particular attention will be paid to creating a situation in which chores are shared fairly, not stereotypically or conveniently.

1 CHORES IN THE FAMILY OF ORIGIN

Purpose This exercise is designed to increase your awareness of past experiences in the division of responsibilities in your household as you were growing up. It will help you to recall the values and changing dynamics in your family during your formative years.

Benefit The way in which we were raised as children plays a significant role in our expectations as adults. Our perceptions of the responsibilities in a relationship are fundamental to that relationship. A successful partnership may be jeopardized by discrepancies in these expectations between partners. This exercise will allow you to recognize, as an adult, some of the ideas about chores and responsibilities you formed as a child.

Directions **Step One:** Each partner will need some paper and a pencil to answer the questions at the end of this exercise; you will share these answers with your partner at a later date. Answer these questions for three age periods: 0–6, 7–12, and 13–18 years. Be sure to answer each question as fully as possible and to the best of your ability. If you have difficulty in recalling the information, ask your parents or another family member for help.

Step Two: After you have completed the questions, read them and your responses again to yourself. Try to understand or become aware of how you are feeling about what you are reading. Be specific about the emotions that come up for you in this context. Make a note of your feelings on a separate sheet of paper.

Step Three: Try to understand how your childhood responsibilities and your feelings about the division of chores in your family of origin affect your ideas toward chores in different environments, including, but not necessarily limited to, work, home, vacation residences, and so on.

Step Four: After 3 days, read your answers again. Make additional notes of your feelings and any questions you may have.

Duration and Frequency This exercise will require several short (15 to 30 minute) sessions spaced over a time period of about a week. Repetition is unnecessary.

Suggestions List all the chores you can remember and do not worry about the specific details of each individual chore. Consider how you felt about one parent or another doing a particular chore. Remember

162

how you felt when you did your chores and how your chores compared to your siblings' chores.

Pitfalls   It may be hard for you to remember your upbringing, especially if you feel very negative about your childhood. However, not trying to remember is the primary pitfall of this exercise.

FAMILY-OF-ORIGIN
CHORES QUESTIONS   What were my father's chores/jobs in the household in which I grew up?

What were my mother's chores/jobs in the household in which I grew up?

What were my own chores/jobs in the household in which I grew up?

What were my siblings' chores/jobs in the household in which I grew up?

2 *UNDERSTANDING EACH OTHER'S FAMILY: CHORES*

Purpose   This exercise is a follow-up to "Chores in the Family of Origin." It will give you the opportunity to learn about your partner's family values and expectations with regard to chores in the family in which she or he was raised.

Benefit   Expectations are important in a relationship, and if you and your partner's expectations about roles in your relationship do not coincide, it may cause difficulties. This is particularly true in the area of chores, in which what two people learned in their families of origin may set up severe disagreements and seeds for conflicts and misunderstandings. This exercise will increase your awareness of your partner's expectations as they were formed in her or his childhood.

Prerequisite   "Chores in the Family of Origin"

Directions   **Step One:** You will need your notes from "Chores in the Family of Origin." Sit comfortably facing each other, and determine who will go first. The listener should put her or his notes aside.

Step Two: Share your answers to the questions from "Chores in the Family of Origin," including your feelings about this information. The listener needs to listen actively and carefully. She or he needs to concentrate on any new information about the partner and the feelings the partner is expressing about her or his family of origin.

Step Three: Take a brief break to give the listener a chance to assimilate the new information about the partner.

Step Four: After a short break, the listener shares (i.e., reflects back) the information she or he has learned about the partner. It is important to be patient, as well as to demonstrate understanding and empathy. As listener, attempt to understand how your partner's experience has shaped her or his current attitude toward the division of chores in your household.

Step Five: Agree upon a time during which you can switch roles and repeat steps 1 to 4 to give the other partner a chance to share her or his answers to "Chores in the Family of Origin."

Duration and Frequency   Each turn of this exercise will require about 30 minutes maximum. No repetitions are necessary.

Suggestions   Listen patiently to one another. Each of you will get a turn. Make sure you have your notes to make sharing easier. Do not censor your information, either about the actual chores that had to be done or not done, or with regard to your feelings about them. The listener is required to be understanding and may not interrupt, ridicule, or criticize.

Pitfalls   Resist the impulse to interrupt your partner. Remember that this may be an uncomfortable process for her or him. Try to avoid an analysis of your partner's difficulties in life based on the information shared. Do not put down your partner's ideas and feelings.

3 *IDENTIFYING CHORES*

Purpose

In every household many jobs need to be performed regularly to ensure the smooth running of the home. This exercise will help you to rank the jobs that need doing and how they will be completed.

Benefit

Everyone has a perception of which jobs are most important, of who is responsible, and of just how these tasks should be completed. Frequently, when these expectations are not met, arguments result. This exercise will give you the opportunity to exchange ideas on this subject with your partner without the usual arguments and hasty conclusions.

Prerequisites

"Chores in the Family of Origin"

"Understanding Each Other's Family: Chores"

Directions

Step One: Each partner individually needs to prepare a list of all the chores that, in her or his opinion, need to be completed at regular intervals. Include daily, weekly, and monthly jobs and note how often you believe they should be carried out. Take a couple of days to compile this list to be sure you are not forgetting any tasks. Make an attempt at ranking chores, listing the most critical tasks first.

Step Two: Get back together for a meeting to compare notes. You will probably find that you have different priorities. Nevertheless, regardless of priority arrangement, prepare a new list based on the two original lists that includes all the chores both of you listed. Call this the agreed-upon "Need to Do List."

Step Three: Next, consider the remaining chores. Whenever one partner lists a chore with which the other does not agree, the first partner should explain why she or he deems this task necessary. Give this partner a fair chance to share her or his feelings about this particular chore and listen attentively. If the partner's presentation convinces you that the chore is important, add it to the list you began in step 2. If you still do not agree, place it on a separate list you will call the "Disputed Chores List."

Duration and Frequency

This exercise can be as brief as 10 to 15 minutes if the partners have good agreement or if they are willing to recognize the other person's viewpoint. If long discussions are necessary to decide on which list to place a given item, this exercise may be lengthy. It should be repeated every time one of the partners thinks of a new chore. These repetitions, however, should be brief.

Suggestions   Both partners need to give serious thought to the listing of chores and need to be willing to include all household chores, no matter how small. Several small, related chores may be grouped together if necessary. Both partners need to use active listening skills and problem-solving strategies liberally to facilitate the process of creating the two lists. The "Need to Do List" should be much longer than the "Disputed Chores List," which would best be empty. Save these lists for future exercises.

Pitfalls   Keep the list reasonable, but do not overlook obvious tasks such as turning off the lights at night or making sure the cat is put out.

4 REVERSING ROLES

Purpose   This exercise will help you to appreciate just what your partner does each week to keep your household running smoothly.

Benefit   Nothing creates awareness and appreciation of another's responsibilities like the actual experience of her or his daily routine. Many people have become so used to expecting their partners to perform certain roles that they do not realize the amount of work involved. Gaining an appreciation of the other person's contributions is important and tends to reduce petty fighting. This exercise is designed to help with this process of once again appreciating each other.

Prerequisite   "Identifying Chores"

Directions   **Step One:** Pick a date on which you have an entire weekend day to do this exercise.

Step Two: Each partner makes a list of the regularly performed chores for which she or he is normally responsible. You may want to refer back to the list you developed in "Identifying Chores." Be specific about how often you do them and when. Restrict the list to the usual chores relevant for the chosen day.

Step Three: Switch lists with your partner. Read each other's lists and clarify any questions.

Step Four: Starting immediately, become responsible for your partner's chores for the entire day. You may not skip any chores that are noted on the partner's list, nor may you do less or more for any one given task.

Step Five: At the end of the day, sit down with one another and discuss your experiences and feelings. If you feel it genuinely, express your appreciation of the partner's usual routine.

Duration and Frequency   This exercise will last 1 day, but may be repeated as often as necessary. It is recommended that the partners consider reversing roles for an entire week to get a true appreciation not only of daily, but also of weekly tasks.

Suggestions   Be honest enough in preparing your list of chores to include only the chores that you truly tend to do on the agreed-upon day. If your partner does not complete the tasks to your usual standards, do not complain. Remember to be helpful and answer any queries your partner may have not only while completing step 2, but also throughout the day. However, in asking questions yourself, do not pretend not to know something to get out of performing a specific task. Ignorance is no excuse in this exercise. Be sure to save the lists—they will be used in a future exercise.

Pitfalls   Do not use any excuses not to complete a chore. Instead, be creative. For instance, if you do not know how to change the oil in the car, take the car to a mechanic, go to the library and get a self-help book, or take the car to the auto mechanics department of a local vocational education school.

5 GOING ON STRIKE

Purpose This exercise will help you understand and appreciate the work that each of you contributes to the household, much like "Reversing Roles," but perhaps more drastically. If you feel that you already appreciate each other's contributions, you may skip this exercise.

Benefit Today, in the majority of relationships, both partners work outside the home. This means that general maintenance and household chores have to be squeezed into the time left for rest and relaxation. Sometimes this results in one or the other partner's feeling cheated, as though she or he is the only one doing the work. This exercise will help you see just how the chores are being accomplished by your partner, and just how large a contribution she or he really makes. However, this exercise can be dangerous for partners who have mismatched responsibilities in the home. So beware and stay in touch with your feelings.

Directions **Step One:** Choose one partner to "go on strike" this week.

Step Two: This partner will not do any chores all week. The other partner can either take over those chores or leave them undone.

Step Three: After 3 days, assess the effects of the plan. At the end of the week, make a further evaluation of the exercise.

Step Four: Next week, reverse roles and repeat the exercise.

Step Five: At the end of the second week, discuss how you felt in both roles. Let each other know what you have learned about respective contributions.

Duration and Frequency The exercise lasts over a period of 2 weeks but requires only a small amount of discussion time.

Suggestions If there is an emergency or unexpected visitors, be ready to postpone the exercise and help out your partner. If the exercise pointed out unfairness in the current distribution of chores, do not despair: The remainder of the exercises in this section are designed to address this. If the exercise helped you realize that you are already sharing chores quite equally and satisfactorily, you may skip to the next section if you wish (though you may still learn some helpful hints from the remaining exercises in this section as well). The main thing to learn in this event is how to show appreciation of one another's contributions.

Pitfalls   If you are on strike, avoid doing any of the chores "just to help out." Do not be negative toward your partner when she or he is the one on strike, and do not take revenge when it is your turn to be on strike. Do not feel obliged to do the partner's chores while she or he is on strike. It may be interesting for both of you to realize the full impact of that partner's usual contribution.

6 *CHORE EXPECTATIONS*

Purpose Everyone has her or his own perception of how a chore should be completed. Therefore it is important that both partners share their expectations of what needs to be done how often and where.

Benefit Frequently we refrain from complaining about chores left undone or incomplete, and tension builds up until an explosion occurs. Alternatively, we do the chore ourselves and then complain about the fact that we "had" to do it. Most often, however, a partner may actually do a chore that was assigned to her or him, but the exact execution of the task did not meet with the other partner's expectation of what should have been done. To avoid all three of these circumstances, it must be clear not only who is to do which chores (the purpose of "Dividing Chores," the next exercise), but also the exact nature of and expectations surrounding each individual chore. This exercise is designed to help you establish clear parameters for the different chores you have already identified.

Directions **Step One:** Examine the "Need to Do List" you prepared in "Identifying Chores." For each chore, both partners need to define in writing their exact expectations as to how this chore should be executed, when it needs to be done, and how often it needs to be done. You may decide to take a couple of days to complete this detailed list. You may have difficulty in coming up with the parameters for a given chore if you have never done it before. In these circumstances, try to imagine how you would like the chore to be done.

Step Two: Together go over the expanded and annotated "Need to Do List," with each of you sharing your specific requirements. If you agree on a specific chore, put it aside—you are finished with it. If you disagree, it becomes important that you listen to each other's needs. Discuss your ideas and attempt to reach an agreement. Once you have reached a compromise, write it down for future reference and to clarify any future misunderstanding. If it is too difficult to reach a compromise about the parameters of a certain chore, skip the chore and return to it later, using the problem-solving skills you learned in section 2 on verbal communication.

Step Three: Let your list sit for a couple of days, then return to it and reevaluate what you have done. If you are still dissatisfied, move to "Dividing Chores" to determine who will be responsible for which chore.

Duration and Frequency   This exercise will take several relatively brief sessions over the course of 2 to 4 days. It may be repeated as often as necessary, that is, as often as you add a new chore to your "Need to Do List."

Suggestions   Listen carefully to your partner's expectations and be willing to compromise. Choose a few chores that are not very important to you and let your partner determine their parameters. Use the active listening skills and problem-solving skills you have learned so far. Be creative in your expectations and definitions as well, and be willing to try new procedures for certain tasks if you have completely different ways of doing something. Keep these lists for future use.

Pitfalls   Avoid being rigidly insistent in your requirements or parameters. A little flexibility buys a lot of goodwill, especially if both of you contribute some!

7 DIVIDING CHORES

Purpose   Chores can be divided in many ways. This exercise will help you determine how to divide chores on the "Need to Do List" with a minimum of frustration and resentment.

Benefit   Several decades ago, in traditional households, responsibility for chores was clearly defined, with the male partner working out of the home and the female partner working in the home. In today's rapidly changing society, responsibilities and family composition are changing as well. In light of such changes, adherence to old values often creates resentment and ill feelings. Lack of adherence to old values, on the other hand, may leave critical tasks unassigned and partners angry that no one is taking responsibility. This exercise will allow you to explore alternative and creative ways to determine how chores might be divided.

Prerequisites   "Identifying Chores"

"Chore Expectations"

Directions   **Step One:** Use the "Need to Do List" you created in "Identifying Chores" defined according to the expectations you agreed on in "Chore Expectations." Determine if there are any chores on this list that one of you is not able to do (e.g., perhaps one of you does not know how to fix a car; breast-feeding a baby will prove to be difficult for a male partner).

Step Two: Discuss why this person is not able to do a particular chore. Explore if there is an alternative means to handle this task if the partner could learn the skills involved, for example, perhaps the person could learn how to change the oil in the car. Do not overlook creative solutions. A partner may well be able to feed the baby in the middle of the night if the mother is willing to pump breast milk before going to sleep!

Step Three: Go back through the list and identify chores you are willing to do. Once both partners have done this, check if any chores are left uncovered. Assess who is able to take care of those chores for which neither partner volunteered. Assess whether this simple process of looking at chores sufficed to divide up chores equally. If you are unable to come to a good division of chores, do the next exercise, "Dividing Chores: Let's Try Again."

Step Four: Implement the division of chores and maintain it for the next 10 days. Then meet again and discuss how the process has worked for both of you. During these 10 days, refrain from nagging one another. If a partner is not completing an assigned chore, leave it undone. That is indeed a better reminder than doing it yourself and then complaining about it. If you are not satisfied with the division of labor after the 10-day trial period, repeat this exercise.

Duration and Frequency

This exercise will require 15 to 45 minutes depending on how willing the partners are to volunteer for chores. The more items that remain uncovered in step 3, the more time will be required to complete the exercise.

Suggestions

Before definitely deciding that you are unable to sign up for a given chore, ask yourself why you are not able to do it. Be patient with each other and show awareness of each other's concerns. Listen carefully to each other's arguments and be willing to search for creative solutions. Use the problem-solving skills you have learned by now. Do not overlook the possibility of sharing chores that both of you either want to do or do not want to do. The lists will be used again—be sure to keep them.

Pitfalls

Do not make the list of jobs you cannot do longer than the list of those you are willing to do. Do not agree to a labor division that is clearly unfair or unbalanced. Be flexible about learning new jobs. Refrain from saying, "It is not my problem."

8 DIVIDING CHORES: LET'S TRY AGAIN

Purpose This exercise will help you decide how to divide household chores equally and accomplish them with a minimum of resentment and frustration. If you successfully divided the chores based on the simple instructions in "Dividing Chores," skip this exercise.

Benefit Although it may be easy to divide chores according to who is able to do them and who is willing to do them, this process alone may be undesirable if it results in an unequal division of labor. If this is the case, this exercise will help you remedy the situation by helping you take a realistic look at the relative labor involved in all the chores you have identified. Once the work is divided equally and each person shares in the assigning of the work load, everyone feels better and there are fewer arguments and less resentment over household chores.

Directions **Step One:** Take the "Need to Do List" and rearrange all the chores it contains according to whether they must be performed daily, weekly, monthly, yearly, or as needed.

Step Two: Separate the daily chores according to time needed to complete them or according to difficulty level. Determine how much time is required to complete each task. Note the chore and the time requirement and difficulty level on a small index card. Repeat this process for the chores of other intervals, keeping separate piles for daily, weekly, monthly, and yearly chores.

Step Three: Select chores that your partner cannot complete, and give those you cannot do to your partner. Assess how many hours of chores each of you has on a daily, weekly, monthly, and yearly basis, based strictly on how chores were divided according to ability. The partner who has fewer hours in any of the time categories now must select chores from the remaining cards until the assigned hours for the two partners are roughly equal.

Step Four: Place the remaining cards in a bag and alternate in selecting them until all work is assigned. Try to keep the time frames approximately equal, but do not be too rigid about this for now. Chores will be reassigned in a few weeks.

Step Five: Each person needs to prepare a list based on the cards she or he drew or was assigned. Retain the cards in a safe place for later use. Discuss any problems you might have with chore assignment or work load at this point.

Step Six: Complete tasks as assigned for a period of 2 weeks, then review the program.

Step Seven: After those 2 weeks, repeat the procedure for the weekly, monthly, yearly, and "as needed" chores if you are not satisfied with how chores are assigned. However, if the original system worked, stick with it.

Duration and Frequency

Because most of the work for this exercise is already done, steps 1 to 5 may not take you more than an hour. Repeat it after no less than 2 weeks or later as needed.

Suggestions

Consider learning some jobs you cannot do. Refrain from complaining if your partner forgets a chore or does not do it exactly as you like it to be done. Be ready to cooperate with your partner if she or he asks for help—this is not a contest. Be willing to compromise and renegotiate. The more open-minded you can be in this process the more likely you will be to reduce the amount of conflict you have over household chores. In calculating time frames and in making chore assignments in general, be honest about your professional work. If one of you works strictly in the home, you need to be willing to do more of the household chores than the partner who works full-time outside of the home. However, even in such a situation, some division of labor is appropriate! Use your problem-solving skills to discuss and reach compromises about these issues. Retain the lists for future use.

Pitfalls

Avoid completing chores your partner forgets to do. Refrain from nagging about chores not done or done inadequately.

9 HIRING OUTSIDE HELP

Purpose This exercise will help you to decide if you should hire someone to complete some of your household chores.

Benefit When both partners work outside the home, sometimes certain chores are postponed and never completed. This results in frustration and resentment. Using some of your salary to pay someone to take care of these chores may be a sensible investment. This exercise will help you explore this possibility.

Prerequisite "Identifying Chores"

Directions **Step One:** Individually examine the "Need to Do List" you previously prepared in "Identifying Chores." Read the list in the attempt to identify any chores that both of you hate, are not very good at, or are very unlikely to complete. Think about whether these might be jobs you would like someone else to do. If there is more than one such item, assign priorities.

Step Two: Together go over your rejected chores lists to determine whether there are any items you agreed upon. Do not discuss any disagreements at this time; focus on agreements instead.

Step Three: Make a new list that contains the chores both of you agree would be nice to have completed by someone else. Divide up the list and make some phone calls to find out what it would cost to hire someone to do the tasks. Decide beforehand how many phone calls you will make per chore to ensure finding the best prices or arrangements. If you wish to make more inquiries feel free, but make no fewer.

Step Four: Once you have investigated prices, go over the list again and discuss the cost, time, and effort involved. Rank items on the list for priority together one final time, remembering to include both partners' wishes.

Step Five: Decide if you would like to proceed in hiring someone to complete at least some of the chores on your "Rejected Chores" list. If you decide to do so, continue to step 6.

Step Six: Randomly decide who will have the responsibility of hiring someone to perform the job. You can use the information you gained from step 3.

Step Seven: Three weeks after you have implemented the plan, review it and assess its success. Decide whether to continue or stop.

Duration and Frequency Steps 1 to 6 should take a few 1-hour sessions over a 2- to 3-day period. The exercise may be repeated whenever necessary as defined in step 7.

Suggestions Be honest about the jobs you want to hire out. Carefully examine the cost and benefits involved. Take plenty of time to investigate the cost of hiring someone to do the chores for you. Listen to your partner's requests and try not to be selfish. It will be helpful to keep the lists for future reference.

Pitfalls Be sure to listen to each other's needs and do not consider hiring someone to do only your jobs and not your partner's.

10 *SURPRISE CHORES*

Purpose   This exercise will allow you to show your appreciation for your partner in a practical way.

Benefit   In every relationship, appreciation of one another is easily forgotten in the hectic schedules of today's world. In this exercise, not only will you learn a way in which to demonstrate your appreciation for your partner's help in the house in a positive and practical way, but your partner will appreciate you for doing it. It will also let you experience part of what your partner usually contributes to the running of the household, increasing your sense of appreciation for her or him. This exercise cannot do anything but help your relationship.

Prerequisite   "Dividing Chores"

Directions   **Step One:** Look over the chore lists developed in "Dividing Chores." Select one chore you are capable of doing. Plan to complete this chore to surprise your partner by doing it for her or him in the following week. Obviously, you need to keep this resolve to yourself to make it a real surprise.

Step Two: Do the chore. Consider how you feel about doing it for your partner. More than likely you will feel very good about doing something nice for your partner. Do not expect anything in return or you will defeat the purpose of the exercise.

Duration and Frequency   The length of time needed for this exercise varies depending on the chore you chose. The exercise may be repeated whenever and as often as you want.

Suggestions   Try to select a chore that your partner will enjoy not having to do, in other words, do not pick your partner's favorite chore. Instead try to pick a chore you know your partner hates. Try to surprise your partner. Have no expectation of reciprocity! As the partner who is being surprised, show enthusiasm and appreciation of your partner's effort, even if she or he did not do your chore perfectly. Relationships involve give-and-take—when you take (i.e., when you receive a surprise such as this one), be grateful and appreciative.

Pitfalls   If your partner fails to recognize your gesture, do not get angry, but do share your disappointment at her or his lack of awareness and appreciation. Do not expect your partner to reciprocate.

SECTION SIX *Finances*

EXERCISES
1. My Family's Financial Attitudes
2. Personal Financial Values
3. Financial Dreams
4. Establishing a Common Household Budget
5. Trimming the Budget
6. Compromising About Budget Expenditures
7. Sharing Logistic Financial Responsibilities
8. Asset Sheets: Where Everything Is
9. Consumer Goals
10. Common Financial Gripes

The exercises in this section center on a topic that commonly results in bitter arguments and disagreements among partners. Given the sensitive nature of this topic, these exercises may be particularly difficult, but at the same time may prove to be some of the most important exercises to attempt to complete successfully. If you can resolve your financial differences, you may well have solved the primary source of your day-to-day disagreements. Given that finances have to do primarily with money earned and money spent, these exercises may be difficult for you to discuss with your counselor. If you do not want to divulge this information to your counselor, you may want to deal with these issues more indirectly in counseling sessions, discussing specific amounts in privacy.

1 MY FAMILY'S FINANCIAL ATTITUDES

Purpose   This exercise will help you recall how financial matters were taken care of in your childhood and how this compares to the financial messages your partner received during childhood.

Benefit   Many of our behaviors and values stem from our families of origin, as was pointed out in previous exercises. Attitudes and beliefs are also expressed in families regarding financial values and financial status. Understanding how financial matters were handled in your families during your own and in your partner's childhood will give you insight into how your respective attitudes toward finances were formed. You may notice that there are some financial beliefs you hold strictly because they were modeled for you during childhood, but that they actually may no longer apply. You may also notice several remarkable differences in your own and your partner's attitudes. Such differences can lead to arguments, and it is crucial to resolve the problems by working toward a compromise with which both of you can live.

Directions   **Step One:** Find a comfortable space and some time to relax. Each of you separately should reflect on the different periods of your life, including your early years, middle childhood, teenage years, and even young adulthood. Consider all of the questions at the end of this exercise for each of those periods and make some notes about what you discover.

Step Two: After a few days, review your answers and add any new thoughts you may have had since the original reflection.

Step Three: Share your answers with your partner, alternating who goes first on each question noted in step 1. Listen attentively and actively to your partner's answers without asking too many questions. You may want to take some notes as your partner speaks.

Step Four: After both of you have reviewed each period and your answers to the list of questions, compare your financial backgrounds and consider how they have influenced your current attitude toward finances. Discuss how your background and personal financial attitudes have entered your current relationship, and situations in which differences in backgrounds and attitudes may have created conflict for the two of you.

Duration and Frequency   This is a lengthy exercise that takes much reflection and thought. It will take about 1 week to complete, but fortunately needs to be done only once.

Suggestions   Take plenty of time reflecting on all the answers in step 1. Answer the questions honestly and try to understand where your own monetary and financial attitudes originated. When discussing and sharing your own background, remain nonjudgmental. Use all the active listening skills you learned in previous exercises in other sections of this book.

Pitfalls   Avoid ridiculing or criticizing your partner about her or his childhood experiences. Remember, there are no right or wrong answers here; this is merely an opportunity to understand the development of your partner's and your own financial attitudes. Do not use this exercise to discuss which attitudes you should or should not adopt in your current relationship. Focus strictly on understanding your backgrounds and personal attitudes. Also, do not criticize or ridicule your partner for having grown up in a household that was richer or poorer than your own.

FAMILY-OF-ORIGIN FINANCIAL QUESTIONS

1. What type of housing did you and your family have?
2. Did your family own or rent a home, condominium, or apartment?
3. Did both of your parents work outside the home, earning money? If so, did you know how much they earned?
4. How would you describe your family's financial status? Were you poor, rich, or somewhere in-between? Did you ever suffer because of lack of money? Did your financial status change over the years?
5. Did you have an allowance? If so, how much did you receive? Were there any restrictions on how you were to spend it?
6. Did you have a savings account, savings bonds, and so forth? If so, was this typical for all of your family members or were you special in this regard?
7. Did your parents talk about money with you and the other children in the family? If so, what were their messages?
8. Did the financial messages change over the years?
9. Which of your own attitudes about money and finances can you identify that you share with at least one of your parents?
10. Which of your own attitudes about money and finances can you identify that you developed specifically in opposition to what at least one of your parents believed?
11. What other thoughts occur to you as you think about money and finances in the context of the family in which you grew up?

2 *PERSONAL FINANCIAL VALUES*

Purpose

This exercise will give you the opportunity to consider your feelings and attitudes, or ethics, about certain financial matters. This exercise is an expansion of "My Family's Financial Attitudes" and significantly builds upon it.

Benefit

Finances play a large part in most relationships, and differing values can lead to serious arguments and misunderstandings. An awareness of what each of you finds most important with regard to finances and money will allow you to compromise more easily with your partner on certain points.

Prerequisite

"My Family's Financial Attitudes"

Directions

Step One: Separately, make a list of your attitudes and feelings about the financial or money-related issues listed at the end of this exercise.

Step Two: After a few days, review your answers and add any new thoughts you have had since the original reflection.

Step Three: Share your answers with your partner, alternating who goes first on each question referred to in step 1. Listen attentively and actively to your partner's answers without asking too many questions. You may want to take some notes as your partner speaks.

Step Four: Compare your and your partner's financial attitudes and feelings and discuss how they have entered your current relationship and situations in which differences in attitudes may have created conflict for the two of you. Write down all major differences you have uncovered between your respective attitudes and feelings about money.

Step Five: Use the problem-solving skills you have learned in previous exercises to discuss and resolve any major differences. If you are unable to resolve your differences, work toward achieving a mutually agreeable compromise.

Duration and Frequency

This is a lengthy exercise that takes much reflection and thought. It will require at least 20 to 30 minutes each for steps 1 and 2, and 30 to 45 minutes for the discussion. If you have difficulty reaching agreement, you may need to schedule a further meeting.

Suggestions   Try to find some solution or compromise for each question perhaps by using the problem-solving techniques you learned previously. Be honest about your own beliefs and refrain from criticizing your partner's if you do not agree. Focus on compromise, not scrutiny. It may be best to start the discussion by highlighting the areas in which you agree.

Pitfalls   Avoid adhering so rigidly to your principles that you cannot effect a compromise. Do not be critical of your partner's beliefs.

FINANCIAL OR MONEY-RELATED ISSUES

1. using credit cards and bank loans for both small and large purchases
2. owning a house or condominium vs. renting a house or an apartment
3. saving a certain sum of money on a regular basis
4. starting a college fund for children (if applicable)
5. spending money on "fun" things
6. spending money on vacations
7. taking financial risks, e.g., investing in the stock market
8. planning for retirement

3 FINANCIAL DREAMS

Purpose   This exercise will allow you to evaluate whether your financial attitudes and beliefs as well as your financial dreams are compatible.

Benefit   There are many reasons why relationship problems arise in the context of finances. Although most grow out of financial difficulties or incompatible attitudes or beliefs, some come strictly from the ideas partners have about how to spend any extra money they have. This extra money may be no more than $10 or may be as much as the grand prize won in a lottery. Disagreements about financial dreams (small or large) can wreak havoc on a relationship. In this exercise you will find out whether you and your partner have compatible financial dreams.

Directions   **Step One:** Individually, sit back and get comfortable. Find a quiet time and place in which you are unlikely to be disturbed.

Step Two: Imagine that you have an extra $500 to spend that you did not know you would have. Become aware of how you feel about this sudden availability of money.

Step Three: Prepare a list of items on which you would consider spending this money. Be creative, but realistic and honest. If you think you would want to put this money in savings, put that down. Do not let any other feedback confuse you. In other words, do not attempt to figure out what your partner would want to do with this money. This is your fantasy—note your own preference only.

Step Four: Get together with your partner and compare your feelings and choices, focusing on how similar or dissimilar they are.

Step Five: If your choices were very different, try to come to a compromise on how to spend the money.

Duration and Frequency   This exercise will take from 20 to 30 minutes and may be repeated as often as you wish.

Suggestions   Be realistic, but be creative. When sharing feelings and choices, be open-minded and noncritical with one another. If you repeat the exercise, you may want to alter the amount of money you fantasize about to see if your compatibilities or differences change depending upon that factor.

Pitfalls   Avoid trying to convince your partner that she or he is spending the money unwisely. If you want to focus on your differences, do so to see if you can reach a compromise position, not to be critical or to argue.

4 ESTABLISHING A COMMON HOUSEHOLD BUDGET

Purpose This exercise will help you delineate how and where you and your partner spend money for your common or shared household.

Benefit Often couples operate in the dark as far as finances are concerned, assuming that the other person is aware of what the monthly expenses are and tracks whether she or he has remained within the budget. When two people share one household, it is crucial for both of them to know where money is spent to avoid fighting over expenditures that were not discussed previously. It is important that partners set up an operating household budget that is agreeable to both. It is likely that partners' differences in financial attitudes will result in differences with regard to how much money is spent or saved. This exercise is designed to help partners negotiate a budget.

Directions **Step One:** Together establish a list of the monthly expenditures that you face both individually and jointly. Specifically, following the items listed in the outline at the end of this exercise (you may need to add additional regular monthly expenses), list the exact dollar amount of your expenses in the appropriate columns. In other words, note whether each expense is incurred only by one partner or shared equally; if an expense is incurred equally by both, place the dollar amount in the "joint" column (e.g., if you live together, the amount for rent or house payment goes in the joint column because that expense is incurred by both partners jointly); if both partners have a similar expense, but pay it separately, note it in both partner columns (e.g., if both of you have car payments, put the respective amounts under each partner).

Step Two: Repeat step 1, using the budget provided on the page following the monthly budget, to create a listing of annual, semiannual, or other expenses that occur at regular intervals other than monthly.

Step Three: After a few days look at both lists again and add any items you may have forgotten. Add up the monthly expenditures at the bottom of the page as indicated. Add the second regular-interval budget in the same manner, but then divide the sum by the interval to obtain an amount that is prorated monthly (e.g., yearly expenditures are divided by 12; semiannual expenditures are divided by 6). Add the prorated monthly amount to the monthly amounts on the monthly budget to get an idea of how much money the two of you spend individually and jointly.

Step Four: Compare the total monthly expenditures to your monthly income. If the monthly income is larger than the monthly expenditures and both partners are satisfied with the way each paycheck is utilized and the way the money is spent, you may skip the next two exercises. If your expenditures are greater than your income, proceed to "Trimming the Budget." If one partner feels cheated (e.g., makes more, but spends less; contributes more to the joint bills than the other partner but earns an equal amount), proceed to "Compromising About Budget Expenditures." If both conditions are true (more expenditure than income and dissatisfaction about how expenses are shared), do both "Trimming the Budget" and "Compromising About Budget Expenditures."

Step Five: After 3 months, review whether your budget is still accurate. Repeat "Trimming the Budget" and "Compromising About Budget Expenditures" as necessary at that time.

Duration and Frequency   This exercise may require several days to complete and needs to be reviewed after 3 months.

Suggestions   Be as honest about your bills as you can be. Be thorough in listing all possible expenditures. Refrain from underestimating costs regardless of how tempting this might be. If you are not sure about certain bills, check your records and calculate an average to get an idea of what to expect. If you do not agree on an amount, look at past bills to verify actual expenses. Anticipate any new bills that may develop in the next 2 to 3 months (e.g., are you planning to buy a new car?). Be sure to keep the completed budgets.

Pitfalls   Do not use this exercise to criticize one another about specific expenses. At this time you merely want to establish how much money you spend on a regular basis. If you have disagreements about the necessity of certain items, wait to resolve these through "Trimming the Budget."

MONTHLY EXPENDITURES BUDGET

Items	Partner A	Partner B	Joint
rent or house payment	_____	_____	_____
electricity bill	_____	_____	_____
water bill	_____	_____	_____
gas bill	_____	_____	_____
phone bill(s)	_____	_____	_____
cable TV bill	_____	_____	_____
garbage removal bill	_____	_____	_____
car payment (car #1)	_____	_____	_____
car payment (car #2)	_____	_____	_____
grocery bills	_____	_____	_____
clothing bills	_____	_____	_____
drugstore bills	_____	_____	_____
lawn or yard upkeep	_____	_____	_____
home repairs	_____	_____	_____
student loan payments	_____	_____	_____
credit card bill #1	_____	_____	_____
credit card bill #2	_____	_____	_____
credit card bill #3	_____	_____	_____
gasoline bill (car #1)	_____	_____	_____
gasoline bill (car #2)	_____	_____	_____
transportation costs	_____	_____	_____
parking cost	_____	_____	_____
lunch money	_____	_____	_____
child support payment	_____	_____	_____
child care bills	_____	_____	_____
pet food bills	_____	_____	_____
entertainment	_____	_____	_____
job-related expenses	_____	_____	_____
health insurance	_____	_____	_____
_____	_____	_____	_____
_____	_____	_____	_____
_____	_____	_____	_____
_____	_____	_____	_____
_____	_____	_____	_____
_____	_____	_____	_____
monthly totals:	_____	_____	_____
add prorated amounts from next page:	_____	_____	_____
grand total expenses:	_____	_____	_____
monthly incomes:	_____	_____	_____

EXPENDITURES BUDGET FOR OTHER INTERVALS

Items	Partner A	Partner B	Joint
Annual			
income tax	_____	_____	_____
property tax	_____	_____	_____
registration (car #1)	_____	_____	_____
registration (car #2)	_____	_____	_____
_____	_____	_____	_____
_____	_____	_____	_____
_____	_____	_____	_____
yearly totals:	_____	_____	_____
(divide total by 12 for) prorated monthly totals:	_____		_____
Semiannual			
insurance (house)	_____	_____	_____
insurance (car #1)	_____	_____	_____
insurance (car #2)	_____	_____	_____
_____	_____	_____	_____
_____	_____	_____	_____
_____	_____	_____	_____
semiyearly totals:	_____	_____	_____
(divide total by 6 for) prorated monthly totals:	_____	_____	_____
Other Intervals			
_____	_____	_____	_____
_____	_____	_____	_____
_____	_____	_____	_____
_____	_____	_____	_____
_____	_____	_____	_____
interval totals:	_____	_____	_____
(divide total by interval length for) prorated monthly totals:	_____	_____	_____
prorated monthly grand totals:	_____	_____	_____

5 TRIMMING THE BUDGET

Purpose   For those who realized through "Establishing a Common Household Budget" that you are consistently overspending, this exercise will help you negotiate areas in which you are willing to trim expenditures.

Benefit   The process of identifying areas in which expenditures can be trimmed can result in great financial relief. However, more important, it may result in a reduction of the stress on the relationship caused by financial difficulties and the worry about making ends meet. Invariably, when household budgets are not balanced, partners fight over who is causing the financial problems. Just as invariably, both partners are to blame. This exercise will help you negotiate about how and where to trim your household budget. If your finances are in severe disarray, you may need a financial consultant to help straighten them out. If you hire a financial consultant, this exercise still can be helpful in the sense that it keeps you negotiating as opposed to blaming and arguing.

Prerequisite   "Establishing a Common Household Budget"

Directions   **Step One:** Take out the budget you prepared in "Establishing a Common Household Budget." Identify all items that are not essential, that is, crucial to continued survival by marking them with a red X. For instance, mark items such as monthly clothing allowances, lunch monies, and so forth with a red X. Mark items that may be essential, but could be reduced by thriftier consumption, with a yellow X. For instance, place a yellow X next to items such as electricity or water bills. For now, ignore essential items that cannot be easily altered, such as rent or house payments, car payments, child support payments, and so forth.

Step Two: Make a list of all red-X items and determine how much money you spend on these items each month. Compare this sum to the difference between your current income and expenditures. If you divide the sum of these items by 2 and that number is as large or larger than the difference (your budget deficit), you may be able to cut enough cost here to balance your budget. If this number is smaller than your budget deficit, you may have to add 50% of yellow-X items until the total becomes larger than the deficit.

Step Three: Each partner should have the list of red-X and yellow-X items identified in step 2. Each partner now goes through the list and marks items that can be eliminated altogether and items in which expenses could be trimmed relatively easily. For instance, often the clothing allowance can be easily cut in half if you are just willing to be a smarter consumer, buy only during sales, or explore second-hand stores (this is particularly true for children's clothing while children are still growing). Lunch money can be saved easily by making sack lunches rather than frequenting restaurants or snack bars. Evaluate each item realistically according to what you personally are willing to do to reduce cost.

Step Four: Compare the cost-reduction measures both of you identified in step 3. Negotiate any differences in opinions by using the verbal communication skills you have learned. Attempt to reach a compromise that results in a balanced budget, even if that means giving up certain items. Be willing to listen to your partner's arguments and focus not on what she or he can do to reduce cost, but rather take responsibility for your own consumer behavior. Optimally, if all costs and income are shared equally, reductions would also be shared in equal proportions.

Duration and Frequency

This exercise can take a long time. If it preoccupies you for more than a total of 10 hours, it may be time to hire a financial consultant. The exercise may also need to be repeated each time the two of you create a new household budget that is not balanced.

Suggestions

Enter this exercise with an open mind and a willingness to compromise. Finances can be worked out only if both partners are willing to listen to each other's arguments and explanations. Remember to put this exercise within the context of the financial attitudes and beliefs you explored earlier. Build compromises around attitudes and beliefs that you share. Use all your active listening and communication skills. Remember to avoid roadblocks to communication and to use "I" messages and "I understand" messages throughout your negotiations. If you run into a particularly difficult negotiation, use the problem-solving procedures you learned in the verbal communication section. Do not hesitate to hire a financial consultant if you cannot find a way to trim your budget on your own.

Pitfalls

This exercise is certain to fail if you walk into it believing that you personally have all the correct answers and that your partner is wrong or inept at dealing with finances.

6 COMPROMISING ABOUT BUDGET EXPENDITURES

Purpose   This exercise is designed to help partners negotiate perceived unfairness in the current household budget. It should be used only if the partners have found a way to balance their budget. If you are still running a deficit, return to "Trimming the Budget" before beginning this exercise.

Benefit   This exercise ascertains whether both partners feel comfortable about their financial contributions and expenditures. There are few things that can upset the relationship balance more than if one partner feels that she or he is being taken advantage of financially by the other. Once both partners feel financially compatible, they can go on with their business of caring for and loving each other.

Prerequisite   "Establishing a Common Household Budget"

Directions   **Step One:** Each partner begins by preparing a list of expenses (based on the household budget developed in "Establishing a Common Household Budget") that this person perceives as unfair to her or him.

Step Two: Write down why you think the current arrangement is unfair. Be very specific and give concrete examples and explanations about what seems to be wrong (at least in your opinion). Let this list and explanations sit for at least 24 hours. Return to it to revise it and add any additional thoughts or take out any blaming statements that may have slipped in. Give this revised list to your partner to read over the next 24 hours.

Step Three: Set an appointment when to meet to discuss the two prepared statements. When the appointed time comes, agree on how long you will meet and under what circumstances you will end the meeting.

Step Four: Begin by choosing who goes first. The first partner then talks about her or his reaction to the prepared statement of the other partner. Talk about the items with which you agree and disagree. Then switch roles, giving the other partner a chance to critique. Remain calm and do not interrupt when it is the other person's turn to speak. Consider all arguments with an open mind and attempt to reach a compromise where conflicts are identified.

Step Five: Hire a consultant if you cannot negotiate fair solutions by yourselves.

Duration and Frequency This exercise can take as little as half an hour or as long as an hour a day for several weeks. Be patient and remain willing to repeat the exercise every time there is a change in your financial situation that results in ambivalent or ill feelings.

Suggestions Be sure to set a limit on how long you will negotiate in step 3. You may set certain prearranged limits. For instance, you may want to agree to meet for no more than 1 hour; you may want to agree that if you cannot reach at least one compromise after 45 minutes that you will quit for today and try again tomorrow; you may agree that if one partner starts blaming or screaming, the session is over for today; you may even agree, if no compromise is reached after several attempts, to hire a consultant.

Do not use this exercise to make the point that you earn more money than your partner. How much money each contributes in exact numbers is less important than the feeling that both of you are doing your best to keep your budget balanced and your financial situation secure. In this exercise, you will need all the active listening skills and positive communication skills you can muster. Problem solving and negotiation are crucial. You may choose to review some of the more important verbal communication exercises before delving into the process of creating fair finances.

Pitfalls It would be wrong to assume that fairness implies that both partners contribute equal amounts or spend equal amounts. Fairness is in the eye of the beholder (or in this case in the eyes of the two beholders). There are other means through which partners can feel comfortable with their financial contributions and responsibilities than by splitting everything 50/50.

7 *SHARING LOGISTIC FINANCIAL RESPONSIBILITIES*

Purpose   This exercise will help you delineate how you and your partner wish to divide responsibilities for paying bills, balancing checkbooks, and general maintenance of finances.

Benefit   Many households today have two incomes, therefore it is important to determine who is responsible for the logistics of writing checks to pay the bills, balancing checkbooks, and otherwise maintaining the shared financial affairs. These decisions are critical even with a balanced budget so that no one can claim that she or he did not pay a given bill because she or he thought that the other person was supposed to pay it. Arguing over money and finances can occur even when the partners have enough money to pay their bills easily if logistics are not clearly outlined and followed. This exercise is designed to help you arrange a logistics schedule of financial management. Although it gives some examples of sharing such logistics, only your creativity will limit the variations you may develop.

Prerequisite   "Establishing a Common Household Budget"

Directions   **Step One:** Take out the monthly budget you developed in "Establishing a Common Household Budget." Take out your other financial records, such as checkbooks, account registers, and savings account registers. Answer the following questions:

1. Do you have two individual checking accounts, with each partner being responsible for one account, or do you have a joint checking account? Or do you have a joint account and two individual checkbooks for the same account?

2. If you have a joint account, what percentage of your paychecks goes into this account? What percentage, if any, goes into separate accounts?

3. Are you relying on one income or two? If you have only one income, do you have a joint account? Who has access to the account?

4. If you have separate accounts, is your partner authorized to write checks from your personal account?

Step Two: Negotiate and decide on procedures that satisfy both of you as to the logistics of paying bills and balancing checkbooks. A few examples are provided here, but different partners will have unique financial situations, and you may have to find your own approach.

Example One: If you have a joint account, you need to decide who writes the checks for this account and who balances the checkbook. Determine a procedure through which you can ascertain that if the other partner has to write a check from this account, it will be entered in the register to make sure that all expenses can be accounted for.

Example Two: If you have a joint account, you may also have your own separate account. Each of you may contribute a negotiated percentage to the joint account and all joint bills are paid from this account. Personal bills are paid from the separate accounts.

Example Three: If you have joint and separate accounts, develop a system of taking turns for dealing with the joint account. Perhaps each partner could be responsible for the account and the payment of bills during 6 months of the year (e.g., one partner takes all the even, the other the odd months, or 6 months on, 6 months off).

Example Four: If you have only separate accounts, figure out a system to pay fair proportions of the joint expenses. For instance, one month, one person may pay all the bills, the next month the other partner is responsible. Or both partners write checks for 50% of the amount for each individual bill so that all bills are paid by two checks, one from each partner. Or one partner makes out a check to the other partner for half of the amount and that partner then pays the full amount of the bill.

Duration and Frequency

This exercise may be completed over several days. You may choose to review the procedures you developed after 3 months to see how well they are working. If necessary, repeat the exercise at that time.

Suggestions

Both partners must be willing to help with the logistics of paying bills and balancing checkbooks. While negotiating the exact procedures, use your active listening and communication skills. Be willing to compromise and keep an open mind. Allow yourselves to be creative even if this results in a procedure that is different from what you or your parents used to do.

Pitfalls

Failure to cooperate in the sharing of the bills will render this exercise a failure. Also entering the negotiation with preconceived notions of how the logistics should be arranged will make you less willing to compromise, and more likely to argue and be critical.

8 ASSET SHEETS: WHERE EVERYTHING IS

Purpose   This exercise will motivate you to list all your assets and will update both of you regarding your joint financial situation.

Benefit   Many people deny the possibility of death and therefore never discuss with their partners critical financial issues that are important for the person to know should one partner die suddenly. Furthermore, in many relationships, one person assumes responsibility for handling all financial affairs, leaving the other partner in the dark about how to pay bills, when to pay them, and how to stay on top of debts and handle other financial obligations. This exercise will bring into the open all the hidden financial procedures and affairs of the two partners. Thus, should one partner suddenly be unable to help (because of illness, death, out-of-town business trips, and so on), the other person will feel confident in her or his ability to take over the financial responsibilities. Having easy and ready access to current financial records not only makes good sense but can be vital during an emergency or a sudden illness.

Prerequisite   "Establishing a Common Household Budget"

Directions   **Step One:** Make copies of the questionnaires that follow this exercise. Each partner individually must complete a copy of the appropriate section of the questionnaire.

Step Two: Both partners must cooperate to complete part 2 of the questionnaire together.

Step Three: Make copies of the resultant list and keep them handy in a few safe places. Both partners need to know where these lists (or information sheets) are kept in case of an emergency. You may add a copy of the budget you prepared in previous exercises to have easy access to this information as well.

Step Four: Update your financial information yearly or more often if needed.

Duration and Frequency   This exercise may be completed quickly if you do not have many financial affairs to record, or it may take a few hours. It should be repeated whenever your financial situation changes in some way, or at least once yearly to review and update information.

Suggestions   Many useful books on the market offer a variety of questionnaires and extensive financial advice. This is a simple exercise to develop an awareness of your financial obligations and affairs. Make an effort to include all your assets and assemble all necessary information should your partner suddenly have to take care of your financial affairs.

Pitfalls   Be aware that, occasionally, a partner will conceal assets from her or his partner. This may prove to be a problem in any emergency situation.

FINANCIAL QUESTIONNAIRE

Part One: Name of Partner _____

Today's Date: _____ Current Age: _____

Years to Retirement: _____

Annual Income: _____ (Source[s]: _____)

Amount in Savings Account: _____

    (Acct #_____; Location: _____)

Amount in Additional Savings Account: _____

    (Acct #_____; Location: _____)

Amount in Additional Savings Account: _____

    (Acct #_____; Location: _____)

Amount in Checking Account: _____

    (Acct #_____; Location: _____)

Amount in Additional Checking Account: _____

    (Acct #_____; Location: _____)

Amount in Retirement Fund: _____

    (Type of Fund: _____; Location: _____)

Amount in Additional Retirement Fund: _____

    (Type of Fund: _____; Location: _____)

Amount in Stock Account: _____

    (Type of Stock: _____; Location: _____)

Amount in Additional Stock Account: _____

    (Type of Stock: _____; Location: _____)

Amount in Bond Account: _____

    (Type of Bond: _____; Location: _____)

Amount in Additional Bond Account: _____

    (Type of Bond: _____; Location: _____)

Other Investments: _____

_____

_____

_____

(describe what they are and where they are; provide account numbers and locations as appropriate)

Safety Deposit Box: _____

_____

_____

(describe its contents and provide its location)

Life Insurance: _____

_____

_____

(describe what type; provide name of beneficiary; give policy number and location)

Home (Address) _____

      Equity: _____

      Bank Loan Account Number: _____ Location: _____

Other Real Estate _____

      Equity: _____

      Bank Loan Account Number: _____ Location: _____

Other Real Estate _____

      Equity: _____

      Bank Loan Account Number: _____ Location: _____

Other Real Estate _____

      Equity: _____

      Bank Loan Account Number: _____ Location: _____

Other Assets: _____

_____

_____

_____

(describe and provide necessary account or policy numbers, locations, and other crucial information)

Bank Loan (for _____)

      Bank Loan Account Number: _____ Location: _____

      Amount Owed: _____ Payment Logistics: _____

Bank Loan (for _____)

      Bank Loan Account Number: _____ Location: _____

      Amount Owed: _____ Payment Logistics: _____

Other Liabilities _____

_____

_____

(describe in detail with all crucial information)

Will: ____ yes ____ no

      If yes, where it is: _____

Additional Information:

_____

_____

_____

Part II: Joint Assets

Today's Date: _____ Current Ages: _____

Annual Joint Income: _____

    (Source[s]: _____)

Amount in Joint Savings Account: _____

    (Acct #_____; Location: _____)

Amount in Additional Savings Account: _____

    (Acct #_____; Location: _____)

Amount in Additional Savings Account: _____

    (Acct #_____; Location: _____)

Amount in Joint Checking Account: _____

    (Acct #_____; Location: _____)

Amount in Additional Checking Account: _____

    (Acct #_____; Location: _____)

Amount in Joint Retirement Fund: _____

    (Type of Fund: _____; Location: _____)

Amount in Joint Stock Account: _____

    (Type of Stock: _____; Location: _____)

Amount in Additional Stock Account: _____

    (Type of Stock: _____; Location: _____)

Amount in Joint Bond Account: _____

    (Type of Bond: _____; Location: _____)

Amount in Additional Bond Account: _____

    (Type of Bond: _____; Location: _____)

Joint Safety Deposit Box: _____

_____

(describe its contents and provide its location)

Other Joint Investments: _____

_____

_____

_____

(describe what they are and where they are; provide account numbers and locations as appropriate)

Joint Life Insurance: _____

_____

_____

(describe what type; provide name of beneficiary; give policy number and location)

Joint Home (Address) _____

    Equity: _____

    Bank Loan Account Number: _____ Location: _____

Other Joint Real Estate _____

    Equity: _____

    Bank Loan Account Number: _____ Location: _____

Other Real Estate _____

    Equity: _____

    Bank Loan Account Number: _____ Location: _____

Other Real Estate _____

    Equity: _____

    Bank Loan Account Number: _____ Location: _____

Other Joint Assets: _____

_____

_____

_____

(describe and provide necessary account or policy numbers, locations, and other crucial information)

Joint Bank Loan (for _____)

    Bank Loan Account Number: _____ Location: _____

    Amount Owed: _____ Payment Logistics: _____

Joint Bank Loan (for _____)

    Bank Loan Account Number: _____ Location: _____

    Amount Owed: _____ Payment Logistics: _____

Other Joint Liabilities _____

(describe in detail with all crucial information)

Will: ____ yes   ____ no

      If yes, where it is: _____

Additional Information:

_____

_____

_____

_____

_____

_____

_____

_____

9 CONSUMER GOALS

Purpose This exercise will help you to develop short-term consumer goals by making a list of the things you wish to purchase in the near and distant future.

Benefit Consumerism and the choice to purchase certain items is often a spontaneous affair. Although spontaneity with regard to large purchases is a dangerous matter for anyone, it is even more likely to cause problems if it occurs within the context of a relationship. When partners use their joint resources to give in to their personal consumer desires, problems develop. For this reason, it is helpful for partners to create consumer goal lists that they can agree on or that they can accept. Such lists not only keep partners oriented toward joint and personal goals, but can also be beneficial when it comes time to purchase gifts for a partner's birthday or other special events.

Directions **Step One:** Each partner individually should review and write down the things she or he would like to have that require money to obtain. Do not restrict yourselves to products, but also include nontangibles such as vacations or savings accounts.

Step Two: Identify which items on the list reflect short-term goals and which represent long-term goals. Also attempt to give an estimated monetary value to each item.

Step Three: Share your personal list with your partner. Look for any overlap in consumer goals. Use common goals derived from the personal lists to begin to develop a joint list that you agree on. Rank-order items within the short-term and long-term categories.

Step Four: Discuss ways to finance the different consumer goals and assess whether any are financially feasible right now. Allow yourselves to dream together, but in the end be realistic about what you can and cannot afford.

Step Five: Keep the lists handy to avoid spontaneous purchases that are of low priority or not mentioned on the list. Also use the lists to make wiser choices about gifts for your partner by choosing from among the items on her or his personal list.

Duration and Frequency This exercise will take between 20 to 30 minutes and may be repeated as often as necessary or desired.

Suggestions   To make the list versatile, include small as well as large items. Differentiate between items you really want and those you believe you cannot live without. In developing the joint list, use your active listening skills and positive communication skills. Do not create a problem where none need exist. For instance, do not fight over whether the airplane or the sailboat should be a higher priority if you cannot afford either in the near future. As always, be respectful of each other's choices; neither criticize nor ridicule. Everyone has different desires, none are better or worse than others. Save these lists for future reference.

Pitfalls   Criticism and ridicule or lack of respect and caring are likely to cause this exercise to fail. Avoid imposing your wants or desires on your partner.

10 *COMMON FINANCIAL GRIPES*

Purpose This exercise will help you identify your most prominent areas of financially related disagreements and will help you negotiate solutions to these conflicts.

Benefit In every relationship in which partners have personal financial attitudes, beliefs, and goals, it is likely that they will criticize one another for the financial choices they make. One partner may claim that the other spends too much money on clothing, whereas that partner claims that the other is too stingy. Such recurrent griping is extremely unnerving for the two partners and leads to petty arguments that could be resolved easily if the partners could look at each other's behavior realistically and could strike a compromise. This exercise is designed to facilitate just such a process.

Prerequisites "My Family's Financial Attitudes"
"Personal Financial Values"
"Consumer Goals"

Directions **Step One:** Each partner individually needs to sit down with a pen and piece of paper to think about her or his common gripes about the partner's ways of dealing with money. Write down all the gripes you have in a truthful, but caring manner. In other words, use your good communication skills in writing (do not blame or criticize, rather phrase your messages in terms of how you feel and with empathic understanding).

Step Two: The two partners exchange lists and then give each other 20 minutes to read them and write a rebuttal. Just as the original list was developed with care and concern, so is the rebuttal phrased in terms of "I" messages and "I understand" messages. The rebuttal is not done defensively, but thoughtfully.

Step Three: When both of you have finished writing your rebuttals, get together to read and discuss your refuting statements to one another. In so doing, choose a first and second partner. The first partner presents her or his first rebuttal. The second partner responds nondefensively. The two partners then discuss the gripe and attempt to reach a compromise. Once one gripe has thus been allayed, the second partner reads her or his first rebuttal and the process of negotiation is repeated.

Duration and Frequency   Each rebuttal discussion will last approximately 10 minutes. Combined with the time for preparing written lists and statements, this results in a length for this exercise of about 40 minutes if each partner gets one turn. The exercise can be repeated until all gripes have received attention.

Suggestions   This exercise will work best if both partners remain nondefensive and open-minded. The verbal communication skills you learned previously will come in handy to write statements and rebuttals that are respectful, caring, and yet communicate effectively the feelings of each partner about the other's behavior and gripe. Begin this exercise with the most minor gripe to get some practice before moving on to financial concerns that are large and highly conflictual. Discontinue the exercise if you find yourselves getting too angry to be respectful of one another's feelings. Cool down and try again later.

Pitfalls   It would defeat the purpose of this exercise to attack or blame the partner for the financial behavior about which you are concerned. Do not expect to find perfect solutions—be willing to compromise or even delay decisions when a solution is not found within 20 minutes at most.

SECTION SEVEN *Parenting*

EXERCISES
1. Do We Want to Be Parents?
2. My Family's Parenting Style
3. What I Liked and Disliked About My Own Parents' Parenting
4. Common Parenting Disagreements
5. Negotiating Parenting Values
6. Negotiating Parenting Goals
7. Negotiating Parenting Discipline Styles
8. Negotiating Children's Chores
9. Having Problems?
10. Solving Problems

The exercises in this section are focused on conflicts about parenting that can cause extreme distress in an intimate relationship. By resolving differences or problems within the realm of parenting, many partners will find their relationship strengthened. The first exercise is appropriate for partners who do not have children but are considering becoming parents. The remainder of the exercises apply only to parents. However, given the many variations present in current society (e.g., one partner having sole responsibility for parenting, having children that are not living with you, having children for whom you are not a biological parent, etc.), both partners will need to discuss whether all exercises are appropriate and if they apply to their current situation. Perhaps parenting is not an issue in your relationship. Discussing the exercises and your circumstances with your counselor may be useful in determining how the exercises can help your relationship.

1 *DO WE WANT TO BE PARENTS?*

Purpose   Whether you are already parents or whether you are planning to be parents someday, this exercise can be helpful. Specifically, if you are still in the planning stages, this exercise can help you determine whether you want children at all. If you already have children, it can help you understand why you chose to have children, if you did not consider this issue consciously at the time you became pregnant. This exercise will help you to define your reasons for wanting children and how you feel about being a parent.

Benefit   To many, the urge to reproduce is instinctual, and we often succumb to it without pausing to examine our motivations for becoming parents. Sometimes we even fail to discuss this decision with our partner and later have hurt feelings when it becomes obvious that we have different opinions or ideas about this important issue. Traditionally, we often feel that when we are in a serious relationship or when we reach a certain age that we should become parents. Clearly defining the expectations and examining the probable impact of parenthood on our lives in advance will help reduce stress later. Awareness of reasons for becoming or not becoming parents will also help partners better understand their reactions to each other when the topic of having children arises.

Directions   **Step One:** If you are thinking about parenthood in the future, take 5 minutes and visualize being a parent; imagine how it would feel and how it would affect your life-style. If you are already a parent, take 5 minutes and visualize what it is like for you right now to be a parent. Is it different from what you anticipated? If yes, how so? How has it affected your life-style?

Step Two: Next, each partner needs to take a sheet of paper and answer the questions that follow this exercise.

Step Three: After 2 to 3 days, look over your answers again and make any additions or corrections.

Step Four: Take turns in sharing your answers alternately with your partner.

Step Five: Take a short break to allow yourselves to assimilate your partner's responses. Then take time to discuss your interpretation of your responses together. If you are not yet parents, use this time to begin arriving at a consensus about this possibility. If you are parents already, be supportive of one another and try to find ways to help each other with the negative aspects of this experience.

Duration and Frequency It will take several days to complete this exercise because you need to take time between step 2 and step 3 to mull over your responses.

Suggestions Be honest—do not give answers that you think the other person wants to hear. Most importantly, do not say you want children because you think your partner wants to hear that. Try to share each idea without interruption. If you are not yet parents, you may want to take time to talk to other parents to be able to answer the questions more realistically. Do not answer according to what you hope would occur; answer according to what you realistically think will occur.

Pitfalls Listen carefully to each other's answers but avoid becoming angry if you do not agree with them. Do not be afraid to be honest about your feelings and thoughts.

PARENTING ASSESSMENT If you are thinking about parenthood in the future:

1. Do I want to become a parent, and if so why (list specific reasons)?
2. What do I **feel** and **think** about being a parent?
3. What specific problems do I anticipate about parenthood?
4. What do I expect will be the best thing about being a parent?
5. What do I expect will be the worst thing about being a parent?
6. How might parenthood change my relationship with my partner?
7. If we have children, how will we be able to keep our special relationship?

If you are already a parent:

1. Did I want to become a parent or did this just happen (list specific reasons)? Would I do it over again?
2. What do I **feel** and **think** about being a parent?
3. What specific problems have I encountered about parenthood?
4. What has been the best thing about being a parent?
5. What has been the worst thing about being a parent?
6. How has parenthood changed my relationship with my partner?
7. Is there something else we could do or could have done to keep our special relationship?

2 *MY FAMILY'S PARENTING STYLE*

Purpose This exercise will help you recall how your own parents dealt with you when you were a child and how that compares to the parenting your partner received during childhood.

Benefit Many of our present behaviors and values stem from our families of origin, as was pointed out in a previous section. Attitudes and beliefs also are expressed in families by how parents raise their children—what procedures they use, what their attitudes are, and what goals they set for their children. Understanding how you and your partner were parented yourselves will give you an insight into how your respective attitudes, goals, and procedures about parenting were formed. You may notice that you hold some parenting behaviors strictly because they were modeled for you during childhood and that they actually may not be the best ones. You may have recognized that you use some strategies as a direct reaction against something your own parents did that you did not like. You may also notice several remarkable differences in your own and your partner's attitudes, goals, and procedures. A recognition of differences can lead to arguments but is crucial to working toward a parenting compromise with which both of you feel comfortable.

Directions **Step One:** Find a comfortable space and some time to relax. Each of you individually should reflect upon the different periods of your life, including your early years, middle childhood, teenage years, and even young adulthood. Consider all of the questions on the questionnaire at the end of this exercise for each of those periods and make thorough notes about what you discover.

Step Two: After a couple of days, review your answers and add any new thoughts you may have had since the original reflection took place.

Step Three: Share your answers with your partner, alternating who goes first on each question referred to in step 1. Listen attentively and actively to your partner's answers without asking too many questions. You may want to take some notes as your partner speaks.

Step Four: Compare your parenting backgrounds and consider how they have influenced your current attitudes, beliefs, and goals about parenting. Discuss how your personal background may have influenced your own parenting style and where differences in backgrounds and attitudes have created conflicts in opinions for the two of you.

Duration and Frequency

This is a lengthy exercise that takes much reflection and thought. Step 1 alone may take a week or so to complete. Step 2 should take no more than an additional hour. Step 3 may take several lengthy sessions. Step 4 may be skipped at this time if it is too difficult, but should be returned to later if skipped now. It is likely to require several meetings of the two partners and may be conducted over the course of an additional week. Fortunately, once completed, this exercise does not have to be repeated per se. However, step 4 may be repeated frequently and spontaneously as you and your partner gain more insight into your parenting and as you work on other exercises in this section.

Suggestions

Take plenty of time reflecting on all the answers in step 1. Answer the questions honestly and try to recreate the atmosphere of your home in your mind as much as possible. You may even want to call a sibling to get her or his perceptions about your parents' styles and attitudes. When discussing and sharing your parenting backgrounds, remain nonjudgmental with one another. Do not criticize the partner's parents regardless of what they did, but be an active and empathic listener. Use all the active listening skills you learned in the verbal communication section. Be sure to keep your responses to the questionnaire for future exercises.

Pitfalls

This exercise can bring forth painful memories for some people. This is true especially if parents were abusive and nonempathic. You may realize for the first time that you did not have the happy childhood you wanted to have. The same may happen to your partner, so empathy and caring are critical in doing step 3 (maybe even step 4). Avoid ridiculing or criticizing your partner about her or his childhood. Remember, there are no right or wrong answers here; this is merely an opportunity to look at your childhoods and parents. Do not use this exercise to discuss which parenting attitudes and goals to adopt in your current relationship with your own child or children (later exercises will help you do this). For now, focus strictly on understanding your own and your partner's backgrounds and personal experiences.

Parenting Questionnaire*

1. Who was the primary parent in your home, i.e., who spent the most time with the children?

2. What were your primary parent's attitudes and beliefs about
   (V) children? For instance, did she or he believe (mark all that apply)
   - that children should be spoiled?

Note: The meaning of the letters V, G, and D will be explained in exercises 5 to 7.

- that children should be seen and not heard?
- that children should take care of their parents?
- that children are the most important aspect of family life?
- that children have the same rights as adults?
- that all children in the household have the same rights and responsibilities regardless of age differences?
- that children cannot understand most important issues (e.g., finances) and are therefore to be kept in the dark about any problems the parents are encountering?
- that children need to be informed of all family problems, including conflicts in the parents' marital relationship?
- that children are basically bad?
- that children are basically good?
- that all children are alike?
- that boys and girls should be treated differently?
- that children's rights should supersede parents' rights?
- that children should always be included in all activities the adults engage in?

(add any other attitudes or beliefs your primary parent held about children, even if they are not specifically listed here)

3. What were your primary parent's goals for her or his
(G) children? In other words, what were the messages that you received about what you ought to or would become once you were an adult? For instance, did your primary parent seem to hope or imply that you and your brothers and sisters would grow up to be (mark all that apply)

- followers?
- leaders?
- independent thinkers?
- free spirits?
- spitting images of their parents?
- unique?
- people who fit in under any circumstances?
- people who have their own opinions?
- people who follow the opinions of others?
- people who adapt or conform?
- people who challenge the system and break some rules every now and then?
- perfect?
- losers or failures?

- people who always win regardless of how they go about doing so?
- people who put the needs of others ahead of their own?
- religious?
- smart?
- achievers?
- just like their parents?
- better than their parents?
- those things the parents themselves could not become?

(add any other goals your primary parent held about her or his children, even if they are not specifically listed here)

4. Did your primary parent have different goals for you and
(G) your siblings—e.g., were there different goals for the male and the female children in the family? Were there different goals for the earlier- and later-born children?

5. Was your primary parent satisfied with your gender or had
(V) she or he hoped for a girl, but you were a boy; or hoped for a boy, but you were a girl?

6. What were the important messages your primary parent gave
(V) you about yourself? Were you a good child or a bad child? A smart child or a dumb child? A wanted child or an endured child?

7. Did your primary parent treat the various children in your
(V) family differently from one another? Did she or he have favorites? Did she or he identify scapegoats?

8. Did your primary parent seem to enjoy being a parent or was she or he a parent only because of having to be?

9. What kind of discipline strategies did your primary parent
(D) use? In other words, did your primary parent (mark all that apply)

- make you feel guilty for misbehavior? If so, under what circumstances and how?
- use corporal punishment (i.e., hit you)? If so, where did she or he hit you and how often? How bad an offense did you have to commit for the parent to resort to hitting?
- use time-outs (i.e., make you stand in a corner or go to a secluded spot in the house) to correct behavior?
- teach you logical or natural consequences (i.e., make you feel the consequences of your misbehavior; e.g., if you refused to wear your coat, you got cold; if you lost your bike, you had to earn money to buy a new one)?
- talk to you to help you understand what you did wrong?

- ignore you when you tried to get her or his attention in inappropriate ways (e.g., if you threw a tantrum in a grocery store, did she or he just walk off and let you come to your senses)?
- reward you in some way if you behaved well?
- let you know she or he appreciated it when you behaved well?
- praise you for good behavior?
- notice good behavior?
- pay attention to you only when you misbehaved?
- make you feel terrible for your behavior?
- hold you or another sibling out as an example of how a child should or should not behave to alter your behavior?
- yell at you to get you to do things?
- humiliate you in front of other people to get you to change your behavior?
- talk poorly about you behind your back?
- ground you or take away privileges as punishment (e.g., took away your allowance; did not allow you to watch TV; refused the nightly bedtime story)?

(add any other means of discipline your primary parent used with her or his children, even if they are not specifically listed here)

10. What kind of philosophy did your parent have about
(V) parenting? In other words, using the definitions below, was
(D) your parent authoritarian, permissive, or authoritative?

Authoritarian: The parent is the boss and the child has to follow the rules and has few rights; discipline is strict and there are few, if any, rewards for good behavior; many rules are applied rigidly and excuses are not tolerated.

Permissive: The child is the boss and decides what she or he wants to do with little interference by the parent; the parent rarely, if ever, punishes the child; there are few rules in the household and they can be easily broken without repercussions for the child.

Authoritative: The parent has clear rules for the child and applies them flexibly and caringly; the parent is willing to talk with the child and pays attention to good behavior; corporal punishment is rarely used; parent and child tend to communicate well and respect each other's rights.

11. Was your primary parent abusive or neglectful? In other
(D) words, did she or he hit you so badly that bruises or other
marks or injuries resulted? Did she or he sometimes forget to
feed you or clothe you? Did she or he fail to support you
emotionally? Did she or he use you sexually (this includes not
only intercourse, but also fondling, masturbation,
inappropriate sexual touching, and similar interactions)?

12. Did your primary parent like you?

13. If there was another parent in the home, what was her or his
involvement with you? If the person was quite involved in
your life, go back and answer questions 2 to 12 for this
parent as well.

14. Did your parents agree on how to discipline you?

15. Did your parents fight over issues related to parenting? For
instance, did they believe that one was more lenient than the
other? Did they complain that one was not sufficiently
involved with the children?

16. Did your parents have certain parenting roles with the
(V) children? For instance, was one parent the disciplinarian
(e.g., did one parent use the other's return from work as a
threat, such as: "Just wait till your father gets home. Then
you'll get a beating!")?

17. Did your parents seem to collaborate on the task of
(V) parenting? In other words, did they make major decisions
about the children together, or was one parent the decider
and the other the follower?

18. What did your parents do when they disagreed about a
parenting decision?

19. Were there times in your life when you got along better or
(D) worse with either parent? For instance, some people get
along fine with their parents as young children, but not as
adolescents. If so, when did you get along, and when did you
fight more? Why do you think you got along differently at
different times? Did your parents agree or disagree about
strategies?

20. Did you prefer one of your parents over the other? If so,
(V) why? What was it that you liked better about one? What did
the other do that made you like her or him less? Did one
parent frighten you, but the other did not?

21. What was the best thing your parents ever did for you? Did
(V) they do this good thing often enough? Did they do this good
thing for you freely, or did you have to earn it in one way or
another?

22. What was the worst thing your parents ever did to you? How
(V) often did this happen and how did you feel about it? Do you
believe other parents do this to their children as well? If so,
should they?

23. What kinds of chores were you responsible for? Do you think
(G) they were appropriate for a child your age?

3 WHAT I LIKED AND DISLIKED ABOUT MY OWN PARENTS' PARENTING

Purpose
This exercise is designed to bring you yet another step closer to understanding how your and your partner's ideas about parenting were formed, and why they may or may not be compatible.

Benefit
The background against which our attitudes, beliefs, and goals about parenting developed influences our own parenting style. We incorporate things our own parents did that we liked into our own repertoire of parenting skills, and we delete those things we did not like. Thus, recognizing what we did and did not like gives us better insight into our own parenting choices. Understanding this information for ourselves and our partners helps us become more tolerant of our differences in parenting styles and paves the way for compromises on parenting issues as we come to recognize the reasons we do things now.

Prerequisite
"My Family's Parenting Style"

Directions
Step One: Take out your completed questionnaire from "My Family's Parenting Style." Go back through your answers with red and green highlighting pens. With the green pen, highlight all the things your parents did that you liked, and with the red pen, highlight all the things they did that you did not like.

Step Two: Exchange questionnaires with your partner so that she or he now is reading about your parenting background. Each partner goes through the answers with a red and a green felt-tip pen. Put a green asterisk next to the items on the partner's questionnaire that you like about your partner's parents' parenting; place a red asterisk next to items you dislike.

Step Three: Take the two questionnaires and compare your likes about your parents' parenting. Circle all items on both questionnaires that you both liked (i.e., all items that are highlighted in green and have a green asterisk at the same time). Make a new list of strategies, attitudes, and beliefs that reflect the parenting issues both of you like about both sets of parents.

Step Four: Now take the two questionnaires and compare your dislikes about your parents' parenting. Circle all items on both questionnaires that you both disliked (i.e., all items that are highlighted in red and have a red asterisk at the same time). Make a new list of strategies, attitudes, and beliefs that reflect the parenting issues both of you dislike about both sets of parents.

Duration and Frequency   This exercise can proceed rather quickly compared to some of the other parenting exercises because you rely largely on work you did in "My Family's Parenting Style." Nevertheless, you should plan on about 1 to 2 hours of work. This exercise does not need to be repeated unless you remember new parenting issues about your own parents.

Suggestions   Be honest about your likes and dislikes, both on your own parents' list and your partner's parents' list. Do not discuss disagreements about what you and your partner mark as likes or dislikes. This exercise serves merely to help identify common likes and dislikes, not to help you make decisions about who has made the right choices.

Pitfalls   Criticizing one another for the choices or criticizing one's parents for their parenting represent the two major pitfalls of this exercise. Refrain from value judgments at this time. Just be honest about what you like and do not like. For now, ignore any items where you disagree (you will be asked to return to these later).

4 COMMON PARENTING DISAGREEMENTS

Purpose   This exercise will help you identify your most prominent areas of disagreements related to parenting and will help you negotiate solutions.

Benefit   In every relationship in which partners have to share responsibility for the care of children, it is likely that they will criticize one another for the parenting choices they make. One partner may claim that the other is too lenient, whereas that partner may feel that the other is authoritarian and unwilling to give in. Such recurrent griping is extremely unnerving for the two partners and can lead to arguments that could be easily resolved if the two partners could look at each other's behavior realistically and strike a compromise. This exercise is designed to facilitate just such a process.

Prerequisite   "My Family's Parenting Style"

Directions   **Step One:** Each partner individually needs to sit down with a pen and piece of paper to think about her or his common gripes about the partner's ways of dealing with the children. Write down all the gripes you have in a truthful but caring manner. In other words, use good communication skills in writing (do not blame or criticize, rather phrase your messages in terms of how you feel and with empathic understanding). You may use the questions in the questionnaire of "My Family's Parenting Style" to help you trigger your memory.

Step Two: The two partners exchange lists and then give each other 20 minutes to read the list and write a rebuttal. Just as the original list was developed with care and concern, so is the rebuttal phrased in terms of "I" messages and "I understand" messages. The rebuttal is not done defensively, but thoughtfully.

Step Three: When both partners have finished writing their rebuttals, they get together to read and discuss their refuting statements to one another. In so doing, choose a first and second partner. The first partner presents her or his first rebuttal, after which the second partner responds nondefensively. The two partners then discuss the gripe and attempt to reach a compromise. Once one gripe has thus been resolved, the second partner reads her or his first rebuttal and the process of negotiation is repeated.

Duration and Frequency Each rebuttal discussion will last approximately 15 to 20 minutes. Combined with the time for preparing written lists and statements, this results in a length of about 40 minutes if each partner gets one turn. The exercise can be repeated until all gripes have been addressed. You may choose to do this exercise over 2 days if a particularly emotional issue arises.

Suggestions This exercise will work best if both partners remain nondefensive and open-minded. The verbal communication skills you learned previously will come in handy to help you write statements and rebuttals that are respectful, caring, and yet communicate effectively your feelings about your partner's behavior and gripes. Begin this exercise with the most minor gripe to get some practice before moving on to major conflicts about parenting that are highly ingrained. Discontinue the exercise if you find yourselves getting too angry to be respectful of one another's feelings. Cool down and try again later.

Pitfalls It would defeat the purpose of this exercise to attack or blame the partner for the parenting behavior about which you are concerned. Do not expect to find perfect solutions—be willing to compromise or even delay decisions when a solution is not found within 20 minutes at most. Later exercises are designed to help you negotiate solutions.

5 NEGOTIATING PARENTING VALUES

Purpose This exercise gives you the opportunity to explore your personal values about parenting. This task represents an expansion of "Do We Want to Be Parents?" and builds upon it in that it asks you to search for some of the same information, but with regard to your own parenting style.

Benefit The values we have as parents clearly determine and influence how we behave as parents. If two parents of the same children have very different values, they invariably fight over who is right and who is wrong when it comes to concrete decision making. Understanding value differences is the first step in developing compromises that are compatible with both parents' value systems.

Prerequisites "My Family's Parenting Style"

"What I Liked and Disliked About My Own Parents' Parenting"

Directions **Step One:** Get out the questionnaire you responded to in "My Family's Parenting Style." You will note that several items have a **(V)** under the item number. Look as these items in detail. They reflect parenting values.

Step Two: Think about how you feel about each item (regardless of how your parents dealt with the item!). Think of any other values you hold about parenting. Based on all of these thoughts and feelings, prepare a list of parenting values that you hold.

Step Three: Compare your own list with your partner's list. Circle or highlight in green items on both lists about which both of you agree. Circle or highlight in red items from both lists where you definitely disagree. Circle in pencil any items about which one of you feels strongly and the other does not really have an opinion.

Step Four: Discuss all items marked in green to become aware of the many values you already share.

Step Five: Discuss all the items marked in pencil, giving the person who feels strongly about each item a chance to voice her or his opinion. The other partner merely listens. Because the listening partner already agreed that she or he does not feel strongly about the topic, the only thing this discussion needs to accomplish is to see whether the listening partner can come to recognize why this item is important to the other person. If, after the discussion, both partners agree that this item is important, mark it in green. Otherwise leave it as is.

Step Six: Discuss the items marked in red by alternating who goes first as you work through the list of these items of disagreement. The partner who goes first presents her or his opinion about each given value. The other listens, using active and empathic listening. After the partner is finished expressing her or his opinion, both partners should attempt to negotiate a compromise. If you find a compromise, put it on the list marked in green and eliminate the original red item. If you cannot negotiate a compromise, try to reach a point where the item can at least be marked in pencil. Through this step try to eliminate all but a few of the red items. Some disagreement will be left—that is normal and to be expected. No two people are likely to agree on everything. In fact, some disagreement is healthy.

Duration and Frequency

This is a lengthy exercise that takes much reflection and discussion. Plan to spend at least 15 minutes per red item and 10 minutes per pencil-marked item. Green items can be dealt with in a minute or so. Preparation of values lists will take about 30 minutes. Repeat this exercise as often as necessary and as you have new ideas.

Suggestions

Try to find some compromise for each red item by using the problem-solving techniques you learned previously. Be honest about your own beliefs and refrain from criticizing your partner's if you do not agree. Focus on compromise, not scrutiny. If you feel yourselves getting close to an argument, stop the exercise and come back to it later when both of you have cooled down. You may want to save your work for future reference.

Pitfalls

Avoid adhering so rigidly to your principles that you cannot effect a compromise. Do not be tempted to criticize your partner's values.

6 *NEGOTIATING PARENTING GOALS*

Purpose

This exercise will provide you a chance to explore your personal goals about parenting. This task represents an expansion of the previous exercises in this section and builds upon them in that it asks you to search for some of the same information, but with regard to your own parenting style.

Benefit

As parents, the goals of parenting that we hold profoundly influence how we treat our children and what messages we give them. Whenever two parents have very different goals for the same child, arguments and fights typically ensue over whose goals are correct. This can translate into problems both in parenting the child as well as difficulties within the intimate relationship between the two partners. The first step toward developing compromises that both parents find acceptable is to gain an understanding of what each partner regards as important in parenting.

Prerequisites

"My Family's Parenting Style"

"What I Liked and Disliked About My Own Parents' Parenting"

Directions

Step One: On the questionnaire you completed in "My Family's Parenting Style," you will notice that several items have a **(G)** under the item number. These items reflect goals that parents have for their children, which in turn influence how parents treat their children.

Step Two: Each partner should think carefully about how she or he feels about each item. The partners should think about how *they* feel about the item, not how their respective parents felt or how they think the other partner feels. Each partner should also consider any other goals that she or he has for each child. Based on all of these thoughts and feelings, each partner should prepare a list of parenting goals that she or he holds.

Step Three: The two lists that were developed should be compared. Circle or highlight in green items on both lists on which both of you agree. Circle or highlight in red items from both lists where you definitely disagree. Circle in pencil any items about which one of you feels strongly and the other does not really have an opinion.

Step Four: Both partners should discuss the items that were circled or highlighted in green to become aware of any goals for your children that are already shared.

Step Five: Discuss any items circled or highlighted in pencil. When doing so, give the person who feels strongly about an item the opportunity to voice her or his opinion while the other partner merely listens. Because the listening partner already stated that she or he does not feel strongly about the given goal, the discussion should focus on determining whether the listening partner can come to recognize why this goal is important to the other person. If after the discussion both partners agree that this is an important goal, mark it in green. Otherwise leave it as is.

Step Six: Discuss the items identified with a red mark by alternating who goes first as you work through the list of items of disagreement. The partner who goes first presents her or his opinion about the given goal. The other listens, using active and empathic listening skills. Attempt to negotiate a compromise. If you find a compromise, put it on the list marked in green and eliminate the original red item. If you cannot negotiate a compromise, try to reach a point where the item can at least be marked in pencil. Try to eliminate all but a few of the red items.

Duration and Frequency

This can be a very lengthy exercise because it requires much reflection and discussion. Plan to spend at least 15 minutes per red item and 10 minutes per pencil-marked item. Green items can be dealt with in a minute or so. Preparation of goals lists will take about 20 minutes. Repeat this exercise as often as necessary when you have new ideas.

Suggestions

Both partners should be careful not to criticize or denounce the other partner's parenting goals. It is important to keep in mind that the exercise is designed for you to learn more about your own and your partner's parenting goals, not to establish who is the better parent. Work on finding compromise solutions for each item marked in red. If you find yourselves getting stuck on any specific goal, skip it for now and go on to the next goal. It will not help anything if this exercise is used to start arguments. Remember, the goal is to compromise and to work together.

Pitfalls

Try not to defend your own goals to such a degree that you do not allow for compromise. Although it may be easy to see one goal as the "right" and only one, it is usually the case that there is no absolute "right" or "wrong" goal. It is very likely that your children have entirely different goals for themselves anyway—remembering this makes compromise just a little bit easier.

7 NEGOTIATING PARENTING DISCIPLINE STYLES

Purpose This exercise gives you the opportunity to explore your personal style of discipline. This task represents an expansion of several previous exercises in this section and builds upon them in that it asks you to search for some of the same information, but with regard to your own parenting style as it is relevant to actual discipline of your child or children.

Benefit The way we treat our children as parents when they behave well or when they misbehave is unique and strongly influenced by our values and goals for parenting. If two parents of the same children have very different goals and values for their offspring, they invariably have different styles and use different techniques to discipline their children. Compromising on goals and values is crucial to developing discipline strategies both parents can live with and that are respectful of the child. In this exercise, the work of "My Family's Parenting Style" and "Personal Parenting Values" is applied to help the partners arrive at compromises about actual techniques or disciplinary strategies that they will use with their children.

Prerequisites "My Family's Parenting Style"
"Negotiating Parenting Values"
"Negotiating Parenting Goals"

Directions **Step One:** Both of you should get out the questionnaire you responded to in "My Family's Parenting Style." You will note that several items have a (**D**) under the item number. Look as these items in detail. They reflect various discipline styles that parents use with their children.

Step Two: Consider how you feel about each of these discipline items. At this point, it is important only how *you* feel about it, not how your parents or your partner feels about it. You may also come up with other disciplining strategies that you use. After thinking about the strategies, develop a list of disciplining strategies that you use or would consider using.

Step Three: Both partners should compare their respective lists. Following the same approach used in "Negotiating Parenting Values" and "Negotiating Parenting Goals," circle or highlight in green those items both of you use or endorse using; circle or highlight in red those items about which you definitely disagree;

227

and circle in pencil any item that one of you uses or endorses, and about which the other has no strong opinion one way or the other.

Step Four: Identify the strategies marked in green and discuss what you like about these strategies and how and where you use them most effectively. These are the strategies you can always fall back on in times of disagreement about how to handle certain situations.

Step Five: Discuss the items marked in pencil. In so doing, give the partner who feels strongly about the use of a strategy the opportunity to discuss why she or he endorses it. While this partner is speaking, the other partner should just listen. Endorsement of the strategy means that the partner is not likely to use this strategy herself or himself, but is willing to tolerate its use with the children by the other partner. If after the discussion both partners at least endorse the item, mark it in green. Otherwise mark it in red.

Step Six: For the items marked in red, alternate who goes first in discussing these strategies about which you disagree. The partner who goes first presents her or his opinion about the given means of discipline while the other partner listens. After the partner has had an opportunity to express her or his opinion about the strategy, both partners should attempt to negotiate a compromise about its use. If a compromise is attained, mark the strategy in green. If no compromise is attained, leave it marked in red. Through this procedure, try to eliminate as many of the strategies or means of discipline marked in red as possible. Because of disagreement, all strategies left marked in red are off-limits from now on. Only strategies marked in green may be used with the children from here on.

Duration and Frequency

This exercise will take quite a bit of time because it requires much contemplation, discussion, and important decision making. You can expect to spend at least 20 minutes per red item, 15 minutes per penciled item, and 1 to 2 minutes per green item. Repeat this exercise as often as you wish as long as red items are left after each discussion. Perhaps you can settle on a compromise later.

Suggestions

Work toward attaining a compromise for each item marked in red. Be honest about your own reasons for wanting to use certain strategies to discipline your children, and refrain from criticizing your partner's preferred strategies if you do not agree with them. Certain strategies, however, should always be off-limits, namely, no child should be beaten, nor should any child be subjected to any form of mental or physical duress. When one partner feels strongly about a certain strategy, that person has veto privilege. A veto leads to a red mark and makes the given strategy off-limits.

Overall, focus on compromise, not scrutiny, and do not overuse your veto power. If you feel yourselves getting close to an argument, stop the exercise and come back to it later when both of you have cooled down.

Pitfalls   Avoid adhering so rigidly to your ideas about discipline that you cannot work out a compromise. Do not be tempted to criticize your partner's means of intervening with the children (as long as the means do not hurt the children in any way, physically or emotionally).

8 *NEGOTIATING CHILDREN'S CHORES*

Purpose This exercise will help you establish agreement about chores you consider appropriate for your child.

Benefit Part of growing up is learning to accept responsibility for our lives. With that in mind, most of us expect our children to begin to take part in the day-to-day running of a household by helping with certain chores. It is important that these chores be age-appropriate so that the child can complete them without undue difficulty and with some sense of pride in her or his achievement. Parents often have difficulty agreeing on which chores should be delegated to children. Such disagreement provides children the perfect opportunity to get out of their chores by seeking support from the parent who seems ambivalent about a chosen chore. Presenting chores and responsibilities to children with a united front helps parents ensure that the children will not be able to play the parents off against each other in order to avoid responsibility.

Directions **Step One:** Each parent lists the chores that she or he thinks the child should be responsible for.

Step Two: Compare your lists to see if you already have some agreement. Mark chores both of you agree about in green. Mark chores on which you disagree in red. If you have plenty of "green" chores, move on to step 3. If you have too few "green" chores, use the problem-solving techniques you learned in the verbal communication section to develop a compromise. Try to develop at least 4 to 5 chores about which you agree.

Step Three: Take "green" chores one by one and discuss your exact expectations of the child, keeping the age and abilities of your child in mind. Discuss expectations until the two of you can agree on how and when the chore must be performed. Repeat this process for each "green" chore.

Step Four: Present the chores to your child or children with a united front. In other words, both partners should sit down with the child or children to convey the message that this is an agreed-upon process. Explain that the child will be expected to do the chore.

Step Five: After a few weeks, review the situation and make any necessary adjustments.

Duration and Frequency   This exercise should take 15 to 30 minutes initially, and may be repeated as often as necessary.

Suggestions   This may be a relatively easy exercise if the two partners share similar attitudes and values. Because previous exercises have established these, you can use that context to facilitate the discussion about chores. Do not settle on chores just because you had to do them when you were a child. Be reasonable and willing to compromise.

Pitfalls   Do not be rigid about your position. There are plenty of chores children can do—you should be able to find at least a few about which both of you can agree.

9 *HAVING PROBLEMS?*

Purpose

This exercise will help you develop skills you can use to initiate discussions with your partner about problems you may experience with your child's behavior so that you may obtain much-needed support in the parenting role.

Benefit

Frequently, one or the other parent feels as though she or he is the only one aware of and willing to deal with a child's behavior problems. Such feelings lead to isolation, frustration, and even anger against the partner who seems uninvolved and nonsupportive. This exercise will help you learn how to involve your partner to share the burden of being a parent. It will help both partners feel less alone in the parenting task and will provide some much-needed adult support, as well as a reality check about the severity of the problem perceived by the parent.

Directions

Step One: Let your partner know of your need to share your frustrations about your child, and set up a time to do so.

Step Two: Both parents should sit comfortably while the partner who initiated the meeting shares the problem, how she or he feels about the problem, and what is happening with the child. The other partner listens and then adds her or his own feelings or comments at the end if necessary.

Step Three: Acknowledge each other's feelings and position vis-à-vis the identified problem and indicate willingness to support one another. Express your mutual appreciation for each other's support in raising your child.

Duration and Frequency

This exercise will take 10 to 30 minutes and may be repeated as often as necessary. The more often you do this exercise, the less time you may need for it and still get the full benefit of feeling supported. This is an exercise you should repeat often.

Suggestions

When expressing your frustrations, be careful to focus on the child and not on your partner. Clearly outline the problem and your reaction to it. As the listener, view the problem from your partner's perspective and empathize with her or his feelings. Remember, the idea of this exercise is to lend support to the partner who feels overburdened by a child or by the parenting role, not to solve the problem (this will be dealt with in the next exercise). Sometimes problems become smaller just by virtue of being shared. Giving support to one another is critical here.

Pitfalls   Beware of blaming your partner for the child's problem. Listen to your partner's feelings and avoid downplaying them or disagreeing with them. The listener should avoid talking too much; doing so prevents the partner from expressing her or his feelings.

10 SOLVING PROBLEMS

Purpose   This exercise will help you develop effective techniques to discuss and solve problems you might encounter with your children. It will help to develop a plan of action that will relieve frustrations and change the disagreeable behavior.

Benefit   Frequently when we have to discuss problems of discipline with our children over and over again, our frustration level is so great that our ability to communicate effectively is impaired. This exercise will help partners develop skills to problem-solve regarding a child's misbehavior. This exercise will result in partners' being more capable of getting support from one another and of developing effective solutions to problems while working together as a parenting team.

Prerequisites   "Negotiating Parenting Values"
"Negotiating Parenting Goals"
"Negotiating Parenting Discipline Styles"
"Having Problems?"

Directions   **Step One:** The parent who is aware of a problem makes an appointment with the partner to discuss it.

Step Two: Both parents should sit comfortably while the partner who initiated the meeting shares the problem, how she or he feels about the problem, and what is happening with the child. The other partner listens and then adds her or his own feelings or comments at the end if necessary.

Step Three: Acknowledge each other's feelings and position vis-à-vis the identified problem and indicate willingness to support one another. Express your mutual appreciation for each other's support in raising your child.

Step Four: Using the problem-solving strategies you learned in the verbal communication section, develop solutions for the problem with which both of you are comfortable. Be sure that these solutions are in line with the parenting values, goals, and discipline strategies you developed for yourselves in the previous exercises in this section. It is best to develop several different acceptable solutions and rank them in order of importance.

Step Five: Take the first solution for the first problem, together present it to the child, and implement it for the next 2 weeks. If it does not work, replace it with the next solution. Continue to enforce the solutions jointly. Remember, it is easier to change behavior if you are consistent and follow through.

Duration and Frequency

This exercise may be very quick (10 to 15 minutes) if the problem is relatively minor or easy to deal with. It may require a significant amount of time if the parents disagree about the problem and need more time to arrive at a compromise. Obviously, this is an exercise that can be repeated as often as necessary when problems arise.

Suggestions

Deal with and solve only one problem at a time, and remember to be positive about behavior changes. Use all of your active listening skills and problem-solving strategies to come up with solutions. Support one another in the parenting role and be responsible for implementing the solutions together. Be willing to compromise and be true to your established parenting values, goals, and chosen strategies.

Pitfalls

Do not try to find the perfect solution. Do not allow the search for a solution to override the joy of feeling supported by the partner and of enjoying the awareness that the parenting task is indeed shared.

SECTION EIGHT *Sexuality*

EXERCISES
1. How I Grew Up: Sexual Knowledge
2. How I Grew Up: Sexual Attitudes and Values
3. What Turns You On . . . Or Off
4. What Turns You On . . . Or Off: Sharing
5. What You Like and Dislike
6. Making Changes
7. Sexual Games
8. Sexual Fantasy: Imagining
9. Sexual Fantasy: Discussing
10. Taking the Initiative

The exercises in this section deal with the area of partners' sexuality. This area is another primary source of conflicts in relationships and often produces emotionally charged verbal exchanges. These exercises are designed to help you explore the problem areas in your sexual relationship in the least conflictual manner possible. Furthermore, they aim to help you resolve these conflicts by guiding you toward compromise and new patterns of sexual relating. Sexuality is a very private topic that often involves considerable stress for individuals, both with regard to engaging in sex and talking about their sexuality. Although the sensitivity and emotionally charged nature of the topic may seem to make sex difficult to talk about with a counselor, they are the very reason why a counselor may be helpful with these exercises.

1 HOW I GREW UP: SEXUAL KNOWLEDGE

Purpose   This exercise will help you identify how you were educated about sexual matters.

Benefit   As you have learned from exercises in previous sections of this book, much of our behavior, values, and attitudes is greatly affected by our experiences as a child in our family of origin. In this respect, our sexuality is no different from other areas. How and from whom you learned about sex, and the accurate and inaccurate information you received, all have had an influence on your sexuality. By identifying your first learning experiences about sexuality, you will gain a greater understanding about the sexual aspects of your personality. This, in turn, may be beneficial to your relationship, particularly if you are experiencing difficulties in this realm.

Directions   **Step One:** Independently think about the sources of your sexual knowledge. Choose a quiet time and place in which you are unlikely to be disturbed. Focus on early recollections of how and when you learned about sex. At this point, focus on the acquisition of knowledge about sex, rather than values or attitudes about sex. Who gave you the information? Was the information correct or incorrect? What was the information passed on to you? Write this information down on paper for later sharing with your partner.

Step Two: Select a partner who will start the exercise. This partner will share with her or his partner the information that was recalled and written down in step 1.

Step Three: As the listener, your role is merely to listen actively and empathically to your partner. Ask questions if it might help your partner's recollection. Neither ridicule or criticize your partner's memories nor pass judgment.

Step Four: Reverse roles and repeat steps 2 to 3. If the first partner took a lot of time, you may want to wait to reverse roles until your next meeting time.

Duration and Frequency   The sharing portion of this exercise will take between 10 to 15 minutes for each partner. There is no need to repeat the exercise until further memories surface.

Suggestions   Be honest about the sources of your sexual knowledge. Focus not only on accurate information, but also on times when you were given misinformation or were misled, intentionally or unintentionally. Be supportive of one another and be sure not to ridicule or tease one another.

Pitfalls   The main danger in this exercise is one or both partners' being too embarrassed to talk about their early recollections. If this proves to be a problem, try to help one another to feel it is safe. Another possible pitfall is the inability to remember the precise sources of sexual knowledge. Do not worry about perfection in this exercise; focus on general memories.

2 HOW I GREW UP: SEXUAL ATTITUDES AND VALUES

Purpose This exercise will help you determine what influence your family of origin has had on your sexual values and attitudes.

Benefit Parents' attitudes toward and values about sexuality are conveyed to children in direct and indirect, overt and covert messages. The messages we received as children about sexuality play a major role in determining our outlook on sexuality as adults. By identifying attitudes toward and values about sexuality in your family of origin, you will gain further understanding about the sexual aspects of your personality. Such understanding may give you greater insights into how you are functioning within the sexual realm of your intimate relationship.

Prerequisite "How I Grew Up: Sexual Knowledge"

Directions **Step One:** Each partner should spend some time thinking about the origins of her or his sexual attitudes and values individually. Find a private place in which you will not be disturbed or distracted. Focus on recollections of your parents' attitudes toward and values about sexuality. Think deeply about the messages they gave you about sex, both overtly and covertly. Focus not only on what was told you about sex, but also on the implicit messages about sexuality.

Step Two: Identify one partner to start the exercise through the following procedure: The partner who did not start "How I Grew Up: Sexual Knowledge" as the speaker will be the first speaker for this exercise. The speaker will then share the information she or he recalled and wrote down in step 1.

Step Three: The listener's role is simply to listen to her or his partner. As listener, you can ask questions if it might help your partner's recollection, but be careful not to criticize or belittle your partner.

Step Four: Switch roles and repeat steps 2 and 3.

Duration and Frequency Between 15 to 30 minutes should be allocated for each partner to share her or his recollections. Repetitions of this exercise are unnecessary unless additional memories or insights arise.

Suggestions Try to be as honest as possible with your partner about the origins of your sexual attitudes and values. Think about how your parents dealt with the issue of sexuality with you, with any siblings, and with each other. This can be an awkward and embarrassing exercise, so both partners should be supportive and patient and should be careful to not belittle or make fun of one another.

Pitfalls   One or both partners could become embarrassed as a result of this exercise. This embarrassment could lead the partner not to participate in the exercise or not to divulge all relevant information. It is important not to push a partner beyond what she or he is able and willing to do at the time. On the other hand, this needs to be balanced by a willingness to take risks and to learn to trust one another. It may take time for both partners to feel comfortable to participate in this exercise. If there are significant difficulties, it may be helpful to discuss these with your counselor. Another possible pitfall is being unable to remember your parents' sexual attitudes and values. It may help to focus on general impressions rather than trying to remember specific examples or comments.

3 *WHAT TURNS YOU ON . . . OR OFF*

Purpose This exercise is designed to help make you aware of what you find sexually stimulating. It will also help you identify and share things you dislike.

Benefit We are often reluctant, for a variety of reasons, to examine intimate details about our sexual tastes, desires, and interests, let alone share them with our partners. Being able to identify and examine your sexual likes and dislikes will help you gain insight into the sexual side of your being. Sharing this information ultimately with your partner can make the sexual aspect of your relationship more gratifying.

Directions **Step One:** Each of you should complete the questionnaire at the end of this exercise. Put an asterisk by those items in which you and your partner no longer engage or never engaged but that you would like at least to try in your relationship. At this point do not share your responses with your partner.

Step Two: After completing the questionnaire, look back at your answers and think carefully about each item. For items that you find delightful, think about what aspects of the act you find enjoyable and desirable. For items that you find disgusting, think carefully what it is about the item that offends you. For any items that you indicated you would like at least to try in your relationship, think about what makes the act desirable or interesting. Make notes about these thoughts.

Duration and Frequency The time to complete this exercise will vary from individual to individual but should take approximately 15 to 20 minutes. Upon completion, you may want to put the questionnaire aside for a few days or a week and look at it again to see if your answers have remained the same.

Suggestions Even if it embarrasses you, try to be honest with this questionnaire. Remember, at this point you will not be sharing it with your partner. At first, put down your immediate reactions to each item. When you think about each item and what appeals to or disgusts you about it, consider again how you rated the item.

Pitfalls Some people may be offended by items on this list. It is important to remember that sexual likes and dislikes vary from individual to individual, and that there are few, if any, absolute rights and wrongs when it comes to sexuality. Be honest with yourself about the items and your responses to them.

QUESTIONNAIRE FOR WHAT TURNS YOU ON . . . OR OFF

Using the following scale, circle the number that best reflects your feelings toward each item. Place an asterisk (*) to the left of any item that you would like to either try or increase the frequency of in your relationship.

	Undesirable			Neutral			Desirable
1. cuddling (nonsexual)	1	2	3	4	5	6	7
2. caressing (nonsexual parts)	1	2	3	4	5	6	7
3. caressing (sexual parts)	1	2	3	4	5	6	7
4. deep kissing (French kissing)	1	2	3	4	5	6	7
5. body kissing	1	2	3	4	5	6	7
6. massage	1	2	3	4	5	6	7
7. missionary position	1	2	3	4	5	6	7
8. oral sex	1	2	3	4	5	6	7
9. anal sex	1	2	3	4	5	6	7
10. rear-entry position	1	2	3	4	5	6	7
11. breast-fondling	1	2	3	4	5	6	7
12. side-by-side position	1	2	3	4	5	6	7
13. mirrors	1	2	3	4	5	6	7
14. masturbation	1	2	3	4	5	6	7
15. changing sexual partners (swinging)	1	2	3	4	5	6	7
16. erotic movies	1	2	3	4	5	6	7
17. erotic literature	1	2	3	4	5	6	7
18. rubber	1	2	3	4	5	6	7
19. leather	1	2	3	4	5	6	7
20. animals	1	2	3	4	5	6	7
21. sadomasochism	1	2	3	4	5	6	7
22. role-playing in costumes	1	2	3	4	5	6	7
23. watching sex in mirrors	1	2	3	4	5	6	7
24. unusual locations (outdoors, etc.)	1	2	3	4	5	6	7
25. bisexual	1	2	3	4	5	6	7
26. homosexual	1	2	3	4	5	6	7
27. ménage à trois	1	2	3	4	5	6	7
28. group sex	1	2	3	4	5	6	7
29. other: _____	1	2	3	4	5	6	7
30. other: _____	1	2	3	4	5	6	7
31. other: _____	1	2	3	4	5	6	7
32. other: _____	1	2	3	4	5	6	7

4 WHAT TURNS YOU ON . . . OR OFF: SHARING

Purpose

This exercise is designed to help make you aware of what you and your partner find sexually stimulating. It will also help you identify and share those things that you and your partner dislike.

Benefit

For most people, sexuality is one of the most private aspects of their being. Most people share it with only one, or a few people. And for many, it is a difficult topic to talk about, even with their partner. However, for true intimacy to evolve in a relationship, it is crucial that partners share their innermost feelings about themselves, including their sexual selves. Sharing of sexual desires, interests, and wishes with partners is often difficult for many people. We are often reluctant, for a variety of reasons, to discuss intimate details about our sexual tastes, desires, and interests with our partners. However, being able to share your likes and dislikes will enhance your sex lives and will result in greater enjoyment of your most intimate moments.

Prerequisite

"What Turns You On . . . Or Off"

Directions

Step One: Select a partner to start this exercise. This partner will start the sharing process by providing her or his response to the first item on the questionnaire in the previous exercise, and discussing any thoughts or feelings she or he may have about it. When this partner is finished speaking, the other partner shares her or his response to the first item. At this point, do not discuss each other's response; just listen and remain open-minded.

Step Two: Continue this process, alternating who goes first on each item until you have worked your way through the entire questionnaire.

Step Three: After you have both reviewed and shared your lists, each partner should identify two things that she or he learned about the partner through this exercise. These items should be shared with your partner following the procedure in step 1.

Duration and Frequency

The time to complete this exercise will vary, but should take at least 45 minutes. Take your time with this exercise, even if it means completing it over two meeting times.

Suggestions

Be as honest as possible with your partner, even if it proves to be embarrassing or difficult. Furthermore, even if you feel shocked or surprised by your partner's responses, try to avoid indicating this.

Remember that your partner is trusting you to respect the intimate information she or he is sharing. Also remember that just because she or he expresses an interest in a behavior does not necessarily mean she or he wants to include it in your relationship.

Pitfalls   This is no time to be critical of your partner. Because this can be a difficult and embarrassing exercise for many people, it is important to be supportive of one another. Do not ridicule or embarrass your partner, rather accept what is told to you without being judgmental. Do not use this exercise as an opportunity to criticize your partner.

5 *WHAT YOU LIKE AND DISLIKE*

Purpose   This exercise is designed to give you the opportunity to share what you like and what you dislike about the sexual aspect of your relationship with your partner.

Benefit   Communication between two people, even close, intimate partners, is difficult and strained at times, particularly about topics that are potentially emotionally volatile. Often, two partners will not share thoughts and feelings with one another for fear of hurting the other person. The flip side of this is that all too often partners will neglect to tell one another about the positive qualities or attributes they see in each other. By sharing both positive and negative thoughts and feelings about the sexual aspect of your relationship, you will create an atmosphere in which both of you will be able to meet your sexual and intimacy needs. This, in turn, will help create a deeper and stronger bond between you.

Directions   **Step One:** Independently, take some time to reflect on the sexual and physical aspects of your relationship. Focus on both the positives as well as the negatives you would like to see changed. As you reflect on these issues, write down two lists: one reflecting the positive aspects of your sexual relationship, the other reflecting aspects you would like to change. Make notes about the items on these lists.

Step Two: Select a partner to start this exercise. Starting with the list of positives, this partner will start the sharing process by describing one thing that she or he likes about the sexual relationship. When this partner is finished speaking, the other partner shares her or his first item from the positive list. At this point, do not discuss your partner's response; just listen and remain open-minded.

Step Three: Continue this process by taking turns on each item on the positive list until you have worked your way through the entire list.

Step Four: After you have completed the positive list, each of you should choose two items from the list of things you would like to change. Share these with your partner, switching back and forth as you did in steps 2 and 3; however, this time the other partner starts the sharing process.

Step Five: After you have shared your two items from the second list, each of you should identify two things that you learned about your partner through this exercise. These things should be shared with one another following the procedure in step 2.

Duration and Frequency

The time to complete this exercise will vary, but should take approximately 30 to 45 minutes. However, take your time with this exercise, even if it means completing it over two meeting times.

Suggestions

Be as honest as possible with your partner, even if it proves to be embarrassing and difficult. Be sure to focus on and highlight the positive aspects that you like about your sexual relationship. Furthermore, even if you feel shocked or surprised by your partner's responses, try to avoid indicating this. Try not to be defensive about your partner's comments. Remember that you are doing this exercise to help one another, not to hurt each other.

Pitfalls

It is important to identify as many positive aspects as possible. This will provide hope to the relationship and help balance out the items that you would like to see changed. Do not take this exercise as an opportunity to criticize your partner. Because this can be a difficult and embarrassing exercise for many people, it is important to be supportive of one another. Do not ridicule or embarrass your partner, rather accept what is told to you without being judgmental.

6 *MAKING CHANGES*

Purpose   This exercise is designed to help you initiate changes in your sexual relationship based on feedback from the previous exercises.

Benefit   The first step in creating change in your relationship is to identify the areas that need to be changed. The next step is to implement the change and assess its impact on the relationship. Too often, couples will get locked into approaching situations in a certain way without trying to change this approach. This style may be acceptable and appropriate if both partners are pleased with the approach and the outcome. However, if one or both partners are dissatisfied, it becomes imperative to make some changes. In many situations, to do otherwise is to threaten the relationship itself. Creating changes in your sexual relationship based on feedback from one another will help the relationship in many ways. First, the value of being heard and listened to cannot be understated. Next, the ability and willingness of both partners to be flexible and adaptive will lend strength to the relationship itself. Last, the changes in the sexual relationship may lead to one or both partners' experiencing greater sexual satisfaction and, thus, make for a stronger, happier relationship.

Prerequisites   "What Turns You On . . . Or Off: Sharing"
"What You Like and Dislike"

Directions   **Step One:** Based on the feedback from the previous exercises, each partner should think of one thing that she or he is willing to change in the sexual relationship. This should be an item that is acceptable to the partner, both morally and physically, and that the other partner expressed an interest in changing. It does not necessarily have to be a big change; it just has to be a change in response to the other partner's feedback. Indeed, at this point, it is better to start with a small, minor change and work your way up to major changes.

Step Two: Each partner should share what this change will be and gain assurance that it is desirable to the other partner.

Step Three: Implement this change on an experimental basis for the next 2 to 3 weeks. After this time, discuss with your partner how each of you experienced the change, determining whether it was satisfying, pleasing, or difficult. If necessary, continue experimenting with this change for another 2 to 3 weeks. If it is agreeable to both partners, the change can become an ongoing part of your sexual relationship.

Step Four: Repeat steps 1 to 3 for other changes that were identified in "What Turns You On . . . Or Off: Sharing" and "What You Like and Dislike," and that are morally and physically acceptable to both partners. Always implement the changes on an experimental basis and evaluate them after a few weeks.

Duration and Frequency

It should take only a few minutes to identify the change, but, depending on the nature of the change, it may take much more time to implement it. Repeat this exercise as often as both partners believe it necessary or desirable. Try to implement, on an experimental basis, as many changes as you can.

Suggestions

At first, choose small and easily implemented changes. Be willing to try new things that your partner finds interesting or desirable. However, do not engage in anything you feel strongly against; this may serve only to worsen the situation.

Pitfalls

Do not expect a great deal at first—change takes time and effort. Be sure to select only items with which each partner is comfortable; this is not an opportunity to force your partner to do something that she or he does not want to do.

7 SEXUAL GAMES

Purpose   The purpose of this exercise is to add a little spice to your sex life.

Benefit   Often, after several years of marriage, partners become preoccupied with day-to-day problems of living, children, work, or finances, and spontaneity disappears from their sexual relationship. This exercise will give a small jump start to pulling a sexual relationship out of the doldrums.

Directions   **Step One:** Choose a game from the list of suggestions at the end of this exercise, or create one of your own games.

Step Two: Play the game, have fun, and enjoy each other's company.

Step Three: After the game, review how it felt to both of you to try such a new experience.

Duration and Frequency   This exercise could take anywhere from 20 to 30 minutes to several hours. Repeat the exercise as often as both partners wish.

Suggestions   At first, pick games that are the least embarrassing or threatening to both partners. After the game, decide if you would like to do it again and when, and how you might change the rules or structure of the game to make it even more enjoyable or exciting. Try different games and see if you can be creative enough to make up your own special game.

Pitfalls   It is important that both partners be comfortable with the chosen game and that the game be stopped at any time either partner becomes uncomfortable. The point of the exercise is to have fun with each other, and being uncomfortable would certainly counteract this purpose.

SEXUAL GAMES   1. strip poker: lose a piece of clothing for each hand lost, or use your clothes in place of poker chips for bets
2. chess: lose a piece of clothing for each piece lost
3. wrestling: in the nude
4. twister: in the nude
5. sex gourmet: place some food on your partner and lick it off
6. adult board game, such as Intimate Partners or Swingers

8 *SEXUAL FANTASY: IMAGINING*

Purpose   This exercise will help you become aware of how fantasizing can increase your sexual pleasure.

Benefit   An ability to fantasize about sexual matters helps prevent your relationship from becoming routine or boring. It can add spice to your sex life!

Directions   **Step One:** You will not have to share this with your partner. Make yourself comfortable in a quiet place with the lights low. Now, in your mind, create a scenario that you find sexually stimulating. Put as much detail into your fantasy as you can. Imagine not only sights, but also sounds and smells.

Duration and Frequency   This exercise will take from 10 to 20 minutes and may be repeated whenever you please.

Suggestions   This exercise should be enjoyable, so make sure you are undisturbed and have plenty of time. If you have difficulty developing a fantasy, try using some adult material.

Pitfalls   Do not let your partner coerce you into sharing your fantasies.

9 SEXUAL FANTASY: DISCUSSING

Purpose This exercise will help you share your fantasies with your partner.

Benefit This exercise will encourage you to have fun sexually with your partner. The excitement it generates will remind you of the fun and thrills in the carefree days early in the relationship, perhaps before children and responsibilities colored your sexual interaction.

Prerequisites "What Turns You On . . . Or Off: Sharing"
"Sexual Fantasy: Imagining"

Directions **Step One:** Review the different fantasies you used in "Sexual Fantasy: Imagining." Pick a partner to go first.

Step Two: The first partner decides which of the different fantasies developed earlier in the questionnaire for "What Turns You On . . . Or Off" she or he would like to use. This partner then checks her or his partner's list to make sure it will be an acceptable interaction.

Step Three: Present your fantasy to your partner either verbally or in writing.

Step Four: The partner reviews the fantasy and has the right to accept it or veto it. Your partner has the right and may choose to alter some parts of the fantasy if they cause displeasure, discomfort, or embarrassment.

Step Five: Jointly decide if you want to act out the fantasy and arrange an appointment for this. If you decided this fantasy is unacceptable, start this exercise over with step 1.

Step Six: After you have acted out the fantasy, discuss the experience and share what made you feel good and anything you found disturbing. Set a date when you will switch roles and repeat the exercise to give the other partner a chance to try out her or his fantasies.

Duration and Frequency There is no time limit for this exercise because it will depend on the fantasy. It may be repeated whenever you please.

Suggestions Keep the first fantasy close to your usual sexual practices and save the more daring fantasies for a later date. If your partner rejects your fantasy, do not feel personally rejected. Discuss what is causing the problem with the fantasy and see if it can be modified to please both of you. Abandon a fantasy only if you have honestly and carefully attempted to find a compromise that pleases both of you.

Pitfalls   Do not let embarrassment spoil your enjoyment, and be ready to alter your fantasy to make your partner comfortable if necessary. Do not force your fantasy if your partner is unwilling.

10 *TAKING THE INITIATIVE*

Purpose   This exercise is designed to help you develop a balance in your sexual relationship that results in an approximately equal number of attempts by both partners to initiate sex.

Benefit   Often one partner feels that she or he is the only partner who initiates sexual encounters in the relationship. Very likely this leads to this partner's perception that the other partner does not desire her or him or that the partner actually rejects her or him when the partner is "not in the mood."

Directions   **Step One:** Together, honestly review your sexual relationship. Determine who initiated the last few encounters. If it seems fairly equal, you probably do not need this exercise. If one person seems to predominate, continue to step 2.

Step Two: Discuss honestly with each other why you do or do not initiate sex with your partner. You may need to examine past relationships, family upbringing, and past experiences. This is a difficult process and you may find it hard to understand why you do what you do and why your partner does what she or he does. If you find this aspect of your sexual relationship too painful to discuss, stop and go on to the next step.

Step Three: Switch roles for 2 weeks, so that the person who usually is the initiator becomes the receiver and the receiver becomes the initiator.

Step Four: After 2 weeks review how this attempt at balancing who initiates sexual encounters went. Remember, this is an extremely difficult exercise. Hence, if the new initiator actually makes advances first only on one occasion or feels uncomfortable at first, do not worry and remember to keep encouraging each other.

Step Five: Alternate weeks, with one or the other partner being the initiator.

Duration and Frequency   This exercise does not really take any time above and beyond the time you usually spend on sexual encounters in your relationship. It merely shifts roles. It may be repeated often, especially if the partners find it successful.

Suggestions   Try to stay relaxed and communicate any fears and embarrassment to each other. Do not expect more of your partner than she or he is willing or able to give at this time. This exercise is difficult, and criticism will defeat its purpose—remember that for this exercise to work, it must feel like a benefit to both of you.

Pitfalls   Avoid teasing each other about your fears or embarrassment. Do not be critical and do not expect too much of your partner.

PART THREE *Bibliography*

BOOKS FOR THE PROFESSIONAL

GENERAL COUPLES COUNSELING ISSUES

Ables, B., & Brandsma, J. (1984). *Therapy for couples: A clinician's guide for effective treatment.* San Francisco: Jossey-Bass.

American Association for Marriage and Family Therapy. (1982). *Ethical principles for family therapists.* Upland, CA: Author.

American Association for Marriage and Family Therapy. (1984). *Family therapy glossary.* Washington, DC: Author.

Bader, E., & Pearson, P.T. (1988). *In quest of the mythical mate: A developmental approach to diagnosis and treatment in couples therapy.* New York: Brunner/Mazel.

Bagarozzi, D., Jurich, A.P., & Jackson, R.W. (1983). *Marital and family therapy: New perspectives in theory, research, and practice.* New York: Human Sciences.

Bardis, P. (1988). *Marriage and family: Continuity, change, and adjustment.* Dubuque, IA: Kendall-Hunt.

Barker, R.L. (1984). *Treating couples in crisis: The fundamentals and practice of marital therapy.* New York: Free Press.

Baucom, D.H., & Epstein, N. (1990). *Cognitive-behavioral marital therapy.* New York: Brunner/Mazel.

Beach, S.R.H., Sandeen, E.E., & O'Leary, K.D. (1990). *Depression in marriage: A model for etiology and treatment.* New York: Guilford.

Berner, R.T. (1992). *Parents whose parents were divorced.* New York: Haworth.

Bjorksten, O.J.W. (1985). *New clinical concepts in marital therapy.* Washington, DC: American Psychiatric Press.

Bockus, F. (1980). *Couple therapy.* Northvale, NJ: Aronson.

Bograd, M. (Ed.). (1991). *Feminist approaches for men in family therapy.* New York: Haworth.

Bornstein, P.H., & Bornstein, M.T. (1986). *Marital therapy: A behavioral-communications approach.* New York: Pergamon.

Boszormenyi-Nagy, I., & Krasner, B.R. (1986). *Between give and take: A clinical guide to contextual therapy.* New York: Brunner/Mazel.

Brehm, S.S. (1992). *Intimate relationships.* New York: McGraw-Hill.

Brock, G.W. (1992). *Procedures in marriage and family therapy.* Boston: Allyn & Bacon.

Brown, E.M. (1991). *Patterns of infidelity and their treatment.* New York: Brunner/Mazel.

Cameron-Bandler, L. (1985). *Solutions.* San Rafael, CA: Future Place.

Carl, D. (1990). *Counseling same-sex couples.* New York: Norton.

Carter, E.A., & McGoldrick, M. (Eds.). (1980). *The family life cycle: A framework for family therapy.* New York: Gardner.

Chasin, R., Grunebaum, H., & Herzig, M. (Eds.). (1990). *One couple, four realities: Multiple perspectives on couple therapy.* New York: Guilford.

Clark, D., & Haldane, D. (1990). *Wedlocked? Intervention and research in marriage.* Cambridge, MA: Blackwell.

Coche, J., & Coche, E. (1990). *Couples group psychotherapy: A clinical practice model.* New York: Brunner/Mazel.

Crosby, J.F. (1991). *Illusion and disillusion: The self in love and marriage.* Belmont, CA: Wadsworth.

Crosby, J.F. (Ed.). (1989). *When one wants out and the other doesn't: Doing therapy with polarized couples*. New York: Brunner/Mazel.

Daniels, P., & Weingarten, K. (1982). *Sooner or later: The timing of parenthood in adult lives*. New York: Norton.

Deschner, J.P. (1984). *The hitting habit: Anger control for battering couples*. New York: Free Press.

Dicks, H.V. (1984). *Marital tensions: Clinical studies toward a psychological theory of interaction*. New York: Routledge.

Dinkmeyer, D., Dinkmeyer, D., Jr., & Sperry, L. (1987). *Adlerian counseling and psychotherapy* (2nd ed.). Columbus, OH: Merrill.

Dryden, W. (1985). *Marital therapy in Britain, Vol. 1: Context and therapeutic approaches*. New York: Taylor & Francis.

Dworkin, S.H., & Guiterrez, F.J. (1992). *Counseling gay men & lesbians: Journey to the end of the rainbow*. Alexandria, VA: American Association for Counseling and Development.

Ellis, A., Sishel, J., Yaeger, R., DiMattia, D., & DiGiuseppe, R. (1989). *Rational-emotive couples therapy*. New York: Pergamon.

Erskine, R., & Moursund, J. (1988). *Integrative psychotherapy in action*. Newbury Park, CA: Sage.

Filsinger, E.E. (1983). *Marriage and family assessment: A source book for family therapy*. Newbury Park, CA: Sage.

Filsinger, E.E., & Lewis, R.A. (1981). *Assessing marriage: New behavioral approaches*. Newbury Park, CA: Sage.

Fincham, F.D., & Bradbury, T.N. (Eds.). (1990). *The psychology of marriage: Basic issues and applications*. New York: Haworth.

Fitzgerald, R.V. (1990). *Conjoint marital therapy*. Northvale, NJ: Aronson.

Fitzpatrick, M.A. (1988). *Between husbands and wives: Communication in marriage*. Newbury Park, CA: Sage.

Framo, J.L. (1982). *Explorations in marital and family therapy*. New York: Springer.

Framo, J.L. (1992). *Family-of-origin therapy: An intergenerational approach*. New York: Brunner/Mazel.

Fredman, N., & Sherman, R. (1987). *Handbook of measurements for marriage & family therapy*. New York: Brunner/Mazel.

Freeman, D.R. (1982). *Marital crisis and short-term counseling: A casebook*. New York: Free Press.

Freeman, D.R. (1990). *Couples in conflict: Inside the counseling room*. Orlando, FL: Open University.

Garland, D.S.R. (1983). *Working with couples for marriage enrichment*. San Francisco: Jossey-Bass.

Gilbert, L. (1985). *Men in dual-career families: Current realities and future prospects*. Hillsdale, NJ: Erlbaum.

Glick, I.D. (1987). *Marital and family therapy* (3rd ed.). Philadelphia: Grune & Stratton.

Goldberg, D.C. (Ed.). (1985). *Contemporary marriage: Special issues in couples therapy*. Pacific Grove, CA: Brooks/Cole.

Goodrich, T.J., Rampage, C., Ellman, B., & Halstead, K. (1983). *Feminist family therapy: A case book*. New York: Norton.

Greenberg, L.S., & Johnson, S.M. (1988). *Emotionally focused therapy for couples*. New York: Guilford.

Grossman, H.Y. (1990). *The experience and meaning of work in women's lives*. Hillsdale, NJ: Erlbaum.

Guerin, P.J. (1987). *The evaluation and treatment of marital conflict: A four-stage approach.* New York: Basic Books.

Gurman, A.S. (Ed.). (1991). *Casebook of marital therapy.* New York: Guilford.

Gurman, A.S., & Kniskern, D. (Eds.). (1981). *Handbook of family therapy.* New York: Brunner/Mazel.

Hafner, R.J. (1986). *Marriage and mental illness: A sex-roles perspective.* New York: Guilford.

Hahlweg, K., & Jacobson, N.S. (1984). *Marital interaction: Analysis and modification.* New York: Haworth.

Haldane, J.D. (1988). *Marital therapy: Research, practice and organization.* New York: Pergamon.

Haley, J. (1987). *Problem solving therapy* (2nd ed.). San Francisco: Jossey-Bass.

Hansen, J.C., & Falicov, C.J. (Eds.). (1983). *Cultural perspectives in family therapy.* Rockville, MD: Aspen.

Hansen, J.C., & L'Abate, L. (Eds.). (1982). *Values, ethics, legalities and the family therapist.* Rockville, MD: Aspen.

Ho, M.K. (1990). *Intermarried couples in therapy.* Springfield, IL: Charles C Thomas.

Hofling, C.K., & Lewis, J.M. (1980). *The family: Evaluation and treatment.* New York: Brunner/Mazel.

Huber, C.H., & Baruth, L.G. (1987). *Ethical, legal and professional issues in the practice of marriage and family therapy.* Columbus, OH: Merrill.

Hughes, M. (1991). *Marriage counseling: An essential handbook.* New York: Continuum.

Humphrey, F.G. (1983). *Marital therapy.* Englewood Cliffs, NJ: Prentice-Hall.

Hurvitz, N., & Straus, R.A. (1991). *Marriage and family therapy: A sociocognitive approach.* New York: Haworth.

Jacob, T. (Ed.). (1987). *Family interaction and psychopathology. Theories, methods, and findings.* New York: Plenum Press.

Jacobson, N.S., & Gurman, A.S. (Eds.). (1986). *Clinical handbook of marital therapy.* New York: Guilford.

Jacobson, N.S., & Margolin, G. (1979). *Marital therapy: Strategies based on social learning and behavior exchange principles.* New York: Brunner/Mazel.

Kelley, H.H., Berscheid, E., Christensen, A., Harvey, J.H., Huston, T.L., Levinger, G., McClintock, E., Peplau, L.A., & Peterson, D.R. (1983). *Close relationships.* New York: Freeman.

Kern, R.M., Hawes, E.C., & Christensen, O.C. (1989). *Couples therapy: An Adlerian perspective.* Minneapolis: Educational Media.

Kershaw, C.J. (1992). *The couple's hypnotic dance: Creating Ericksonian strategies in marital therapy.* New York: Brunner/Mazel.

L'Abate, L. (1985). *Handbook of family psychology and therapy.* Pacific Grove, CA: Brooks/Cole.

L'Abate, L. (Ed.). (1992). *Programmed writings: A self-administered approach for interventions with individuals, couples, and families.* Pacific Grove, CA: Brooks/Cole.

Lachkar, J. (1992). *The narcissistic/borderline couple: A psychoanalytic perspective on marital therapy.* New York: Brunner/Mazel.

Lauer, R.H., & Lauer, J.C. (1991). *Marriage and family: The quest for intimacy.* Madison, WI: Brown.

Lederer, W.J., & Jackson, D.D. (1968). *The mirages of marriage.* New York: Norton.

Lewis, J.M. (1989). *The birth of the family: An empirical inquiry.* New York: Brunner/Mazel.

Lieberman, R.P., Wheeler, E.G., De Visser, L.A., Kuehnel, J., & Kuehnel, T. (1980). *Handbook of marital therapy: A positive approach to helping troubled relationships.* New York: Plenum Press.

Madanes, C. (1981). *Strategic family therapy.* San Francisco: Jossey-Bass.

Marks, S.R. (1986). *Three corners: Exploring marriage and the self.* Lexington, MA: Heath.

McGoldrick, M., & Gerson, R. (1985). *Genograms in family assessment.* New York: Norton.

McGoldrick, M., Pearce, J.K., & Giordano, J. (Eds.). (1982). *Ethnicity and family therapy.* New York: Guilford.

McWhirter, D., & Mattison, A. (1983). *The male couple: How relationships develop.* Englewood Cliffs, NJ: Prentice-Hall.

Minuchin, S., & Fishman, H.C. (1981). *Family therapy techniques.* Cambridge, MA: Harvard University Press.

Moses, A.E., & Hawkins, R.O. (1983). *Counseling lesbian women and gay men.* St Louis: Mosby.

Neidig, P., & Friedman, D.H. (1984). *Spouse abuse: A treatment program for couples.* Champaign, IL: Research Press.

Nichols, W.C. (1988). *Marital therapy: An integrative approach.* New York: Guilford.

Noller, P. (1984). *Nonverbal communication and marital interaction.* Oxford: Pergamon.

Noller, P., & Fitzpatrick, M.A. (Eds.). (1988). *Perspectives on marital interaction.* Philadelphia: Multilingual Matters Limited.

Ohlsen, M.M. (1979). *Marriage counseling in groups.* Champaign, IL: Research Press.

O'Leary, K.D. (1987). *Assessment of marital discord.* Hillsdale, NJ: Erlbaum.

Paolino, T.J., & McCrady, B.S. (Eds.). (1978). *Marriage and marital therapy: Psychoanalytic, behavioral, and systems theory perspectives.* New York: Guilford.

Patterson, G.R. (1990). *Depression and aggression in family interaction.* Hillsdale, NJ: Erlbaum.

Sager, C.J., Brown, H.S., Crohn, H., Engle, T., Rodstein, E., & Walker, L. (1983). *Treating the remarried family.* New York: Brunner/Mazel.

Satir, V.M. (1988). *The new peoplemaking.* Palo Alto, CA: Science & Behavior Books.

Satir, V.M., & Baldwin, M. (1983). *Satir: Step by step.* Palo Alto, CA: Science & Behavior Books.

Scanzoni, J., Polonko, K., Teachman, J., & Thompson, L. (1989). *The sexual bond: Rethinking families and close relationships.* Newbury Park, CA: Sage.

Schaap, C. (1982). *Communication and adjustment in marriage.* Lisse, Netherlands: Swets & Zeitlinger.

Scharff, D. (1982). *The sexual relationship: An object relations view of sex and the family.* London: Routledge & Kegan Paul.

Scharff, D., & Scharff, J.S. (1991). *Object relations couple therapy.* Northvale, NJ: Aronson.

Scharff, J.S. (1989). *Foundations of object relations family therapy.* Northvale, NJ: Aronson.

Scott, J., Sr. (1989). *Marital therapy: A hypnoanalytic approach.* Manchester, NH: Irvington.

Segraves, R.T. (1982). *Marital therapy: A combined psychodynamic-behavioral approach.* New York: Plenum Press.

Sherman, R., & Fredman, N. (1986). *Handbook of structured techniques in marriage and therapy.* New York: Brunner/Mazel.

Sherman, R., Oresky, P., & Rountree, Y. (1992). *Solving problems in couples and family therapy.* New York: Brunner/Mazel.

Sholevar, G.P. (Ed.). (1981). *Handbook of marriage and marital therapy.* Jamaica, NY: Spectrum.

Sperry, L., & Carlson, J. (1991). *Marital therapy: Integrating theory and technique.* Denver: Love.

Stahmann, R., & Hiebert, W.J. (1987). *Premarital counseling: The professional's handbook.* New York: Free Press.

Stahmann, R., Hiebert, W.J., & Klemer, R.H. (1984). *Counseling in marital and sexual problems: A clinician's handbook.* New York: Free Press.

Stoltz-Loike, M. (1992). *Dual career couples: New perspectives in counseling.* Alexandria, VA: American Association for Counseling and Development.

Strean, H.S. (1985). *Resolving marital conflicts: A psychodynamic perspective*. New York: Wiley.

Stuart, R.B. (1980). *Helping couples change: A social learning approach to marital therapy*. New York: Guilford.

Tseng, W., & Hsu, J. (1991). *Culture and family: Problems and therapy*. New York: Haworth.

Vesper, J.H., & Brock, G.W. (1991). *Ethics, legalities, and professional practice issues in marriage and family therapy*. Boston: Allyn & Bacon.

Walters, M., Carter, B., Papp, P., & Silverstein, O. (1988). *The invisible web: Gender patterns in family relationships*. New York: Guilford.

Weeks, G.R. (Ed.). (1989). *Treating couples: The intersystem model of the Marriage Council of Philadelphia*. New York: Brunner/Mazel.

Weeks, G.R., & L'Abate, L. (1982). *Paradoxical psychotherapy: Theory and practice with individuals, couples, and families*. New York: Brunner/Mazel.

Wile, D.B. (1981). *Couples therapy: A nontraditional approach*. New York: Wiley.

Willi, J. (1982). *Couples in collusion*. New York: Aronson.

Willi, J. (1984). *Dynamics of couple therapy*. New York: Aronson.

Wolinsky, M.A. (1990). *A heart of wisdom: Marital counseling with older and elderly couples*. New York: Brunner/Mazel.

Wolman, B.B., & Stricker, C. (Eds.). (1983). *Handbook of marital and family therapy*. New York: Plenum Press.

PARENTING ISSUES

Abidin, R.P. (1982). *Parenting skill: Workbook and trainer's manual*. New York: Human Sciences.

Abidin, R.R. (Ed.). (1980). *Parent education and intervention handbook*. Springfield, IL: Charles C Thomas.

Ambert, A. (1992). *The effect of children on parents*. New York: Haworth.

Backett, K.C. (1982). *Mothers and fathers: Studies of negotiation of parental behavior*. New York: St. Martin's.

Berman, P.W., & Pedersen, F.A. (Eds.). (1987). *Men's transitions to parenthood: Longitudinal studies of early family experience*. Hillsdale, NJ: Erlbaum.

Bornstein, M.H. (Ed.). (1991). *Cultural approaches to parenting*. Hillsdale, NJ: Erlbaum.

Buchholz, E.S. (Ed.). (1983). *Ego and self psychology: Group interventions with children, adolescents, and parents*. Northvale, NJ: Aronson.

Cochran, M., Larner, M., Riley, D., Gunnarsson, L., & Henderson, C.R. (1990). *Extending families: The social networks of parents and their children*. New York: Cambridge University Press.

Cohen, R.S., Cohler, B.J., & Weissman, S.H. (Eds.). (1984). *Parenthood: A psychodynamic perspective*. New York: Guilford.

Dreikurs, R., & Grey, L. (1968). *A new approach to discipline*. New York: Hawthorn.

Dreikurs, R., & Soltz, V. (1964). *Children: The challenge*. New York: Hawthorn.

Fedders, C., & Elliot, L. (1987). *Shattered dreams*. New York: Harper & Row.

Fraiberg, S.H. (1958). *The magic years*. New York: Scribner.

Gordon, T. (1970). *PET: Parent effectiveness training*. New York: Wyden.

Gordon, T., & Sands, J. (1978). *P.E.T. in action*. New York: Bantam Books.

Koblinsky, S. (1983). *Sexuality education for parents of young children: A facilitator training manual*. Fayetteville, NY: Ed U Press.

Lang, F.A. (1988). *Parent-group counseling: A counselor's handbook and practical guide*. New York: Free Press.

Painter, G., & Corsini, R.J. (1990). *Effective discipline in the home and school.* Muncie, IN: Accelerated Development.

Painter, G., & Corsini, R.J. (1992). *Action guide for effective discipline in the home and school.* Muncie, IN: Accelerated Development.

Paul, J.L. (1980). *Understanding and working with parents of children with special needs.* Fort Worth, TX: Holt, Rinehart & Winston.

Pillari, V. (1991). *Scapegoating in families: Intergenerational patterns of physical and emotional abuse.* New York: Brunner/Mazel.

Pillemer, K., & McCartney, K. (1991). *Parent-child relations throughout life.* Hillsdale, NJ: Erlbaum.

Popkin, M.H. (1983). *Active parenting handbook.* Atlanta: Active Parenting.

Powell, D.R. (1988). *Parent education as early childhood intervention: Emerging directions in theory, research and practice.* Norwood, NJ: Ablex.

Schaefer, C.E., & Briesmeister, J.M. (Eds.). (1989). *Handbook of parent training: Parents as co-therapists for children's behavior problems.* New York: Wiley.

Schultz, J.E. (1991). *Early childhood materials and equipment.* Wichita, KS: SEED.

Stern, D.N. (1990). *Diary of a baby.* New York: Basic Books.

Trotzer, J.P., & Trotzer, T. (1986). *Marriage and family: Better ready than not.* Muncie, IN: Accelerated Development.

SEXUALITY ISSUES

Araoz, D.L. (1982). *Hypnosis and sex therapy.* New York: Brunner/Mazel.

Brake, M. (Ed.). (1982). *Human sexual relations: Toward a redefinition of sexual politics.* New York: Pantheon.

Cole, E., & Rothblum, E.D. (Eds.). (1988). *Women and sex therapy.* Binghamton, NY: Harrington Park.

Fisher, S. (1989). *Sexual images of the self: The psychology of erotic sensations and illusions.* Hillsdale, NJ: Erlbaum.

Geer, J.H., & O'Donohue, W.T. (Eds.). (1987). *Theories of human sexuality.* New York: Plenum Press.

Hawton, K. (1985). *Sex therapy: A practical guide.* New York: Oxford University Press.

Kantor, D., & Okun, B.F. (Eds.). (1989). *Intimate environments: Sex, intimacy, and gender in families.* New York: Haworth.

Kaplan, H.S. (1979). *Disorders of sexual desire and other new concepts and techniques in sex therapy.* New York: Brunner/Mazel.

Kaplan, H.S. (1981). *The new sex therapy: Active treatment of sexual dysfunctions.* New York: Brunner/Mazel.

Kaplan, H.S. (1983). *The evaluation of sexual disorders: Psychological and medical aspects.* New York: Brunner/Mazel.

Kaplan, H.S. (1987). *The illustrated manual of sex therapy* (2nd ed.). New York: Brunner/Mazel.

Kaplan, H.S. (1989). *How to overcome premature ejaculation.* New York: Brunner/Mazel.

Killman, P., & Mills, K.H. (1983). *All about sex therapy.* New York: Plenum Press.

Krohne, E.C. (1982). *Sex therapy handbook: A clinical manual for the diagnosis and treatment of sexual disorders.* Manchester, NH: Luce.

Leiblum, S.R., & Rosen, R.C. (1988). *Sexual desire disorders.* New York: Guilford.

Leiblum, S.R., & Rosen, R.C. (1989). *Principles and practice of sex therapy: Update for the 1990's* (2nd ed.). New York: Guilford.

LoPiccolo, J., & LoPiccolo, L. (Eds.). (1978). *Handbook of sex therapy*. New York: Plenum Press.

Masters, W.H., Johnson, V.E., & Kolodny, R.C. (1992). *Human sexuality* (4th ed.). New York: HarperCollins.

McKinney, K., & Sprecher, S. (1991). *Sexuality in close relationships*. Hillsdale, NJ: Erlbaum.

Nadelson, C.C., & Marcotte, D.B. (Eds.). (1983). *Treatment interventions in human sexuality*. New York: Plenum Press.

Neistadt, M.E., & Freda, M. (1988). *Choices: A guide to sex counseling with physically disabled adults*. Melbourne, FL: Krieger.

Schepp, K.F. (1986). *Sexuality counseling: A training program*. Muncie, IN: Accelerated Development.

Schiller, P. (1980). *The sex profession: What sex therapy can do*. Washington, DC: Chilmark House.

Schoeneswolf, G. (1989). *Sexual animosity between men and women*. New York: Aronson.

Weeks, G.R., & Hof, L. (Eds.). (1987). *Integrating sex and marital therapy*. New York: Brunner/Mazel.

Weinstein, E., & Rosen, E. (1988). *Sexuality counseling: Issues and implications*. Pacific Grove, CA: Brooks/Cole.

Wincze, J.P., & Carey, M.P. (1991). *Sexual dysfunction: A guide for assessment and treatment*. New York: Guilford.

BOOKS FOR THE LAYPERSON

GENERAL RELATIONSHIP ISSUES

Arond, M.A., & Parker, S.L. (1987). *The first year of marriage.* New York: Warner.

Arp, D., & Arp, C. (1989). *Sixty one-minute marriage builders.* Brentwood, TN: Wolgemuth & Hyatt.

Augburger, D.A. (Ed.). *Marriages that work.* Scottsdale, PA: Herald.

Barnes, B., & Barnes, E. (1988). *Growing a great marriage.* Eugene, OR: Harvest House.

Beaver, D. (1983). *Beyond the marriage fantasy: How to achieve true marital intimacy.* San Francisco: Harper.

Beck, A.T. (1988). *Love is never enough.* New York: Harper & Row.

Bell, R.S. (1990). *Modern marriage: How they keep it together.* Kansas City, MO: Tivoli.

Besson, C.T. (1987). *Growing together.* Grand Rapids, MI: Baker.

Betcher, W., & McCauley, R. (1990). *The seven basic quarrels of marriage: Recognize, defuse, negotiate and resolve your conflicts.* New York: Random House.

Blumstein, P., & Schwartz, P. (1983). *American couples.* New York: Morrow.

Brady, L.G. (1986). *How to get the most from your marriage without a therapist: Guidelines for intimate relationships.* Chula Vista, CA: Brady.

Brandon, N. (1983). *If you could hear what I cannot say.* New York: Bantam Books.

Bright, B., & Bright, V. (1990). *Managing stress in marriage: Help for couples on the fast track.* San Bernadino, CA: Heres Life.

Brumbaugh, J.A. (1989). *It's a matter of life or death: Wrong thinking about marriage leads to destruction!* Oviedo, FL: Committee for the Restoration of the Family.

Bryant, J. (1987). *Success in marriage—guaranteed!!! The secret of making friends and keeping them.* Saint Petersburg, FL: Socratic.

Bundschuh, R., & Gilbert, D. (1988). *Romance rekindled: The art of loving your spouse.* Eugene, OR: Harvest House.

Carr, J.B. (1988). *Crisis in intimacy.* Pacific Grove, CA: Brooks/Cole.

Cirner, R., & Cirner, T. (1985). *Ten weeks to a better marriage.* Ann Arbor, MI: Servant.

Cline, V. (1987). *How to make a good marriage great: Ten keys to a joyous relationship.* New York: Walker.

Coleman, P.W. (1990). *The forgiving marriage: Resolving anger and resentment and rediscovering each other.* Chicago: Contemporary.

Cowan, C., & Kinder, M. (1986). *Smart women/foolish choices: Finding the right men and avoiding the wrong ones.* New York: NAL-Dutton.

Cowan, C., & Kinder, M. (1990). *Husbands and wives: The guide for men and women who want to stay married.* New York: NAL-Dutton.

Davies, D. (1987). *ABC of marital success.* New York: Adebara & Honeycomb.

Davis, K., & Grossbard-Shechtman, A. (Eds.). (1986). *Contemporary marriage: Comparative perspectives on a changing institution.* New York: Russell Sage Foundation.

Delis, D.C. (1990). *The passion paradox.* New York: Bantam Books.

Denham, H.R., Jr. (1983). *Marriage renewal source book.* Brentwood, TN: JM Productions.

Dinkmeyer, D., & Carlson, J. (1984). *Time for a better marriage.* Circle Pines, MN: American Guidance Services.

Dinkmeyer, D., & Carlson, J. (1989). *Taking time for love: How to stay happily married*. New York: Prentice-Hall.

Donovan, M.E., & Ryan, W.P. (1991). *Love blocks: Breaking the patterns that undermine relationships*. New York: Viking Penguin.

Dotterweich, K. (1990). *Be-good-to-your-marriage therapy*. St. Meinrad, IN: Abbey.

Driscoll, R. (1990). *The binds that tie: Overcoming stalemates and standoffs in love relationships*. New York: Free Press.

Edwards, B.L. (1989). *How to have a happy marriage*. La Vergne, TN: Atlantis.

Ford, E. (1983). *Choosing to love*. Minneapolis: Winston.

Gerstel, N., & Gross, H. (1984). *Commuter marriage: A study of work and family*. New York: Guilford.

Goldberg, H. (1991). *What men really want*. New York: NAL-Dutton.

Good, P. (1987). *In pursuit of happiness*. Chapel Hill, NC: New View.

Gullotta, T.P., Adams, G.R., & Alexander, S.J. (1986). *Today's marriages and families: A wellness approach*. Pacific Grove, CA: Brooks/Cole.

Helmering, D.W. (1986). *Happily ever after: Why men and women think differently*. New York: Warner.

Hendrix, H. (1989). *Getting the love you want: A guide for couples*. New York: Harper & Row.

Hine, J.R. (1985). *How to have a long, happy healthy marriage*. Petaluma, CA: Interprint.

Hinton, A.P. (1985). *Keep the home fires burning: How to have an affair with your spouse*. New York: Simon & Schuster.

Hof, L., & Miller, W. (1980). *Marriage enrichment: Philosophy, process and program*. New York: Prentice-Hall.

Houghton, A.B. (1988). *Partners in love: Ingredients for a deep and lively marriage*. New York: Walker.

Kalashian, S., & Makowski, S. (1988). *Making marriage work: A handbook*. Riverview, FL: Alafia.

Klagsbrun, F. (1985). *Married people: Staying together in the age of divorce*. New York: Bantam Books.

Knight, G.W. (1984). *The second marriage guidebook*. Brentwood, TN: JM Productions.

Kriedler, W.J. (1984). *Creative conflict resolution*. Glenview, IL: Scott, Foresman.

Lane, C., & Stevens, L.A. (1989). *How to help your own troubled marriage*. Madison, TN: L S Records.

Lazarus, A.A. (1985). *Marital myths: Two dozen mistaken beliefs that can ruin a marriage (or make a bad one worse)*. San Luis Obispo, CA: Impact.

Lerner, H.G. (1989). *The dance of intimacy: A woman's guide to courageous acts of change in key relationships*. New York: HarperCollins.

Liebowitz, M.R. (1983). *The chemistry of love*. Boston: Little, Brown.

Loughary, J., & Ripley, T. (1987). *Working it out: A guide for dual career couples*. Eugene, OR: United Learning.

Luecke, D.L. (1981). *The relationship manual for couples*. Columbia, MD: Relationship Institute.

Mace, D., & Mace, V. (1983). *How to have a happy marriage*. Nashville: Abingdon.

Mace, D.R. (1983). *Close companions: The marriage enrichment handbook*. New York: Continuum.

Malone, P.T. (1987). *The art of intimacy*. New York: Prentice-Hall.

Maslin, B., & Nir, Y. (1987). *Not quite paradise: Making marriage work*. New York: Fawcett.

Matthews, A.M. (1990). *Why did I marry you, anyway? A practical guide to the first years of marriage*. New York: Pocket Books.

McCray, W.A. (1990). *Saving the Black marriage* (2nd ed.). Chicago: Black Light Fellowship.

McDonough, Y.Z., & Yahm, H. (1990). *Tying the knot: A couple's guide to emotional well-being from engagement to the wedding day*. New York: Viking Penguin.

Meier, P.D. (1988). *You can save your marriage*. Grand Rapids, MI: Baker.

Messina, J. (1986). *Marriage work-out: A marital enhancement workbook*. Tampa, FL: Advanced Development Systems.

Mickey, P.A., & Proctor, W. (1987). *Tough marriage: How to make a difficult relationship work*. New York: Bantam.

Minirth, F.B. (1991). *Passages of marriage*. Nashville: Nelson.

O'Connor, W.J. (1989). *Connecting: Working together for health and happiness*. Cream Ridge, NJ: Healing Acres.

O'Neill, G., & O'Neill, N. (1975). *Open marriage: A new lifestyle for couples*. New York: Evans.

Orbach, S., & Eichenbaum, L. (1983). *What do women want?* New York: Basic Books.

Ortlund, A. (1984). *Building a great marriage*. Tarrytown, NY: Revell.

Owen-Towle, T. (1987). *Staying together: Forty ways to make your marriage work*. Carmel, CA: Sunflower Ink.

Peterson, Y. (1979). *Marital adjustment in couples of which one spouse is,physically handicapped*. Saratoga, CA: R & E.

Pransky, G.S. (1990). *Divorce is not the answer: You can save your marriage*. Blue Ridge Summit, PA: TAB.

Pratt, V.A. (1989). *Coming alive: How mates help each other solve problems and find freedom and intimacy*. Kingston, RI: Green Twig.

Rankin, P., & Rankin, L. (1986). *Your marriage: Making it work*. Batavia, IL: Lion.

Reilly, C.C. (1989). *Making your marriage work: Growing in love after falling in love*. Mystic, CT: 23rd.

Rock, M.A. (1989). *The marriage map: Understanding and surviving the stages of marriage*. New York: Dell.

Ruben, H.L. (1987). *Supermarriage: Overcoming the predictable crises of married life*. New York: Bantam Books.

Scarff, M. (1988). *Intimate partners: Patterns in love and marriage*. New York: Ballantine.

Schwartz, R., & Schwartz, L.J. (1986). *Becoming a couple*. Lanham, MD: University Press of America.

Sell, C.M. (1982). *Achieving the impossible: Intimate marriage*. Portland, OR: Multnomah.

Shupe, A., Stacey, W.A., & Hazelwood, L.R. (1987). *Violent men, violent couples*. Lexington, MA: Heath.

Smith, R.K., & Tessina, T.B. (1987). *How to be a couple and still be free*. North Hollywood, CA: Newcastle.

Stuart, R.B., & Jacobsen, B. (1989). *Weight, sex, and marriage*. New York: Simon & Schuster.

Swain, C. (1982). *Enriching your marriage: A tune-up for partners in love*. Bountiful, UT: Horizon.

Tannen, D. (1990). *You just don't understand: Women and men in conversation*. New York: Morrow.

Tapley, W. (1987). *Happily ever after is no accident*. Lima, OH: CSS of Ohio.

Treat, S.R. (1987). *How to succeed in marriage*. Cleveland: Pilgrim.

Vaughan, P. (1990). *The monogamy myth: A new understanding of affairs and how to survive them*. New York: Newmarket.

Viscott, D. (1987). *I love you, let's work it out*. New York: Simon & Schuster.

Walter, J.A. (1988). *Communicating closeness: The missing link*. Houston: Texas Medical Publications.

Watson, E.U. (1986). *Personal change for marriage, sex, and social happiness*. Pittsburgh: Dorrance.

Wegscheider-Cruse, S. (1988). *Coupleship: How to build a relationship*. Deerfield, FL: Health Communications.

Weiner-Davis, M. (1992). *Divorce-busting: A revolutionary and rapid program for staying together*. New York: Summit.

Weitzman, L. (1983). *The marriage contract: A guide to living with lovers and spouses*. New York: Free Press.

Welwood, J. (1990). *Journey of the heart: Intimate relationships and the path of love*. New York: HarperCollins.

White, H.E., Jr. (1983). *Making marriage successful*. Manchester, NH: Irvington.

Woods, R. (1988). *How to communicate with your spouse*. Salt Lake City: Deseret.

Woolfolk, J. (1982). *Honeymoon for life: How to live happily ever after*. Chelsea, MI: Scarborough House.

PARENTING ISSUES

Adams, D. (1990). *The child influencers: Restoring the lost art of parenting*. Cuyahoga Falls, OH: Home Team.

Aigaki, D.M. (1987). *Trouble in paradise: A survival manual for couples who are parents*. Napa, CA: Dry Creek.

Albert, L. (1989). *Quality parenting*. New York: Ballantine.

Alexander, Z. (1989). *Good lovers make great parents: Pairing and caring with faith, hope, and love*. Grand Rapids, MI: Baker.

Bagley, C., & Verma, G.K. (1983). *Multicultural childhood*. Brookfield, VT: Gower.

Bigner, J.J. (1989). *Parent child relations: An introduction to parenting* (3rd ed.). New York: Macmillan.

Bluestein, J., & Colling, L. (1990). *Parents in a pressure cooker, parent workbook: A guide to responsible and loving parent-child relationships*. Rosemont, NJ: Programs for Education.

Brooks, J. (1987). *The process of parenting* (2nd ed.). Palo Alto, CA: Mayfield.

Brown, B.M. (1990). *Stress busters for kids: A parent's guide to helping kids cope with stress*. Vienna, VA: Brown.

Bruns, J.M. (1990). *The defiant ones: A manual for raising kids*. Pacific Palisades, CA: Calgre.

Clarke, J.I., & Dawson, C. (1989). *Growing up again: How to parent yourself so you can parent your children*. San Francisco: Harper.

Craig, J.E. (1984). *Handling the everyday hassles of childrearing: A practical guide for parents*. San Antonio: Watercress.

Dinkmeyer, D., & McKay, G.D. (1989). *The parent's handbook* (rev. ed.). Circle Pines, MN: American Guidance Service.

Dinkmeyer, D., & McKay, G.D. (1990). *Parenting teenagers: Systematic training for effective parenting*. New York: Random House.

Eden, A.N. (1982). *Positive parenting: How to raise a healthier and happier child (from birth to three years)*. New York: NAL-Dutton.

Ehrensaft, D. (1987). *Parenting together: Men and women sharing the care of their children*. New York: Free Press.

Feisinger, P.R. (1988). *What do we do now? The complete guide for all new parents and parent-to-be!* Chatsworth, MA: CCC.

Firestone, R.W. (1989). *Compassionate child-rearing: An in-depth approach to optimal parenting.* New York: Plenum Press.

Galinsky, E. (1987). *The six stages of parenthood.* Redding, MA: Addison-Wesley.

Galinsky, E., & David, J. (1991). *The preschool years: Family strategies that work—From experts and parents.* New York: Ballantine.

Glover, B., & Shepherd, J. (1989). *The family fitness handbook.* New York: Viking Penguin.

Goldstein, R. (1990). *Everyday parenting: The first five years.* New York: Viking Penguin.

Goldstein, R. (1991). *More everyday parenting: The six-to-nine-year-old.* New York: Viking Penguin.

Gordon, T. (1991). *Discipline that works: Promoting self-discipline in children.* New York: Plume.

Gordon, T., & Sands, S. (1984). *PET in action.* New York: Bantam.

Greenspan, S., & Greenspan, N.T. (1989). *The essential partnership: How parents and children can meet the emotional challenges of intimacy and childhood.* New York: Viking Penguin.

Gruber, B. (1989). *Parent communication.* Torrance, CA: Frank Schaffer.

Harris, J.M. (1989). *You and your child's self-esteem: Building for the future.* New York: Carroll & Graf.

Hill, M. (1987). *Sharing child care in early parenthood.* New York: Routledge.

Hotchner, T. (1988). *Childbirth and marriage: The transition to parenthood.* New York: Avon.

Ikeler, B. (1986). *Parenting your disabled child.* Louisville, KY: Westminster/John Knox.

Kersey, K. (1983). *The art of sensitive parenting: The 10 master keys to raising confident, competent and responsible children.* Reston, VA: Acropolis.

Kimball, G. (1991). *Fifty-fifty parenting: Equality in current family styles.* New York: Free Press.

Krumboltz, J.D., & Krumboltz, H. (1972). *Changing children's behavior.* New York: Prentice-Hall.

Magid, R. (1987). *When mothers and fathers work: Creative strategies for balancing career and family.* New York: AMACOM.

Main, F. (1986). *Perfect parenting and other myths: New ways to encourage responsible, cooperative, and happy children.* Minneapolis: CompCare.

McGinnis, J., & McGinnis, K. (1991). *Parenting for peace and justice.* Los Angeles: Orbis.

Mesle, B.J., & Mesle, C.R. (1981). *Parenting together.* Scottsdale, PA: Herald.

Messina, J.J. (1987). *Tools for parents with developmental disabilities.* Tampa, FL: Advanced Development Systems.

Miller, A. (1990). *For your own good: Hidden cruelty in childrearing & the roots of violence.* New York: Farrar-Straus-Giroux.

Mitchell, W., & Conn, C.P. (1989). *The power of positive parenting.* Tarrytown, NY: Gleneida.

Mollan, R. (1991). *Yes they can! A handbook for effectively parenting the handicapped.* Buena Park, CA: Reality Productions.

Moore, C. (1990). *A reader's guide for parents of children with mental, physical, or emotional disabilities.* Rockville, MD: Woodbine House.

Neely, M., & Haines, J. (1989). *Parents' work is never done: Helping children from 16–30 grow toward psychological well-being.* Far Hills, NJ: New Horizon.

Oberlander, J.R. (1988). *Slow and steady, get me ready: A parents' handbook.* Fairax Station, VA: Bio-Alpha.

Olds, S.W. (1989). *The working parents' survival guide.* New York: Prima.

Olkin, S.K. (1991). *Positive parenting fitness: The parents' resource guide to nutrition, stress reduction, total exercise, and practical information.* Garden City Park, NY: Avery.

Peshawaria, R. (1991). *Managing behavior problems in children: A guide for parents.* New York: Advent.

Popkin, M.H. (1987). *Active parenting: Teaching courage, cooperation and responsibility*. New York: HarperCollins.

Proschel, M., & Sprung, B. (Eds.). (1983). *Beginning equal: A manual about non-sexist childrearing for infants and toddlers*. New York: Women's Action Alliance.

Samalin, N., & Jablow, M.M. (1988). *Loving your child is not enough: Positive discipline that works*. New York: Viking Penguin.

Schaefer, C.E. (1991). *Teach your child to behave: Disciplining with love from birth through eight years*. New York: Plume.

Schaefer, C.E., & Millman, H.L. (1984). *How to help children with common problems*. New York: Van Nostrand Reinhold.

Sears, W. (1986). *Becoming a father: How to nurture and enjoy your family*. Franklin Park, IL: La Leche League International.

Sears, W., & Sears, M. (1991). *300 questions new parents ask: Answers about pregnancy, childbirth, and infant and child care*. New York: Plume.

Siegel, S. (1990). *Parenting your adopted child: A complete and loving guide*. New York: Prentice-Hall.

Tannen, D. (1986). *That's not what I meant! How conversational style makes or breaks your relations with others*. New York: Morrow.

Tannen, D. (1990). *You just don't understand: Women and men in conversation*. New York: Ballantine.

Weinhaus, E., & Friedman, K. (1991). *Stop struggling with your child: Quick-tip parenting solutions for you & you kids*. New York: HarperCollins.

Whelan, E.M. (1980). *A baby?... Maybe: A guide to making the most fateful decision of your life*. New York: Macmillan.

SEXUALITY ISSUES

Ables, B.S. (1987). *For couples only*. Atlanta: Humanics.

Baldwin, D.M. (1991). *Understanding male sexual health*. New York: Hippocrene.

Barbach, L. (1976). *For yourself: Fulfillment of female sexuality—A guide to orgasmic response*. New York: NAL- Dutton.

Barbach, L. (1983). *For each other: Sharing sexual intimacy*. New York: Doubleday.

Barbach, L., & Levine, L. (1981). *Shared intimacies*. New York: Bantam.

Berger, R.E., & Berger, D. (1987). *Biopotency: A guide to sexual success*. Emmaus, PA: Rodale.

Bing, E., & Colman, L. (1989). *Making love during pregnancy*. New York: Farrar-Straus-Giroux.

Botwin, C. (1985). *Is there sex after marriage?* Boston: Little, Brown.

Brecher, E.M. (1986). *Love, sex, and aging: A Consumer's Union report*. Boston: Little, Brown.

Brednel, H.J. (1987). *Sensuality sex: To understand yourself and choose to be your creative, released, sexual self*. Fort Worth, TX: Center for Creative Living.

Chartham, R. (1987). *The sensuous couple* (2nd ed.). New York: Ballantine.

Clark, D. (1978). *Loving someone gay*. New York: NAL-Dutton.

Davis, J. (1984). *Making love: A woman's guide*. New York: NAL-Dutton.

DeBetz, B., & Baker, S.S. (1986). *Erotic focus*. New York: NAL-Dutton.

Devine, M., & Routh, D. (1989). *Real intimacy: Extended lovemaking in the committed relationship*. Virginia Beach, VA: Donning.

Dunkell, S. (1980). *Loveliness: How we make love*. New York: NAL-Dutton.

Finz, I., & Finz, S. (1980). *Whispered secrets: The couple's guide to erotic fantasy*. New York: NAL-Dutton.

Goldberg, H. (1983). *The new male-female relationship.* New York: Morrow.

Haldane, S. (1985). *Couples dynamics: A guide to emotional-sexual enhancement.* Manchester, NH: Irvington.

Hayden, N. (1983). *How to satisfy a woman every time and have her beg for more.* New York: NAL-Dutton.

Helmering, D.W. (1990). *Husbands, wives and sex.* Holbrook, MA: Adams.

Henderson, J. (1987). *The lover within: Opening to energy in sexual practice.* Barrytown, NY: Station Hill.

Hite, S. (1981). *The Hite report.* New York: Dell.

Kahn, E.J., & Rudnitsky, D.A. (1990). *Love codes: How to decipher men's secret signals about romance.* New York: Plume.

Kennedy, A.P., & Dean, S. (1988). *Touching for pleasure: A twelve step program for sexual enhancement.* Chatsworth, CA: Chatsworth.

Levy, H.S., & Ishihara, A. (1989). *The Tao of sex.* Lower Lake, CA: Integral.

Lillibridge, E.M. (1984). *The love book for couples: Building a healthy relationship.* Atlanta: Humanics.

Masters, R. (1988). *Understanding sexuality: The mystery of our lost identities.* Grants Pass, OR: Foundation of Human Understanding.

McCarthy, B., & McCarthy, E. (1990). *Couple sexual awareness: Building sexual happiness.* New York: Carroll & Graf.

Miles, H.J. (1985). *Sexual happiness in marriage.* New York: Jove.

O'Connor, D. (1986). *How to make love to the same person for the rest of your life.* New York: Bantam Books.

O'Connor, D. (1990). *How to put the love back in making love.* New York: Bantam Books.

Pearsall, P. (1988). *Super marital sex.* New York: Ivy.

Pietropinto, A. (1990). *Not tonight dear: How to reawaken your sexual desire.* New York: Doubleday.

Raley, P.E. (1985). *Making love better: Have an affair with your partner.* New York: St. Martin's.

Ransohoff, R. (1990). *Venus after forty: Sexual myths, men's fantasies, and truths about middle aged women.* Far Hills, NJ: New Horizon.

Rosenthal, S.H. (1987). *Sex after forty.* Los Angeles: Tarcher.

Sandowski, C.L. (1989). *Sexual concerns when illness or disability strikes.* Springfield, IL: Charles C Thomas.

Semmens, J. (1989). *Mid-life sexuality: Enrichment and problem-solving.* Durant, OK: Essential Medical Information Systems.

Sutton, W.L. (1981). *Sex for the handicapped man: An educational booklet.* Inglewood, CA: Sutton.

Valois, R.F., & Kammermann, S.K. (1992). *Your sexuality.* New York: McGraw-Hill.

Wells, C.G. (1990). *Right brain sex: Creative visualization to balance sexual pleasure.* New York: Prentice-Hall.

Westheimer, R. (1986). *Dr Ruth's guide for married lovers.* New York: Warner.

Westheimer, R. (1986). *Dr Ruth's guide to good sex.* New York: Warner.

White, B. (1984). *Making love: A man's guide.* New York: NAL-Dutton.

Williams, W. (1988). *Rekindling desire: Bringing your sexual relationship to life.* Oakland, CA: New Harbinger.

Womack, W., & Straus, F.F. (1986). *The marriage bed: Renewing love, friendship, trust and romance.* Seattle: Madrona.

Wong, B.M. (1982). *TSFR: The Taoist way to total sexual fitness for men.* Princeton, NJ: Golden Dragon.

FINANCES

Amling, F., & Droms, W.G. (1986). *The Dow Jones-Irwin guide to personal financial planning.* Homewood, IL: Business One Irwin.

Aubert, E.J., & Stephens, M. (1988). *Personal financial planning made easy.* New London, NH: Advanced Financial Planning Group.

Barker, B. (1987). *Answers: A practical kit to organize your personal and financial matters.* New York: HarperCollins.

Berg, A.G. (1988). *How to stop fighting about money and make some: A couple's guide to financial success.* New York: Newmarket.

Berg, A.G. (1990). *Your wealth building years: Financial planning for 18 to 38 year olds.* New York: Newmarket.

Blue, R. (1989). *The debt squeeze: How your family can become financially free.* Pomona, CA: Focus on the Family.

Burkett, L. (1989). *The complete financial guide for young couples.* Wheaton, IL: Victor.

Burkett, L. (1990). *Financial workbook: A family budgeting guide.* Chicago: Moody.

Cobb, C.G. (1981). *The bad times primer: A complete guide to survival on a budget.* Los Angeles: Times Press.

Dorfman, M.S., & Adelman, S.W. (1986). *Life insurance and financial planning.* Homewood, IL: Irwin.

Dunton, L. (1988). *About your future.... Financial planning will make the difference.* San Diego: National Center for Financial Education.

Esperti, R.A., & Peterson, R.L. (1988). *Loving trust: The right way to provide for yourself and guarantee the future of your loved ones.* New York: Viking Penguin.

Esperti, R.A., & Peterson, R.L. (1991). *Loving trust: The smart, flexible alternative to wills and probate.* New York: Viking Penguin.

Evans, M.K. (1991). *How to make your (shrinking) salary support you in style for the rest of your life.* New York: Random House.

Farmer, R.W., & Ling, R.V. (1990). *The baby's budget book: Financial planning for new parents: Everything you should buy and how much you should plan to spend during your child's first year of life.* Carollton, TX: Shadetree.

Felton-Collins, V. (1990). *Couples and money: Why money interferes with love and what to do about it.* New York: Bantam.

Forte, I. (1987). *I'm ready to learn about money.* Nashville: Incentive.

Freeman, M.H., & Graf, D.K. (1980). *Money management: A consumer's guide to savings, spending, and investing.* New York: Macmillan.

Fries, M., & Taylor, C.H. (1984). *The prosperity handbook: A guide to personal and financial success.* Fairfield, IA: Communications Research.

Ghica, G. (1988). *Financial advice for middle class America: A do it yourself investment guide.* Huntington Beach, CA: G & G.

Givens, C.J. (1988). *Wealth without risk: How to develop a personal fortune without going out on a limb.* New York: Simon & Schuster.

Givens, C.J. (1990). *Financial self defense.* New York: Simon & Schuster.

Givens, C.J. (1992). *More wealth without risk.* New York: Simon & Schuster.

Hom, T. (1991). *Smart, successful and broke: The six step action plan to get you out of debt and into money.* New York: Dell.

Hopper, J.A., & Berry, D. (1988). *Understanding your finances: A practical handbook.* Seattle: Law Forum.

Howard, A.H. (1991). *Money grows on trees.* West Monroe, LA: Howard.

Morris, D.E. (1988). *Retire rich! How to plan a secure financial future.* New York: Simon & Schuster.

Myers, T.S. (1991). *How to keep control of your life after 50: A guide for your legal, medical, and financial well-being.* New York: Free Press.

Nichols, H.S. (1987). *The parents' guide: Money sense.* Reston, VA: Acropolis.

Ortalda, R.A. (1990). *How to live within your means and stay financially secure.* New York: Simon & Schuster.

Pahl, J. (1989). *Marriage and money.* New York: St. Martin's.

Perry, R.D. (1987). *Money problems.* Elgin, IL: Cook.

Peterson, J.L., & Peterson, R.K. (1985). *The family budget.* Orem, UT: Cedar Fort.

Peterson, J.R. (1989). *Turn chaos into cash: A complete guide to organizing and managing your personal finances.* Crozet, VA: Betterway.

Pond, J. (1987). *Personal financial planning forms and checklists.* Boston: Warren, Gorham, & Lamont.

Porter, S. (1986). *Sylvia Porter's love and money.* New York: Avon.

Porter, S. (1989). *Sylvia Porter's your financial security: Making your money work at every stage of your life.* New York: Avon.

Porter, S. (1990). *Sylvia Porter's your finances in the 1990's.* New York: Prentice-Hall.

Quinn, J.B. (1991). *Making the most of your money: A comprehensive guide to financial planning.* New York: Simon & Schuster.

Roberts, W. (1991). *How to save money on just about everything.* Laguna Beach, CA: Strebor.

Salitra, R. (1989). *Effective budgeting techniques: A simple, yet thorough, step-by-step guide to help you gain control over your financial life and future.* Plantation, FL: Bighorn.

Seymour, H. (1987). *How to live on a whole lot less.* Salt Lake City: Olympus.

Steinberger, R.P., & Steinberger, P.W. (1991). *The complete personal budgeting workbook.* Alexandria, VA: American Association of Educated Consumers.

Wagner, J.L. (1987). *Teaching your child money management: A complete step-by-step workbook for the parent.* Orange, CA: Insight Communications.

Webster, D.E. (1987). *How to save money when you build your house: A guide for people who want to build their own house on a limited budget.* Rose Hill, KS: Triangle.

Weisbrod, A. (1989). *Becoming one financially.* Elgin, IL: David C. Cook.

HOUSEHOLD MANAGEMENT ISSUES

Barling, J. (1990). *Employment, stress and family functioning.* London: Wiley.

Gilbert, L. (1988). *Sharing it all: The rewards and struggles of two-career families.* New York: Plenum Press.

Hochschild, A., & Machung, A. (1989). *The second shift: Working parents and the revolution at home.* New York: Viking.

Komarovsky, M. (1987). *Blue-collar marriage.* New Haven, CT: Yale University Press.

McGoldrick, M., Anderson, C., & Walsh, F. (Eds.). (1989). *Women in families: A framework for family therapy.* New York: Norton.

Piotrkowski, C.S. (1979). *Work and the family system.* New York: Macmillan.

Rice, D. (1979). *Dual-career marriage: Conflict and treatment.* New York: Free Press.

Sekaran, U. (1986). *Dual-career families.* San Francisco: Jossey-Bass.

Smith, A.D., & Reid, W.J. (1985). *Role-sharing marriage.* New York: Columbia University.

Stromberg, A.H., & Harkess, S. (Eds.). (1987). *Women working* (2nd ed.). Mountain View, CA: Mayfield.

Ulrich, D., & Dunne, H. (1986). *To love and work: A systemic interlocking of family, workplace, and career.* New York: Brunner/Mazel.

Voydanoff, P. (1987). *Work and family life.* Newbury Park, CA: Sage.